HONOLULU

THE MINI ROUGH GUIDE

There are more than one hundred Rough Guide travel,
phrasebook, and music titles, covering destinations
from Amsterdam to Zimbabwe, languages from Czech
to Thai, and musics from World to Opera and Jazz

Forthcoming titles include

Indonesia • New England • St Lucia • Toronto

Rough Guides on the Internet

www.roughguidoc.com

Rough Guide Credits

Text editor: Andrew Taber
Typesetting: James Morris
Cartography: Maxine Burke

Publishing Information

This first edition published January 1999 by
Rough Guides Ltd, 62–70 Shorts Gardens, London WC2H 9AB

Distributed by the Penguin Group:

Penguin Books Ltd, 27 Wrights Lane, London W8 5TZ
Penguin Books USA Inc., 375 Hudson Street, New York 10014, USA
Penguin Books Australia Ltd, 487 Maroondah Highway,
PO Box 257, Ringwood, Victoria 3134, Australia
Penguin Books Canada Ltd, 10 Alcorn Avenue,
Toronto, Ontario, Canada M4V 1E4
Penguin Books (NZ) Ltd, 182–190 Wairau Road,
Auckland 10, New Zealand

Typeset in Bembo and Helvetica to an original design by Henry Iles.
Printed in Spain by Graphy Cems.

© Greg Ward. 288pp, includes index
A catalogue record for this book is available from the British Library.
ISBN 1-85828-402-3

The publishers and authors have done their best to
ensure the accuracy and currency of all the information
in *The Rough Guide to Honolulu*, however, they can
accept no responsibility for any loss, injury or
inconvenience sustained by any traveler as a result of
information or advice contained in the guide.

HONOLULU

THE MINI ROUGH GUIDE

by Greg Ward

THE ROUGH GUIDES

We set out to do something different when the first Rough Guide was published in 1982. Mark Ellingham, just out of university, was traveling in Greece. He brought along the popular guides of the day, but found they were all lacking in some way. They were either strong on ruins and museums but went on for pages without mentioning a beach or taverna. Or they were so conscious of the need to save money that they lost sight of Greece's cultural and historical significance. Also, none of the books told him anything about Greece's contemporary life – its politics, its culture, its people, and how they lived.

So with no job in prospect, Mark decided to write his own guidebook, one which aimed to provide practical information that was second to none, detailing the best beaches and the hottest clubs and restaurants, while also giving hard-hitting accounts of every sight, both famous and obscure, and providing up-to-the-minute information on contemporary culture. It was a guide that encouraged independent travelers to find the best of Greece, and was a great success, getting shortlisted for the Thomas Cook travel guide award, and encouraging Mark, along with three friends, to expand the series.

The Rough Guide list grew rapidly and the letters flooded in, indicating a much broader readership than had been anticipated, but one which uniformly appreciated the Rough Guide mix of practical detail and humor, irreverence and enthusiasm. Things haven't changed. The same four friends who began the series are still the caretakers of the Rough Guide mission today: to provide the most reliable, up-to-date and entertaining information to independent-minded travelers of all ages, on all budgets.

We now publish more than 100 titles and have offices in London and New York. The travel guides are written and researched by a dedicated team of more than 100 authors, based in Britain, Europe, the USA and Australia. We have also created a unique series of phrasebooks to accompany the travel series, along with an acclaimed series of music guides, and a best-selling pocket guide to the Internet and World Wide Web. We also publish comprehensive travel information on our Web site: **www.roughguides.com**

Help Us Update

We've gone to a lot of trouble to ensure that this Rough Guide is as up to date and accurate as possible. However, things do change, and restaurants and hotels in the resort areas appear and disappear almost daily. All suggestions, comments and corrections are much appreciated, and we'll send a copy of the next edition (or any other Rough Guide if you prefer) for the best letters.

Please mark letters: "Rough Guide Honolulu Update" and send to:

Rough Guides, 62–70 Shorts Gardens, London WC2H 9AB, or
Rough Guides, 375 Hudson St, New York, NY 10014.
Or send email to: mail@roughguides.co.uk

Online updates about this book can be found on
Rough Guides' Web site (see opposite)

The Author

Greg Ward has worked for Rough Guides since 1985, in which time he has also written Rough Guides to Hawaii, Maui, the Big Island, Southwest USA, and Brittany and Normandy, edited and co-written *The Rough Guide to the USA*, edited the India guide (as well as many others), and contributed to books on China, Mexico, California, France, Spain and Portugal. He also helped set up and develop the company's desktop publishing system, and has worked on travel guides for Fodors and Dorling Kindersley.

Acknowledgements

Heartfelt thanks above all to Samantha Cook, for happy times in Hawaii, New Orleans and London; to Jules Brown, Alison Cowan and Cefn Ridout for coming along; and to my parents, for their endless support. I'd also like to thank the many people who made researching this book such fun, especially Julie Blissett, Steven Boyle, Barbara Campbell, Linda Chun, Alex Pangas, James Richmond, and Connie Wright. At Rough Guides, I'm very grateful to Andrew Taber for efficient and informed editing, James Morris for production, Link Hall for fonts, Russell Walton for proofreading, Maxine Burke for maps, and Eleanor Hill for picture research.

CONTENTS

Introduction

Although **Oahu** is only the third largest of the Hawaiian islands – its six hundred square miles are dwarfed by the four thousand square miles of the aptly-named Big Island – it's home to almost 900,000 people, or roughly eighty percent of the state's population. Half of those in turn live along a narrow strip of Oahu's southeast coast, in the city of **Honolulu**, while the economic powerhouse that keeps the whole Hawaiian economy going is even smaller and more crowded still – the tiny, surreal enclave of **Waikīkī**, three miles east of downtown.

After a century of mass tourism to Hawaii, the very name of Waikīkī continues to epitomize beauty, sophistication and glamor. Of course, squeezing enough tower blocks to hold 100,000 hotel beds into a mere two square miles leaves little room for unspoiled tropical scenery. The legendary **beach**, however, remains irresistible, and Waikīkī offers a full-on resort experience to match any in the world. Around six million visitors per year spend their days on the sands of Waikīkī, and their nights in its hotels, restaurants and bars; for many of them, barring the odd expedition to the nearby Ala Moana shopping mall, the rest of Honolulu might just as well not exist.

All of which suits the average citizen of Honolulu, for whom Waikīkī is a small and seldom-visited suburb, just fine. Honolulu is a distinctive and remarkably attractive city in its own right. The setting is gorgeous, right on the Pacific Ocean, and reaching back into a succession of spectacularly lush valleys cut into the dramatic *pali* (cliffs) of the Ko'olau Mountains. **Downtown Honolulu**, centered around a group of administrative buildings that date from the final days of the Hawaiian monarchy, nestles at the foot of the extinct **Punchbowl** volcano, now a military cemetery. As well as boasting top-quality museums such as the **Bishop Museum** and the **Academy of Arts**, it also offers superb **rainforest hikes**, especially in **Makiki** and **Mānoa** valleys, just a mile or so away. Immediately to the west stands the livelier **Chinatown**, and five miles further is the **airport**, just before the sheltered inlet of **Pearl Harbor**.

Thanks to massive immigration, the **population** of modern Hawaii is among the most ethnically diverse in the world, and Honolulu's status as a major international crossroads makes it an extraordinarily cosmopolitan city to visit. Only perhaps 2 percent of its inhabitants are pure Hawaiians, while another 20 percent claim at least some Hawaiian blood. The rest of the population includes the 26 percent who identify themselves as Caucasian, 16 percent Japanese, and 15 percent Filipino, though as over half of all marriages are classified as inter-racial such statistics grow ever more meaningless. In addition, almost as many tourists these days travel eastward to reach Hawaii, especially from Japan and Korea, as travel west from North America. Once there, you'll find that almost everyone speaks English. As a rule the Hawaiian language is only encountered in the few words – such as *aloha* ("love"), the all-purpose island greeting – that have passed into general local usage.

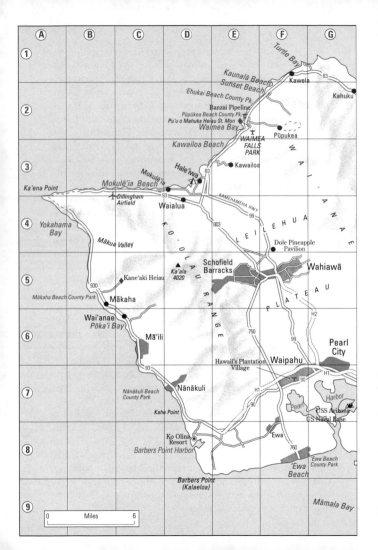

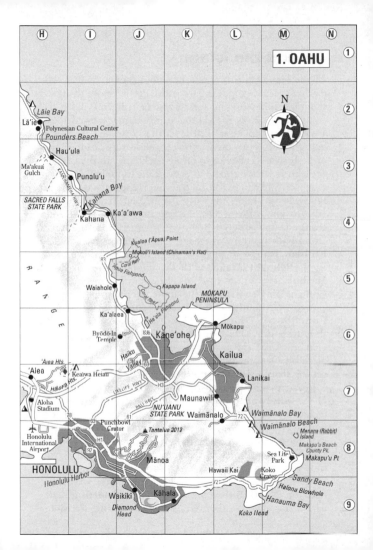

Around the island

All the Hawaiian islands are the summits of a chain of submarine volcanoes, poking from the Pacific more than two thousand miles off the west coast of America. Each has continued to grow for as long as it remained poised above a stationary "hot spot" in the earth's crust, and then, as it has drifted away to the northwest and lost its steady supply of fresh lava, has begun to erode back beneath the ocean.

Oahu is what's known as a "volcanic doublet" in that it consists of two separate but overlapping volcanoes. Roughly speaking, the island is shaped like a butterfly, with its wings formed by the volcanoes of the **Wai'anae Range** in the west – which first emerged from the waves around six million years ago – and the wetter, higher **Ko'olau Range** in the east. In between lies the narrow, flat **Leilehua Plateau**, with the triple lagoon of **Pearl Harbor** at its southern end. The symmetrical outline of Oahu is only spoiled by the more recent eruptions that elongated its southeast coastline, producing craters such as **Punchbowl**, **Diamond Head** and **Koko Head**, and thrusting the island out towards Molokai and Maui. Geologists see the fact that volcanic activity was taking place on Oahu as little as ten thousand years ago as suggesting that further eruptions may still be possible.

Just across the Ko'olaus from Honolulu, the green cliffs of the **windward coast** are magnificent, lined with safe, secluded beaches and indented with remote time-forgotten valleys. Towns such as **Kailua**, **Kane'ohe** and **Lā'ie** may be far from exciting, but you're unlikely to tire of the sheer beauty of the shoreline drive – so long as you time your forays to miss the peak-hour traffic jams.

Mere mortals can only marvel at the winter waves that make the **North Shore** the world's premier **surfing** destination; for anyone other than experts, entering the water at that time is almost suicidal. However, **Waimea**, **Sunset** and **'Ehukai** beaches are compelling spectacles, little **Hale'iwa** makes a refreshing contrast to Waikīkī, and in summer you may manage to find a safe spot for a swim.

Although the **west** or **leeward** coast of Oahu also holds some fine beaches – including the prime surf spot of **Mākaha** – it remains very much off the beaten track. There's just one route in and out of this side of the island, and the locals are happy to keep it that way.

As you travel around, keep in mind that no one owns any stretch of beach in Hawaii. Every beach in the state – defined as the area below the vegetation line – is regarded as public property. That doesn't mean that you're entitled to stroll across any intervening land between the ocean and the nearest highway; always use the clearly signposted "public right of way" footpaths. Whatever impression the large oceanfront hotels may attempt to convey, they can't stop you using "their" beaches; they can only restrict, but not refuse to supply, parking places for non-guests.

Climate and when to go

Of all the major US cities, Honolulu is said to have both the lowest average maximum temperature and the highest minimum, at 85°F and 60°F respectively. Neither fluctuates more than a few degrees between summer and winter. Waikīkī remains a balmy tropical year-round resort, and the only seasonal variation likely to make much difference to travelers is the state of the **surf** on the North Shore. For surfers, the time to come is from October to April, when mighty winter waves scour the sand off many beaches and come curling in at heights of twenty feet or more. In summer, the surf-bums head off home, and some North Shore beaches are even safe for family swimming.

As for room rates, **peak season** in Waikīkī runs from December to March, and many mid-range hotels lower their prices by ten or twenty dollars at other times. Waikīkī is pretty crowded all year, though, and there are few savings to be made by coming in summer.

BASICS

Getting there from the US and Canada

Almost all flights to Hawaii from North America land at Honolulu Airport. Virtually every large US airline flies to the city, with United being the major player; in addition, the state's own Hawaiian Airlines runs services to and from the western states.

The **journey time** from LA or San Francisco to Honolulu is roughly five and a half hours.

Fares and cutting costs

There is no high or low season for flights to Hawaii, and fares remain relatively consistent year-round. However, at **peak periods** – June to August, and around Christmas, the New Year and Thanksgiving – services tend to be booked long in advance, and you might have to pay a slight premium. Flying on a weekday rather than a weekend saves anything from $50 to $200 on a round trip.

The simplest way to save money is to buy a **package** deal including both flight and accommodation. If you buy a flight only, through a **specialist flight agent**, aim to pay around $300 for a round-trip to Honolulu from the West Coast, more like $600 from New York.

AIRLINES AND FLIGHT AGENTS IN NORTH AMERICA

Airlines

Air Canada ✆1-800/776-3000; *www.aircanada.ca*
Aloha ✆1-800/367-5250; *www.alohaair.com/aloha-air*
American Airlines ✆1-800/433-7300; *www.americanair.com*
Canadian Airlines ✆1-800/665-1177 (Can), ✆1-800/426-7000 (US); *www.cdnair.ca*
Continental ✆1-800/231-0856; *www.flycontinental.com*
Delta ✆1-800/221-1212; *www.delta-air.com*
Hawaiian ✆1-800/367-5320; *www.hawaiianair.com*
Northwest ✆1-800/225-2525; *www.nwa.com*
TWA ✆1-800/221-2000; *www.twa.com*
United ✆1-800/241-6522; *www.ual.com*

Flight Agents

American Travel Association ✆1-800/243-2724
Cheap Tickets Inc ✆1-800/377-1000
Council Travel ✆1-800/226-8624; *www.ciee.org*
Educational Travel Center ✆1-800/747-5551; *www.edtrav.com*
Now Voyager ✆212/431-1616; *www.nowvoyagertravel.com*
Skylink ✆1-800/AIR-ONLY
STA Travel ✆1-800/777-0112 or 1-800/781-4040; *www.sta-travel.com*
Travel Avenue ✆1-800/333-3335; *www.travelavenue.com*
Travel Cuts Toronto ✆416/979-2406; *www.travelcuts.com*
Travel Information Center of Hawaii ✆1-800/266-3646
Worldtek Travel ✆1-800/243-1723

Flights from the West Coast

All the airlines quote round-trip fares **from the West Coast to Honolulu** at $300 to $500. **Los Angeles** is generally the cheapest departure point, and is served by six carriers: Hawaiian, United, American, Continental, Northwest and Delta.

Hawaiian Airlines flies from five mainland US cities to Honolulu. Daily flights leave from **San Francisco** at 8.40am, from **Seattle** at 8.50am, from **Los Angeles** at 8.55am, noon and 5.25pm, from **Las Vegas** at 9.10am (with an additional flight on Sunday at 2.50pm) and from **Portland** at 9.10am.

United flies to Honolulu from **San Francisco** at 9.15am, 11.40am 2.10pm and 7pm daily, and from **Los Angeles** at 8.30am, 11.30am, 2.25pm and 6pm.

Of the **other operators** who fly to Honolulu from the West Coast, Delta offers four daily flights from LA and one daily from San Francisco; both American and Continental have two daily flights from LA and one from San Francisco; and Northwest has two services from LA, two from Seattle and one from San Francisco.

Flights from the East Coast

There are no non-stop flights from the **East Coast** to Hawaii, so most visitors fly via California. American and United, however, fly direct to Honolulu **from Chicago**, as do American and Delta **from Dallas**, Northwest **from Detroit** and **Minneapolis**, Delta **from Atlanta**, and TWA **from St Louis**; all take 8–10 hours.

NORTH AMERICAN TOUR OPERATORS

American Airlines FlyAAway Vacations ✆1-800/321-2121
Continental Airlines Vacations ✆1-800/634-5555
Delta Vacations ✆1-800/654-6559; *www.deltavacations.com*.

Fun Sun Vacations, Toronto, ON ✆416/979-2359
Globus/Cosmos, Littleton, CO ✆303/797-2800 or
1-800/221-0090
Pacific Quest, Hale'iwa, HI 96712 ✆1-800/776-2518
Pleasant Hawaiian Holidays, Westlake Village, CA
✆1-800/242-9244; www.2hawaii.com
Questers Worldwide Nature Tours, New York, NY
✆212/251-0444 or 1-800/468-8668
Sierra Club, San Francisco, CA ✆415/977-5522
Sunscapes Travel, Inc, Bellevue, WA ✆425/643-1620 or
1-800/229-8376
Tauck Tours, Westport, CT ✆203/226-6911 or
1-800/468-2825
TWA Getaway Vacations ✆1-800/GETAWAY
United Vacations ✆1-800/328-6877
World of Vacations, Etobicoke, ON ✆416/620-8050

Flights from Canada

Getting to Honolulu from any **Canadian** city apart from
Vancouver will almost certainly require you to change
planes in the US. From **Toronto** United offers routings via
San Francisco for around CDN$1150, or from **Vancouver**
for CDN$600–750; better from Vancouver is Northwest,
with fares starting at CDN$580, via Seattle. Flying from
either **Toronto** or **Montréal**, you can go via Chicago or
Dallas with American (CDN$1250); via Detroit or
Minneapolis on Northwest (CDN$1150); or via Atlanta on
Delta (CDN$1250).

Air Canada flies daily to Honolulu from **Toronto**
(CDN$1100) via **Vancouver** (CDN$650). Canadian has
daily non-stop flights to Honolulu from **Vancouver**, with
fares around CDN$650, and flights three times weekly

(Tues, Wed & Fri) from **Toronto** starting around CDN$985. Through trips from **Montréal**, via Vancouver, start at around CDN$1020.

Canadians flying to Hawaii need passports, but not visas.

Insurance

Your existing insurance may offer full cover when you're away from home. Some homeowners' policies are valid on vacation, and credit cards such as American Express often include medical or other insurance, while most Canadians are covered for medical mishaps overseas by their health plans. Reasonably priced **travel insurance** policies are offered by Access America (✆1-800/284-8300); Carefree Travel Insurance (✆1-800/323-3149); Travel Guard (✆1-800/826-1300; *www.noelgroup.com*); and Travel Insurance Services (✆1-800/937-1387).

Getting there from Australia and New Zealand

There's no shortage of flights from Australia and New Zealand to **Honolulu**, and very little price difference between airlines. Both Qantas and Air New Zealand operate daily services, with journey times of around nine hours.

Fares vary seasonally by around AUS/NZ$200–300. **Low** season counts as mid-January through February, and all of October and November; **high** season runs from mid-May to August and December to mid-January; and **shoulder** season is the rest of the year.

From Australia, most flights to Honolulu are out of **Sydney**, **Brisbane** or **Melbourne**, with daily non-stop services on Qantas for around AUS$1450 in low season or AUS$1599 in high season. For a little less, Air New Zealand fly via Auckland, while Air Pacific can take you via a stopover in Fiji.

From New Zealand, the best deals to Honolulu are on Air New Zealand out of Auckland, costing from NZ$1499 in low season up to NZ$1799 in high season, whether you fly non-stop, or via Fiji, Tonga or Papeete. Air Pacific, via Fiji, and Qantas, via Sydney, both offer low season fares of NZ$1599.

AIRLINES AND AGENTS IN AUSTRALIA AND NEW ZEALAND

Airlines

Air New Zealand ✆13/2476 (Aus); ✆09/357 3000 (NZ)
Air Pacific ✆1-800/230 150 (Aus); ✆09/379 2404 (NZ)
Cathay Pacific ✆13/1747 (Aus); ✆09/379 0861 (NZ)
Qantas ✆13/1211 (Aus); ✆0-800/808 767 (NZ)
Singapore Airlines ✆13/1011 (Aus); ✆09/379 3209 (NZ)

Flight agents

Anywhere Travel, Sydney ✆02/9663 0411
Brisbane Discount Travel, Brisbane ✆07/3229 9211
Budget Travel, Auckland ✆09/366 0061
Destinations Unlimited, Auckland ✆09/373 4033
Flight Centre, Sydney ✆13/1600
Flight Centre, Auckland ✆09/309 0171
Northern Gateway, Darwin ✆08/8941 1394
STA Travel ✆1-300/300 900 (Aus); ✆00/366 6673 (NZ)

Specialist agents

Creative Tours, Sydney ✆02/386 2111
Hawaiian Island Golf Tours, Sydney ✆02/968 1778
Padi Travel Network, Sydney ✆02/9417 2800
Sydney International Travel Centre, Sydney ✆02/9299 8000
USA Travel, Adelaide ✆08/8272 2010

Entry requirements

Australian and New Zealand passport holders who stay less than ninety days in the US do not require visas, so long as they have an onward or return ticket. For longer stays, a US multiple-entry visa costs AUS\$26. You'll need an application form – available from the US visa information service (©1-902/262 682) – one signed passport photo and your passport. For details, contact the US Embassy (Aus: 21 Moonah Place, Canberra ©02/6214 5600; NZ: 29 Fitzherbert Terrace, Thorndon, Wellington).

Insurance

Companies worth trying for **travel insurance** are Cover More, Level 9, 32 Walker St, North Sydney (©1-800/251 881), and Ready Plan, 141 Walker St, Dandenong, Victoria (©1-800/337 462), or 10th Floor, 63 Albert St, Auckland (©09/379 3208). Adventure sports tend not to be included in general policies, so if you plan to go snorkeling or scuba diving without a licence, check with the company first and, if necessary, get extra cover.

Getting there from Britain and Ireland

Much the quickest and cheapest route from the UK to Hawaii is to fly via the mainland United States or Canada, so your options are more or less the same as they are for North Americans.

With a ten-hour flight across the Atlantic to the West Coast, and a five-hour flight over the Pacific, that makes for a very long journey. If you fly straight to the West Coast, however, it's just possible to get to Honolulu on the same day you set off (thanks to the ten- or eleven-hour time difference; see p.221).

Three airlines fly non-stop **from London** to the US West Coast and on to Honolulu: United via Los Angeles and San Francisco, and American and Air New Zealand via Los Angeles only. It's also possible to fly to LA with Virgin and then pick up a flight to Honolulu on Delta, or to fly to LA or San Francisco with either Virgin or British Airways, and connect with flights on to Honolulu on Hawaiian Airlines. Northwest can get you to Honolulu via Amsterdam and LA.

Delta is the only American airline to fly **from Ireland** direct to the US, with daily services to Atlanta from Dublin and Shannon; there's a daily non-stop flight on to Honolulu from Atlanta, but you can't connect with it the same day as you fly from Ireland.

As for **fares**, a typical round-trip ticket from London to Honolulu costs around £450 from January to March (peak season in Hawaii), up to more like £750 in July and August.

FLIGHT AGENTS AND AIRLINES

Agents

Bridge The World ©0171/916 0990
Campus Travel ©0171/730 2101
Council Travel ©0171/437 7767
STA Travel ©0171/361 6262
Trailfinders ©0171/938 3366
Travel Bug ©0161/721 4000
USIT ©01/679 8833 (Dublin); ©01232/324073 (028/9032 4073 from April 22, 2000) (Belfast)

Airlines

Air Canada ©0181/897 1331; ©061/471244 (Shannon)
Air New Zealand ©0181/741 2299
American Airlines ©0345/789789
British Airways ©0345/222111; ©1800/626747 (Dublin)
Continental ©0800/776464
Delta ©0800/414767; ©01/678 8080 (Dublin)
Hawaiian Airlines ©01753/664406
Northwest ©01293/561000
United Airlines ©0845/844 4777
Virgin Atlantic ©01293/747747

Entry requirements

Passport-holders from **Britain**, **Ireland** and most European countries do not require visas for trips to the United States of less than ninety days. Instead you simply fill in the **visa**

waiver form handed out on incoming planes. Immigration control takes place at your point of arrival on US soil, which, if you're flying from Britain, will not be in Hawaii. For further details, contact the **US embassy** in Britain (5 Upper Grosvenor St, London W1A 1AE; ℡0171/499 9000; visa hotline ℡0891/200290) or Ireland (42 Elgin Rd, Ballsbridge, Dublin; ℡01/472 2068).

There is no British or Irish **consulate** in Hawaii.

TOUR OPERATORS IN BRITAIN AND IRELAND

American Holidays ℡01/679 8800
Destination Pacific ℡0171/253 2000
The Hawaiian Dream ℡0181/470 1181
Hawaiian Travel Centre ℡0171/304 5730
Page & Moy ℡0116/250 7000
United Vacations ℡0181/750 9648

Insurance

Travel insurance, including medical cover, is essential in view of the high costs of health care in the US. Both STA and Campus Travel offer reasonable policies, as do Columbus Travel Insurance (℡0171/375 0011) and Endsleigh Insurance (℡0171/436 4451).

Arriving in Honolulu

The runways of Honolulu's **International Airport**, roughly five miles west of the downtown area, extend out to sea on a coral reef. The main Overseas Terminal is connected to the Inter-Island and Commuter terminals by the free Wikiwiki shuttle service. All the terminals are located on a loop road, which is constantly circled by a wide array of hotel and rental-car pick-up vans, taxis and minibuses.

Virtually every arriving tourist heads straight to Waikīkī; if you don't have a **hotel reservation** use the courtesy phones in the baggage claim area, where you'll also find boards advertising room rates. Several competing **shuttle buses**, such as the ABC Shuttle Service (©988-9293), pick up regularly outside the terminals, and will carry passengers to any Waikīkī hotel ($7 one-way, $12 round-trip). A **taxi** will cost around $20, and a stretch limo as little as $25.

In addition, **TheBus** #19 and #20 run to Waikīkī from the airport, leaving from outside the departure lounge of the Overseas Terminal. The ride costs $1 one-way, but you have to be traveling light: TheBus won't carry large bags, cases or backpacks. There are **lockers** at the airport for large items.

The nine-mile – not at all scenic – **drive** from the airport to Waikīkī can take anything from 25 to 75 minutes; the quickest route is to follow H-1 as far as possible, running inland of downtown Honolulu, and then take the Waikīkī exit.

Transport and tours

Although Oahu boasts "TheBus," an exemplary and very comprehensive bus service, it's much easier to explore the island at your own pace with a **rental car**. However, with limited parking and heavy traffic, a car is a liability in Waikīkī itself, so think carefully before renting one for your entire stay.

TheBus

A network of over sixty **bus** routes, officially named **TheBus** and radiating out from downtown Honolulu and the Ala Moana Shopping Center, covers the whole of Oahu (call ℂ848-5555 for route information). All journeys cost $1 (ages 6 19 50¢), with free transfers to any connecting route if you ask as you board. One of the best sightseeing routes is TheBus #52 or #55, which circles the whole of the Ko'olau Range, including the North Shore and the Windward Coast, for just $1. The only disadvantage is that passengers are not allowed to carry large bags or bulky items, which rules out using TheBus to get to or from the airport.

The **Oahu Discovery Passport**, available from ABC stores in Waikīkī (and deliberately under-publicized, following complaints from commercial tour operators), offers four days' unlimited travel on TheBus for $10, while **monthly passes**, obtainable at 7–11 and Foodland stores, cost $25.

THE BUS ROUTES

The following is a selection of TheBus routes most useful for tourists. For a complete list, pick up brochures from the satellite city hall at the Ala Moana Center, or call TheBus information line (daily 5.30am–10pm; ©848-5555), which can tell you not only which bus to take but when the next one will arrive.

#2 Waikīkī to downtown Honolulu and Bishop Museum.
#8 Waikīkī to Ala Moana.
#19 Waikīkī to Honolulu Airport via downtown.
#20 Waikīkī to Pearl Harbor via downtown and Honolulu Airport.
#22 Waikīkī to Hanauma Bay and Sea Life Park.
#51 Ala Moana to Mākaha and Leeward Coast.
#52 "Circle Isle" clockwise; Ala Moana to Hale'iwa and the North Shore.
#55 "Circle Isle" counterclockwise; Ala Moana to Kāne'ohe and the Windward Shore.
#58 Ala Moana to Waikīkī and Sea Life Park.

Other bus companies

Rival companies operate a number of alternative bus services from Waikīkī. The open-sided and overpriced **Waikīkī Trolley** tours a circuit of Honolulu's main attractions – 'Iolani Palace, the Bishop Museum, Ala Moana, and so on – at half-hourly intervals, with the first departure from Waikīkī's Royal Hawaiian Shopping Center at 8am daily, and the last at 4.30pm. You can get on and off as often as you choose for a daily rate of $18, under-12s pay $8; better-value five-day passes cost $30, $10 for under-12s.

The similar **Aloha Tower Trolley** offers a loop trip between the main Waikīkī hotels and Honolulu's Aloha

Tower Marketplace, passing by way of the Bishop Museum, Hilo Hattie's and Chinatown, every fifteen minutes between 8.30am and 11pm daily ($1 one-way).

Car rental

All the major **car rental** chains have outlets at the airport, and many have offices in Waikīkī as well. Reservations can be made using the national toll-free numbers listed below, but check first to see if you can get a better room-and-car deal through your hotel. With so much competition, it's hard to quote specific prices, but a target rate for the cheapest economy car with unlimited mileage should be around $33 per day or $170 per week. No companies rent cars to anyone under 21.

While renting a car enables you to explore Oahu in much greater depth than would otherwise be possible, **driving** in Honolulu itself is not a pleasant experience. The **traffic** on major roads, such as H-1 along the northern flanks of the city, and Likelike Highway and the Pali Highway

CAR RENTAL CHAINS

Alamo ✆1-800/327-9633 (US, Can & HI); 0800/272200 (UK)

Avis ✆1-800/331-1212 (US & Can); 1-800/831-8000 (HI); 0181/848 8733 (UK); 1-800/225 533 (Aus); 09/526 2847 (NZ)

Budget ✆1-800/527-0700 (US, Can & HI); 0800/181181 (UK); 1-300/362 848 (Aus); 09/375 2222 (NZ)

Dollar ✆1-800/800-4000 (US & Can); 1-800/367-7006 (HI); 01895/233300 (UK)

Hertz ✆1-800/654-3011 (US, Can & HI); 0181/679 1799 (UK); 13/3039 (Aus); 09/309 0989 (NZ)

National ✆1-800/227-7368 (US, Can & HI); 01345/225525 (UK)

across the mountains, can be horrendous, and **parking** is always a problem. Waikīkī hotels charge guests around $6–10 per night to **park**. There are meters on the back streets of Waikīkī, near the Ala Wai Canal; and downtown, the largest metered parking lot is on the edge of Chinatown at Smith and Beretania streets.

Bike and scooter rental

Lots of Waikīkī-based companies – such as Aloha Funway (☎942-9696), which has seven locations; Island Scooters (☎924-6743), which has six; and Adventure Rentals, adjoining the *Island Hostel* at 1946 Ala Moana Blvd (☎944-3131) – rent out **scooters** and **bicycles**, with typical rates for both of $15 per day (8am–6pm) or $20 for 24 hours.

Taxis and limousines

Honolulu **taxi** firms include Charley's (☎531-1333), Sida's (☎836-0011) and The Cab (☎422-2222). Alternatively, you could rent a **limousine** with tinted windows – for $42.50 per hour, or $26.50 for a one-way airport ride – from Continental (☎226-4466). Handi-Cabs of the Pacific (☎524-3866) provides transportation for **disabled visitors**.

Bus tours

Countless operators in Waikīkī, such as Polynesian Adventure Tours (☎833-3000), Ē Noa Tours (☎591-2561), and Roberts (☎539-9400), advertise **bus tours** of Honolulu and Oahu. The standard choice is between a half-day **city tour**, including Pearl Harbor, for around $12–20, and a full-day **island tour** starting at $22 (not including Waimea Falls Park; see p.120), or up to $55 including the park and a picnic. Most companies also offer tours to other attractions on Oahu, such as the Polynesian Cultural Center and Sea Life Park. Low-priced **ticket agencies** include Magnum Tickets & Tours, 2134 Kalākaua Ave (℃923-7825) and Aloha Express, at the *Waikīkī Circle Hotel*, 2464 Kalākaua Ave (℃924-4030).

Each weekend, Hawaii Ghost Tours runs two three-hour narrated bus tours of "haunted" Oahu, aimed primarily at tourists on Friday night and locals on Saturday (reservations essential; ℃596-2052).

Walking tours

Both Waikīkī and downtown Honolulu are compact enough to explore on foot on your own, but you can get a great sense of their histories and hidden byways by joining an expert-led **walking tour**.

Honolulu Time Walks runs a regular program of entertaining and informative tours, on topics such as Haunted Honolulu, Old Waikīkī, Mark Twain's Honolulu, and Scandals and Sinners ($7–8; ℃943-0371). Note that all *Sheraton* hotel guests can join a free Time Walks tour of Waikīkī each Wednesday at 9am.

Similar tours are also conducted by Kapi'olani Community College, with specialities including Hawaiian royalty, plantation life, and the history of Chinatown ($5–10; reserve at ℃734-9245). Other Chinatown tours are arranged by the Chinese Chamber of Commerce (Tues 9.30am; $5; ℃533-3831), and the Hawaii Heritage Center (Fri 9.30am; $4; ℃521-2749).

The American Legion organizes one-hour walking tours of the National Cemetery of the Pacific in Punchbowl Crater (adults $15, under-10s free; includes Waikīkī hotel pickup; ℃946-6383).

HIKING

Descriptions of Oahu's most enjoyable **hiking trails** can be found on the following pages:

Diamond Head p.44	Maunalaha Trail p.71
Hau'ula p.108	Pauoa Flats Trail p.72
Kahana Valley p.106	Pu'u 'Ōhi'a Trail p.72
Makiki Valley Trail p.70	Sacred Falls p.108
Mānoa Falls p.75	

For more energetic **hiking**, the Hawaii chapter of the Sierra Club sponsors treks and similar activities on weekends (℃538-6616), while the Hawaii Nature Center arranges hikes most weekends (see p.70; ℃955-0100). Oahu Nature Tours (℃924-2473 or 1-800/861-6018) runs hiking and birdwatching excursions ranging from a sunrise walk up Diamond Head (daily 6.30–8am; $20) to a four-hour hike in the Ko'olau rainforest (daily 2–6 pm; $37). Likehike (℃455-8193) is a gay **hiking** club that runs group hikes on alternate Sundays.

On Saturdays, the Clean Air Team (℃948-3299) runs a free **Diamond Head walk**, meeting at 9am in front of the Honolulu Zoo.

Flight-seeing tours

Finally, if you want to see Oahu from the **air**, take a **helicopter tour** from Honolulu Airport with either Papillon (℃836-1566 or 1-800/367-7095) or Makani Kai (℃834-5813). Both charge around $80 per person for twenty minutes over Waikīkī, and up to $200 for an hour-long island tour. Another option is a **glider** flight from Dillingham Airfield on the North Shore with Soar Hawaii ($60–150; ℃637-3147).

Information and maps

Vast quantities of written information are available about Hawaii. Tourism is big business, and plenty of people and organizations are eager to tell you what's on offer.

For information **by mail** before you arrive, contact the head office of the **Hawaii Visitors Bureau (HVB)**, #801, Waikīkī Business Plaza, 2270 Kalākaua Ave, Honolulu, HI 96815 (©923 1811, fax 924-0290). The HVB also runs a **visitor center** (Mon–Fri 8am–5pm) in Waikīkī, on the fourth floor of the Royal Hawaiian Shopping Center, on Lewers Street end of Kalākaua Avenue. However, you're unlikely to need to visit it: free listings magazines and leaflets are everywhere you turn, including the Arrivals hall at the airport, and all the hotels have information desks.

An ever-increasing amount of information is also available on the **Internet** and World Wide Web. The official HVB site, *www.gohawaii.com*, has links to dozens of accommodation options, activity operators, and the like. The best site for current news and listings is run by the *Honolulu Star Bulletin* newspaper, at *www.starbulletin.com*.

Maps

Much the best **map** of Oahu is published by the University of Hawaii for $3.95. Decent free maps also abound – you'll get a map booklet with your rental car, for example. These can be useful for pinpointing specific hotels and restaurants, but only the University of Hawaii map is at all reliable for minor roads.

Hawaii Visitors Bureaus overseas

Australia
℅02/9955 2619,
fax 9955 2171

Canada
℅604/669-6691,
fax 669-6075

New Zealand
℅09/379 3708,
fax 309 0725

United Kingdom
℅0181/941-4009,
fax 941-4011

For extreme detail, TMK Maps publishes a full-color gazetteer of street maps that covers Honolulu and all of Oahu, available in all the city's major bookstores for $9.95.

Costs, money and banks

Although it's possible to have an inexpensive vacation in Honolulu, prices in Hawaii are consistently higher than in the rest of the US. With 85 percent of the state's food and 92 percent of its fuel having to be shipped in, the cost of living is around forty percent above the US average.

How much you spend per day is, of course, up to you, but it's hard to get any sort of breakfast for under $6, a cheap lunch easily comes to $10, and an evening meal in a restaurant, with drinks, is likely to be $25–30. Even the cheapest hotel is likely to charge well over $60 for a double room, and a rental car with gas won't cost less than $25 per day. It's easy to spend $75 per person per day before you do anything; pay for a snorkel cruise, let alone a helicopter ride, and you've cleared $100.

The state **sales tax** of 4.17 percent on all transactions is almost never included in the prices displayed. Hotels impose an additional six percent tax, making a total of more than ten percent on accommodation bills.

Money and banks

US dollar **travelers' checks** are the best way to carry significant quantities of money, for both American and foreign visitors, as they offer the security of knowing that lost or stolen checks will be replaced. Foreign currency, whether cash or travelers' checks, can be hard to exchange, so foreign travelers should change their money into dollars at home.

For many services, it's taken for granted that you'll be paying with a **credit card**. Hotels and car rental companies routinely require an imprint whether or not you intend to use it to pay. The two major **banks** are the Bank of Hawaii, which belongs to the Plus network of **ATM machines**, and the First Hawaiian Bank, which belongs to both Plus and Cirrus. The main Bank of Hawaii branch in Waikīkī is at 2220 Kalākaua Ave, while the First Hawaiian Bank is nearby at 2181 Kalākaua Ave.

Telephones

Telephone connections on and between the Hawaiian Islands and to the rest of the US are generally efficient and reliable. The **area code** for the entire state of Hawaii is ✆808. Calls from anywhere on Oahu to anywhere else on the island count as local; you don't need to dial the area code and it costs a flat-rate 25¢ on payphones. Calling any of the other islands, you have to prefix ✆1-808 before the number. For **directory assistance** for any Oahu number, call ✆1-411; for the rest of Hawaii call ✆1-808/555 1212.

Hotels impose huge surcharges, so it's best to use a **phone card** for long-distance calls. All the US phone companies issue cards; other possibilities include Global Link prepaid phone cards, sold in Global Link stores in the US (call ✆1-800/864-3311 to find the nearest outlet), the UK's Swiftcall service (✆0171/488 2001), Telstra (✆1-800/626 008) in Australia, or NZ Telecom (✆04/382 5818) in New Zealand.

To make an international call to Hawaii, dial your country's international access code, then 1 for the US, then 808 for Hawaii. To place an international call from Hawaii, dial 011 then the relevant country code (Britain is 44, Ireland is 353, Canada is 1, Australia is 61 and New Zealand is 64).

TELEPHONES |

Mail services

Mail services from Hawaii can be slow; allow a week for anywhere in the US, two weeks or more for the rest of the world.

Honolulu's main **post office**, 3600 Aolele St, Honolulu, HI 96820 (Mon–Fri 7.30am–8.30pm, Sat 8am–2.30pm;), at the airport, is the only one that accepts **general delivery** (poste restante) mail. There are other post offices at 330 Saratoga Rd in Waikīkī (Mon, Tues, Thurs & Fri 8am–4.30pm, Wed 8am–6pm, Sat 9am–noon); at the Ala Moana shopping mall (Mon–Fri 8.30am–5pm, Sat 8.30am–4.15pm); and downtown in the Old Federal Building at 335 Merchant St (Mon, Tues, Thurs & Fri 8am–4.30pm, Wed 8am–6pm). Call ✆423-3990 for all information concerning post offices and mail service on Oahu.

THE GUIDE

Waikīkī

On any one day, half of all the tourists in the state of Hawaii are crammed into the tiny, surreal enclave of **WAIKĪKĪ**, three miles east of downtown Honolulu. Effectively, it's an island in its own right, a two-mile-long, quarter-mile-wide strip sealed off from the rest of the city by the Ala Wai Canal and almost completely surrounded by water. Its incredible profusion of skyscrapers, jostling for position along the shoreline, hold enough hotel rooms to accommodate over 100,000 guests. There are also hundreds of restaurants, and stores providing anything the visitor could possibly want.

Long before Kamehameha the Great built a thatched hut here at the start of the nineteenth century, Waikīkī – the name means "spouting water" – was a favored residence of the chiefs of Oahu. They coveted not only its waterfront coconut groves and well-stocked fishponds, but also the mosquito-free swamps and wetlands that lay immediately behind them. Such land was then a rare and valuable resource, being ideal for growing *taro*, which is cultivated like rice in semi-submerged fields, and whose roots are pounded to create the Hawaiian staple food, *poi*. By the end of the century, however, with Hawaii annexed by the United States, the wetlands were considered all but useless. Waikīkī's value lay instead in its being the best beach within easy reach of Honolulu. When the *Moana* hotel went up in 1901, signalling the start of the tourist boom, a handful of inns were already dotted among the luxurious homes of elite missionary and merchant families.

Waikīkī, however, only began to regain a significant population during the 1920s, when a vast program of land reclamation was instigated. The Ala Wai Canal was dug to divert the mountain streams, and the central area was filled in with chunks of coral sawed from the reef that then ran the full length of the shoreline. Since then, Waikīkī has mushroomed beyond belief. By looking beyond the towering blocks to Diamond Head or the mysterious valleys that recede into the mountains, it's easy to remember that this is a Pacific island. But in Waikīkī itself, there's precious little left of the real Hawaii.

As long as you're prepared to enter into a spirit of rampant commercialism, you'll have a great time in Waikīkī. You could survive with little money by buying snacks from the omnipresent ABC convenience stores, but if saving money is your main priority there's no point staying long in Waikīkī – there's very little to see, and the only alternative to swimming and sunbathing is to shop until you drop.

WAIKĪKĪ BEACH

Viewed objectively, **Waikīkī Beach** would rank pretty low on a list of Hawaii's best beaches. Elsewhere on Oahu, it's not hard to find a stretch of deserted, palm-fringed, tropical shoreline – a tranquil contrast to Waikīkī, where you can hardly see the sand for the sunbathers, and the traffic on Kalākaua Avenue outroars the surf. Somehow, however, the ruckus barely seems to matter. Waikīkī Beach may be crowded, but it's crowded with enthusiastic holiday-makers, wringing every last ounce of pleasure from being on one of the world's most famous beaches.

Glance at the ocean, and you'll be caught up in the ever-changing action. At the water's edge, families splash about while oblivious honeymoon couples gaze hand-in-hand at the horizon; beyond them, circling surfers await the next wave; and, out in the deep-water channel, cruise liners, merchant ships and aircraft carriers make their stately way towards the docks of Honolulu and Pearl Harbor.

Meanwhile, the beach itself plays host to a constant parade of characters: undiscovered starlets parade about in the latest swimsuits; overexcited children dart between seniors lounging on fancy deckchairs; and determined European backpackers doggedly search for the perfect plot of sand.

Waikīkī's natural setting is just as beguiling as its melee of activity. Off to the east, the sharp profile of Diamond Head spears the ocean, while straight back inland the lush green Koʻolau Mountains soar between the skyscrapers. In the early evening especially, as the sun sinks far out to sea and the silhouettes of the palm trees grow ever starker, the overall effect is magical.

Few visitors, however, realize that Waikīkī Beach is almost entirely **artificial**. The landscaping that created Waikīkī changed the ocean currents so that its natural beaches were swept away; ever since, the hotels have had a considerable stake in importing sand. So much was shipped in – much of it from Pāpōhaku Beach on Molokai – that the contours of the sea bottom have been permanently altered. As a result, the **surfing** conditions at what is generally acknowledged to be the birthplace of the sport are no longer all that spectacular – which is why the experts head straight up to Oahu's North Shore, covered on p.117.

Public access is guaranteed on every single beach in Hawaii; whatever it may look like, no hotel ever owns the beach adjacent to it.

Central Waikīkī Beach

Although Waikīkī Beach officially stretches the full length of the Waikīkī shoreline, from the Ala Wai Harbor in the west to within a couple of hundred yards of Diamond Head, each of its many distinct sections has its own name. The **center** of the beach – the segment that everyone still calls Waikīkī Beach – is the point near Duke Kahanamoku's statue (see p.38), where the buildings on the ocean side of Kalākaua Avenue come to a halt and the sidewalk turns into a beachfront promenade. Swimmers here enjoy the best conditions of the entire seafront, with softly shelving sands, and waters that are generally calm.

....

Surfboards can be rented at several beach stands in central Waikīkī, for $8–10 an hour (no deposit required), or up to $25 including instruction.

....

Royal-Moana Beach

To the **west**, central Waikīkī Beach merges with **Royal-Moana Beach**, which fronts the *Royal Hawaiian* and *Sheraton Moana* hotels. It can sometimes be a struggle to walk along this narrow, busy strip because of the crowds, but the swimming is, again, excellent. It's also the best spot for **novice surfers**: head slightly to the right as you enter the water to reach the easy break known as Canoes' Surf (so called because these gentle waves were all the heavy old *koa* canoes could ride). The waves are slightly stronger further left, at the Queen's Surf break.

....

Giving directions, Honolulu residents often say "'Ewa" rather than "west;" 'Ewa is a small town west of Pearl Harbor.

....

Halekūlani (Gray's) Beach

A raised walkway in front of the *Halekūlani Hotel*, where the sea comes right over the sand, leads west from Royal-Moana Beach into another small section known as **Halekūlani Beach**, or, in memory of the small inn that previously stood here, **Gray's Beach**. There's still plenty of sand on the seabed, so the swimming is fine. Inconspicuous footpaths squeeze through to the beach from Kalia Road on either side of the *Halekūlani*.

Fort DeRussy and Kahanamoku beaches

Beyond Gray's Beach, the wide swathe of sand fringing the military base constitutes **Fort DeRussy Beach**. It's a bit of an effort to plod along here, and the ocean floor at this point is sharp and rocky. With few swimmers around, the beach is used mainly by windsurfers. The westernmost section of the Waikīkī shorefront, **Kahanamoku Beach**, flanks the *Hilton Hawaiian Village* (reviewed on p.147). Thanks to its carefully sculpted shelf of sand it's ideal for family bathing, but lacks the glamor or excitement of central Waikīkī.

Kūhiō Beach

Large segments of the long beach that runs **east** of central Waikīkī did not even exist until well after World War II. Until 1922, the shoreline at what's now broad **Kūhiō Beach** was dominated by the oceanfront home of Prince Kūhiō (see p.37). When he donated the land to the city after his death, it held only sporadic patches of sand, and several structures stood *makai* (on the ocean side) of Kalākaua Avenue as recently as 1970.

Now, however, Kūhiō Beach is one of Waikīkī's busiest areas. On the whole, inshore swimming is safe and comfortable, though there's a danger of blundering into deep spots where the former river bed has been exposed by underwater drifts. Both the **Kapahulu Groin**, which extends the line of Kapahulu Avenue out into the ocean, and the long **Slippery Wall**, parallel to the beach roughly fifty yards out, help to keep the sand in and the sea calm, thereby creating a sheltered inshore bathing area. However, the tops of these semi-submerged features are slippery with seaweed, and the water to either side is shallow, so diving off is not recommended. Daredevil locals boogie-board just outside the wall, but don't be tempted to join them unless you really know what you're doing.

Kapi'olani Park Beach

East of the Kapahulu Groin, at the end of the built-up section of Waikīkī, comes a gap in the beach where the sand all but disappears and the waters are not suitable for bathing. Beyond that, to either side of the Waikīkī Aquarium (described on p.42), **Kapi'olani Park Beach** is the favorite beach of many local families and fitness freaks, and is also known for having a strong gay presence. Its lawns offer plenty of free shade, and make a perfect picnic spot. Waikīkī's only substantial stretch of reasonably unspoiled coral reef runs a short distance offshore, shielding a pleasant, gentle swimming area. The most used segment, nearest to Waikīkī, is **Queen's Surf Beach Park**.

Not far past the Aquarium stands the solemn concrete facade of the decaying **War Memorial Natatorium**. This curious combination of World War I memorial and swimming pool, with seating for 2500 spectators, was opened with a 100-metre swim by Duke Kahanamoku (see p.38) on August 24, 1927 – his 37th birthday. During its inaugural championships, Johnny "Tarzan" Weissmuller set world records over 100, 400 and 800 metres.

Ironically, the Natatorium has never recovered from being taken over for training purposes by the US Navy during World War II, and is now in a sorry state. Plans to restore it have caused much concern in recent years, with opponents arguing that the last thing this relatively quiet section of Waikīkī needs is a major tourist attraction. As it is, you may be able to wander in, but don't try to use it.

Sans Souci Beach

East of the Natatorium, palm-fringed **Sans Souci Beach** commemorates one of Waikīkī's earliest guesthouses, built in 1884 and twice stayed in by Robert Louis Stevenson. As well as being sheltered enough for young children, the beach also offers decent snorkeling, unusual for Waikīkī, where most of the reef has been suffocated by dumped sand.

The *New Otani Kaimana Beach* hotel (see p.144), now occupying the site of the Sans Souci, marks the return of buildings to the shoreline, and is as far as most visitors would consider strolling along Waikīkī Beach. However, beyond it lies the **Outrigger Canoe Club Beach**, which was leased in 1908 by the Outrigger Canoe Club on the condition that its waters be set aside for surfing, canoeing and ocean sports. The club headquarters were later replaced by the first of the *Outrigger* chain of hotels, but the ocean remains the preserve of surfers and snorkelers.

Kaluahole Beach

As Kalākaua Avenue heads out of Waikīkī beyond the Outrigger Canoe Club Beach, curving away from the shoreline to join Diamond Head Road and skirt the base of the volcano, it passes a little scrap of sandy beach known as **Kaluahole Beach** or **Diamond Head Beach**. Though too small for anyone to want to spend much time on the beach itself, it does offer some quite good swimming, and makes a good launching-point for windsurfers.

Diamond Head Beach Park

The coast immediately to the east of Kaluahole Beach, officially **Diamond Head Beach Park**, is much too rocky and exposed for ordinary swimmers. It is, however, noteworthy as the site of the 55-foot **Diamond Head Lighthouse**, built in 1899 and still in use. The area also has a reputation as a nudist hangout, especially popular with gay men. A short distance further on, the highway, by now raised well above sea level, rounds the point of Diamond Head; the island of Molokai to the east is visible across the water on clear days. As a rule, only keen surfers pick their way down to the shoreline from the three roadside lookouts that constitute **Kuilei Cliffs Beach Park**.

Kaʻalāwai Beach

Opposite the intersection where Diamond Head Road loops back inland and Kāhala Avenue continues beside the ocean, **Kaʻalāwai Beach**, at the end of short Kulumanu Place, is a narrow patch of white sand popular with snorkelers and surfers. It is brought to a halt by Black Point, where lava flowing from Diamond Head into the sea created Oahu's southernmost point.

WAIKĪKĪ ON FOOT

Most of the **walking** you do in Waikīkī is likely to be by necessity rather than choice; it's not an exciting place to explore on foot, and offers little in the way of conventional sightseeing. Its roads may once have been picturesque lanes that meandered between the coconut groves and *taro* fields,

Street names of Waikīkī

Waikīkī's unfamiliar street names may seem easier to remember if you know the stories that lie behind them:

Helumoa Road: Literally "chicken scratch", it crosses the site of a *heiau* used for human sacrifices, where chickens scratched for maggots amid the corpses.

Ka'iulani Avenue: The young Princess Victoria Ka'iulani (1875–99) was immortalized in a poem by Robert Louis Stevenson.

Kālaimoku Street: Kamehameha the Great's Prime Minister, Kālaimoku, who died in 1827, also styled himself "William Pitt" in honor of his British equivalent.

Kalākaua Avenue: Originally named Waikīkī Road, and renamed in honor of David Kalākaua, the "Merrie Monarch" (1836–91; see p.233), in 1905.

Kālia Road: Kālia was a fishing village that stood between Waikīkī and what's now downtown Honolulu.

Kūhiō Avenue: Prince Jonah Kūhiō Kalaniana'ole (1871–1922), or "Prince Cupid", bequeathed much of the eastern end of Waikīkī to the city after his death.

Lili'uokalani Avenue: Queen Lili'uokalani was the last monarch to rule over Hawaii (1838–1917; see p.233).

Nāhua Street: Chiefess Nāhua once owned an oceanfront estate in Waikīkī.

'Olohana Street: The captured English sailor, John Young (1745–1835; see p.81), was known as 'Olohana to the Hawaiians after his naval cry of "All hands on deck".

Tusitala Street: Named after author Robert Louis Stevenson, whose Hawaiian name was taken from the Samoan word for "storyteller."

Uluniu Avenue: Literally "coconut grove", it marks the site of a cottage owned by King David Kalākaua.

but they're now lined by dull concrete malls and hotels, and a building erected before 1970 is a rare sight. In addition, the daytime **heat** can make walking more than a few blocks uncomfortable.

However, vestiges of the old Waikīkī are still scattered here and there, together with a couple of museums of Hawaiian history, and the lawns of Kapi'olani Park to the east make a welcome break from the bustle of the resort area.

West from the Duke Kahanamoku statue

The logical place to start a walking tour of Waikīkī is right in the middle, on seafront **Kalākaua Avenue**. The central stretch of Waikīkī Beach here is marked by a statue of **Duke Kahanamoku** (1890–1968), which is always wreathed in *leis*. The archetypal "Beach Boy", Duke represented the US in three Olympics, winning swimming golds in both 1912 and 1920. His subsequent exposition tours popularized the Hawaiian art of surfing all over the world, and as Sheriff of Honolulu he continued to welcome celebrity visitors to Hawaii until his death in 1969. He owed his unusual Christian name to his father, who was also called "Duke" because he had been born on the day that Queen Victoria's second son, the Duke of Edinburgh, visited Honolulu in 1869.

Slightly west of the statue, alongside a small police station, in a railed but otherwise unmarked enclosure, stand four large boulders known as the **sacred stones of Ulukou**. These are said to embody the healing and spiritual powers of four magician-priests from Tahiti, who set them in place before returning to their homeland in the fourteenth century.

Still further west, the wedge of the **Sheraton Moana Surfrider** forces Kalākaua Avenue away from the ocean. Though not Waikīkī's first hotel, the *Moana* is the oldest left standing, and since 1983 it has been transformed back to a close approximation of its original 1901 appearance. Like all Waikīkī hotels, the *Moana* is happy to allow non-guests in for a peek; the luxurious settees of its long Beaux Arts lobby make an ideal spot to catch up with the newspapers.

Follow Kalākaua Avenue west from here, and you'll come to the **Royal Hawaiian Shopping Center**, Waikīkī's most upmarket mall (though not a patch on Honolulu's Ala Moana Center; see p.201), and across from that the tackier open-air **International Marketplace**, which has a bargain food court (see p.161). Once the site of an ancient *heiau*, and later of the ten-thousand-strong royal Helumoa coconut grove – of which a few palms still survive – the beachfront here is today dominated by the **Royal Hawaiian Hotel**, also known as the "Pink Palace". Its Spanish-Moorish architecture was all the rage when it opened in 1927, with a room rate of $14 per night, but its grandeur is now somewhat swamped by a towering new wing.

Fort DeRussy and the US Army Museum

Map 3, A7. US Army Museum Tues–Sun 10am–4.30pm; free.
On the map, the military base of **Fort DeRussy** looks like a welcome expanse of green at the western edge of the main built-up area of Waikīkī. In fact, it's largely taken up by parking lots and tennis courts, and is not a place to stroll for pleasure. At its oceanfront side, however, the **US Army Museum** is located in a low concrete structure which, as **Battery Randolph**, housed massive artillery pieces that were directed by observers stationed atop Diamond Head during World War II. Displays here trace the history of warfare in Hawaii back to the time of Kamehameha the Great, with the bulk of the collection consisting of the various guns and cannons that have been used to defend Honolulu since the US Army first arrived, four days after annexation in 1898. One photo shows a young, giggling Shirley Temple perched astride a gun barrel during the 1930s, but the mood

swiftly changes with a detailed chronicling of the pivotal role played by the state during the Pacific campaign against Japan.

East from the Duke Kahanamoku statue

Heading **east** from the Duke Kahanamoku statue, you come first to the *Hyatt Regency Waikīkī* hotel, whose central atrium holds a vast waterfall surrounded by palm trees. A couple of blocks along, the gimmick at the *Pacific Beach Hotel* is its Oceanarium, a multi-story fish tank that reaches from the lobby up through the upstairs restaurants (see p.165).

The Damien Museum

Map 3, I6. 130 Ohua Ave; Mon–Fri 9am–3pm; free; ©923-2690.

Father Damien, the nineteenth-century Belgian priest who ranks with Hawaii's greatest heroes, is commemorated in the simple **Damien Museum**, one block east of the *Pacific Beach Hotel*. This unobtrusive shrine sits beneath a schoolroom behind the angular modern Catholic church of **St Augustine**.

Although he established churches all over Hawaii, Damien's fame derives principally from his final sojourn in the leper colony at **Kalaupapa** on the island of Molokai. When he arrived there in 1873, Kalaupapa was by all accounts a place of misery and despair. For eight years, real or suspected sufferers of what's now known as Hansen's Disease had been shipped there against their will, and abandoned to fend for themselves. Damien gave them their first medical and pastoral care, irrespective of religious background, but eventually succumbed to the disease himself on April 15, 1889, at the age of 49. The museum evokes his life and work with an assortment of mundane trivia, such as receipts for cases of soda and barrels of flour, and his prayerbooks and vestments. Its most powerful punch is saved until last: a series of harrowing photos of Damien on his deathbed, ravaged by disease.

KAPI'OLANI PARK

Beyond the eastern limit of central Waikīkī, as defined by Kapuhulu Avenue, lies Hawaii's first-ever public park, **Kapi'olani Park**, which was established in 1877. Locals flock to this much-needed breathing space, with joggers pounding the footpaths, and practitioners of t'ai chi weaving slow-motion spells beneath the trees. Tourists pour in from 9am on Tuesdays, Wednesdays and Thursdays, for the free **Kodak Hula Show**, which starts at 10am. This kitsch relic of bygone days culminates with grass-skirted *hula* "maidens" (some of whom have participated since it began in 1937) holding up letters to spell out A-L-O-H-A H A W A I I. The adjoining **Waikīkī Shell** hosts large concerts, especially in summer, while the Royal Hawaiian Band performs on the park's **bandstand** on Sundays at 2pm.

Honolulu Zoo

Map 4, I4. Daily 8.30am–5.30pm, last admission 4.30pm; closed Christmas and New Year's Day, adults $6, ages 6–12 $1.

The **Honolulu Zoo** occupies a verdant wedge on the fringes of Kapi'olani Park. With its main entrance barely a minute's walk from the bustle of Waikīkī, its luxuriant tropical undergrowth and blossoming trees, set against the backdrop of Diamond Head, are as much of an attraction as the animals, which range from wallowing hippos and gray kangaroos to some unfortunate monkeys trapped on tiny islands in a crocodile-infested lagoon. The zoo's pride and joy, the African Savanna exhibit, was designed to re-create the swamps and grasslands of Africa. This it manages to do reasonably successfully. In this world of reddish mud live "black" rhinos, which are, in fact, the color of their surroundings.

Waikīkī Aquarium

Map 4, I5. Daily 9am–5pm, closed Christmas day and
Thanksgiving; adults $6, seniors and students $4, ages 13–17
$2.50, under-12s free.

A few minutes walk east of the zoo, along the Kapi'olani
Park waterfront, stands the slick, but disappointingly small,
Waikīkī Aquarium. Windows in its indoor galleries offer
views into the turquoise world of Hawaiian reef fish, among
them the lurid red frogfish – an ugly brute that squats splay-
footed on the rock waiting to eat unwary passersby – and a
teeming mass of small sharks. One whole tank is devoted to
Hanauma Bay (see p.94). Outside, the mocked-up "edge of
the reef", complete with artificial tide pools, feels a bit
pointless with the real thing just a few feet away. Nearby is
a long tank of Hawaiian monk seals, dog-like not only in
appearance but also in their willingness to perform tawdry
tricks for snacks. As well as a description of traditional fish-
farming, there's a display of the modern equivalent, in
which *mahi mahi* fish grow from transparent eggs to glisten-
ing six-footers in what appear to be lava lamps.

DIAMOND HEAD

Map 2, H7. Diamond Head State Monument daily 6am–6pm; free.

The craggy 760-foot pinnacle of **Diamond Head**, immediately southeast along the coast from Waikīkī, is
Honolulu's most famous landmark. It's among the youngest
of the chain of volcanic cones – others include Punchbowl
(see p.68) and Koko Head (p.96) – that stretch across southeast Oahu. All were created by brief, spectacular blasts of
the Ko'olau vent, which reawakened a few hundred thousand years ago after slumbering for more than two million
years. The most recent of the series date back less than ten
thousand years, so geologists consider further eruptions

possible. Diamond Head itself was formed in a matter of a few days or even hours: the reason its southwestern side is so much the highest is that the trade winds were blowing from the northeast at the time.

Ancient Hawaiians knew Diamond Head as either Lei'ahi ("wreath of fire," a reference to beacons lit on the summit to guide canoes), or Lae'ahi ("brow of the yellow-fin tuna"). They built several *heiaus* in and around it, slid down its walls to Waikīkī on *hōlua* land-sleds as sport, and threw convicted criminals from the rim. Its modern name derives from the mistake of a party of English sailors early in the nineteenth century, who stumbled across what they thought were diamonds on its slopes and rushed back to town with their pockets bulging with glittering but worthless calcite crystals.

For most of this century, Diamond Head was sealed off by the US military, who based long-range artillery here during World War I, and after Pearl Harbor used the bunkers to triangulate the guns of Waikīkī's Fort DeRussy. Only in the 1960s, was it reopened as the Diamond Head State Monument public park.

Access to the crater is via a short road tunnel that drills through the surrounding walls from its *mauka* side. The entrance is around two miles by road from Waikīkī; it's not a particularly pleasant walk, so most people either drive or take the bus. Buses #22 and #58 from Waikīkī climb up Monsarrat Avenue past the zoo to join Diamond Head Road, and stop not far from the tunnel; if you're driving, you can also follow the shoreline highway below the mountain and climb the same road from the bottom.

Once inside, the lawns of the crater interior are oddly bland, almost suburban in fact. Often parched, but a vivid green after rain, they're still dotted with little-used military installations. There have been suggestions that these should be replaced by tennis and golf facilities, but the prevailing wisdom is to allow the place to return to nature in due course.

DIAMOND HEAD

The hike to the rim

The reason most people come to Diamond Head is to **hike** the hot half-hour trail up to the rim, for a superb panorama of the whole southern coast of Oahu. It's a more demanding climb than you may be led to expect, so be sure to wear suitable footwear, and bring a flashlight.

The paved footpath climbs slowly from the central parking lot across the crater floor, then meanders up the inside walls. Many of the holes visible but out of reach on the hillside are ancient burial caves. Before long, you're obliged to enter the vast network of military bunkers and passageways that riddle the crater. Immediately after passing through the first long, dark tunnel – watch out for the bolts poking from the ceiling – a tall, narrow flight of yellow-painted stairs leads up between two high walls to the right. It's also possible to head left here to join a path along the outside – a reasonably safe option as long as you follow the contours, and bear in mind that several people have fallen while attempting to scramble straight up.

If you continue up the steps instead, you soon come to another tunnel, then climb a dark spiral staircase through four or so cramped tiers of fortifications, equipped with eye-slit windows and camouflaged from above. Beyond that, a final outdoor staircase leads to the summit, where you get your first sweeping views of Waikīkī and Honolulu. In theory an official geodetic plate marks the highest point, but however often it's replaced it soon gets stolen again.

On days when a *kona* (southwest) wind is blowing, planes landing at Honolulu Airport approach from the east, passing low enough over Diamond Head for you to see the passengers inside.

For details of free Diamond Head guided hikes, see p.20.

Downtown Honolulu

Downtown Honolulu, the administrative heart, first of the kingdom, and now of the state of Hawaii, stands a few blocks west of the original city center. Most of the compact grid of streets where the port grew up is now taken up by Chinatown, while downtown generally focuses on the cluster of buildings that surround **'Iolani Palace**, home to Hawaii's last monarchs. This is certainly a presentable district, with several well-preserved historic buildings, but it's not a very lively one. On weekday lunchtimes, office workers scurry through the streets, but the rest of the time the contrast with the frenzy of Waikīkī is striking. With few shops, bars or restaurants to lure in outsiders, the whole place is usually empty by 8pm

'IOLANI PALACE

Map 5, H5. Call ©522-0832 to join a reservation-only tour; Tues–Sat every 15min 9am–2.15pm; adults $8, ages 5-12 $3, under-5s not admitted.

'Iolani Palace was the official home of the last two monarchs of Hawaii. It was built for **King David Kalākaua** in 1882, near the site of a previous palace that had been destroyed by termites, and he lived here until his death in 1891. For his sister and successor, **Queen Lili'uokalani**, it

45

was first a palace, and then, after her overthrow in 1893 (see p.233) a prison. Until 1968, by which time the termites had pretty much eaten up this palace too, it was the Hawaiian state capitol. Since the completion of the new Capitol in 1969, it has been preserved as a museum.

Although the palace has become a symbol for the Hawaiian sovereignty movement, and is occasionally the scene of large pro-independence demonstrations, the official **tours** are firmly apolitical. Guides revel in the lost romance of the Hawaiian monarchy without quite acknowledging that it was illegally overthrown by the United States. The fact that visitors have to shuffle around in cotton booties to protect the hardwood floors adds to the air of unreality.

Apart from its *koa*-wood floors and staircase, the palace contains little that is distinctively Hawaiian. In the largest of its **downstairs** rooms, the **Throne Room**, Kalākaua held formal balls to celebrate his coronation and fiftieth birthday, and Lili'uokalani was tried for treason for allegedly supporting moves for her own restoration. The *kapu* stick that separates the thrones of Kalākaua and his wife Kapi'olani was made from a narwhal tusk given to Kalākaua by a sea captain. Other reception rooms lead off from the grand central hall, with all available wall space taken up by formal portraits of Hawaiian and other monarchs. Though the plush **upstairs** bedrooms feel similarly stately and impersonal, there's one touching moment: the glass case in the front room, containing a quilt made by Queen Lili'uokalani during her eight months under house arrest.

A grass-covered mound in the garden marks the original resting place of King Kamehameha II and Queen Kamamalu. Their remains, brought here by George Byron (the cousin of the poet) after they died of measles in England in 1824, were later moved to the royal mausoleum in Nu'uanu (see p.78).

'IOLANI PALACE

The palace's **ticket office** is housed in the castellated 'Iolani Barracks on the west side of the grounds, an odd structure that predates the palace by about fifteen years. Before becoming king – the monarch was by this time an elective rather than a hereditary position – Kalākaua is said to have encouraged his soldiers in a mutiny to embarrass his predecessor King Lunalilo, whom he regarded as too pro-Western. If you arrive without a reservation and can't get on the next tour, you can watch a video about the palace instead.

QUEEN LILI'UOKALANI STATUE

Map 5, H4.

Beyond the impressive banyan tree at the foot of the palace steps, a walkway separates the grounds of 'Iolani Palace from the State Capitol to the north. In its center, a statue of **Queen Lili'uokalani** looks haughtily towards the state's present-day legislators. Festooned with *leis* and plumeria blossoms, she's depicted holding copies of her mournful song *Aloha 'Oe*, the Hawaiian creation chant known as the *Kumulipo*, and her draft Constitution of 1893, which precipitated the coup d'état against her.

THE STATE CAPITOL

Map 5, H4.

Hawaii's **State Capitol** – a bizarre edifice, propped up on pillars, in which the two legislative chambers are shaped like volcanoes – is a confused child of the 1960s. It took little more than twenty years for the flaws in its design to force its closure for extensive and very expensive rebuilding. That work has now been completed, though public tours have yet to recommence. In front of the main entrance, there's a peculiar cubic statue of Father Damien (see p.40), modeled in black metal and wearing a black cloak, created by Marisol Escobar in 1968. Well-tended memorials to Hawaiians who died in Korea and Vietnam stand in the grounds to the west.

HONOLULU HALE

Map 5, J5.

The seat of Honolulu's city government – **Honolulu Hale**, opposite the eastern end of the 'Iolani Palace walkway – is a more successful architectural experiment than the State Capitol. An airy 1920s melding of Italianate and Spanish Mission styles, with whitewashed walls, ornate patterned ceilings, and red-tiled roofs, it boasts a grand central atrium that's packed with colorful murals and sculptural flourishes. Various anterooms often host temporary exhibitions of local art or history; even when there's nothing on, visitors are free to stroll through.

WASHINGTON PLACE

Map 5, H3.

Though **Punchbowl Crater** looms large as you look north from the Capitol, and you may be able to spot visitors on the rim, it's a long way away by road; for a full account, see p.68. Much closer at hand, across Beretania Street, is the white-columned, Colonial-style mansion of **Washington Place**. During the 1860s, Queen Lili'uokalani lived here as plain Mrs Dominis, wife to the governor of Hawaii under King Kamehameha V. After her dethronement she returned as a private citizen once more, and died here in 1917. Five years later it became, as it remains, the official residence of the governor of Hawaii, and is not open to the public.

ST ANDREW'S CATHEDRAL

Map 5, G3.

Behind Washington Place and a short distance to the east rises the central tower of **St Andrew's Cathedral**. Work began on this Gothic-influenced Episcopal church in 1867, in realization of plans formed ten years previously by King Kamehameha IV, with the aim of encouraging Anglican missionaries to counterbalance the prevailing Puritanism of their American counterparts. Kamehameha IV had become a staunch Anglophile during an extended visit to Europe. After he died (on St Andrew's Day 1863 – hence the name of the cathedral), his widow Queen Emma (see p.78) kept up the connection. Construction finished in 1958, with the completion of the Great West Window, a stained-glass rendition of the story of Hawaiian Christianity.

THE KAMEHAMEHA STATUE

Map 5, H6.

The flower-bedecked gilt figure of **Kamehameha the Great** (1758–1819), the first man to rule all the islands of Hawaii, stares northwards across King Street towards ʻIolani Palace from outside Aliʻiolani Hale. Kamehameha is depicted wearing the royal cloak (ʻahuʻula), loincloth (malo), sash (kāʻei), and feather helmet (mahiole), and clutching a spear.

The work of Thomas R Gould, an American sculptor based in Florence, the statue was commissioned by the Hawaiian legislature in 1878 to celebrate the centenary of the arrival of Captain Cook. On its way to Hawaii, however, it was lost when the ship that was carrying it caught fire off the Falkland Islands, so a second copy was cast and despatched. That arrived in 1880, and was unveiled by King Kalākaua at his coronation in 1883; surplus insurance money from the lost statue paid for the sequence of four panels depicting scenes from Kamehameha's life around its base. Meanwhile, a whaling captain bought the original statue from a curio shop in Port Stanley, and brought it to Hawaii in return for an $875 reward. It was packed off to Kamehameha's birthplace on the Big Island.

Ceremonies are held at King Kamehameha's statue on June 11 each year, to mark Kamehameha Day, a state holiday.

ALIʻIŌLANI HALE

Map 5, H6. Judiciary History Center Tues–Thurs 10am–3pm; free.

Since it was erected in 1874, **Aliʻiōlani Hale** – "House of the Heavenly King" in Hawaiian – has been Hawaii's first library and National Museum; it was also the first building taken over by the conspirators who overthrew the monarchy in 1893. Throughout its history, however, its main function has been as the home of the state's Supreme Court. The first floor houses the fascinating **Judiciary History Center**, which outlines the history of Hawaiian law from the days of the ancient *kapu* (see p.241) onwards, and chronicles the role played by the Supreme Court in replacing the tradition under which all land was held in common with the concept of private ownership. There's also an intriguing scale model of Honolulu in 1850.

KAWAIAHAʻO CHURCH

Map 5, J5.

Although **Kawaiahaʻo Church**, just east of ʻIolani Palace near the junction of Punchbowl and King streets, was erected less than twenty years after the first Christian missionaries came to Hawaii, it was the fifth church to stand on this site. According to its Protestant minister, Rev Hiram

Bingham, each of the four predecessors was a thatched "cage in a haymow". This one, by contrast, was built with thousand-pound chunks of living coral, hacked from the reef. It's not especially huge, but the columned portico is grand enough, topped by a four-square clock-tower.

Inside, broad balconies run down both sides of the nave, lined with royal portraits. Below, plaques on the walls honor early figures of Hawaiian Christianity. The plushest pews – at the back of the church, upholstered in velvet and marked off by *kahili* standards – were reserved for royalty.

In the gardens on the *mauka* side of the church, a fountain commemorates the site of a spring formerly known as *Ka wai a Ha'o*, "the water of Ha'o". A rare treasure in this barren region, it was used exclusively by *ali'i nui*, or high chiefs, such as chiefess Ha'o.

The small mausoleum in the grounds fronting the church holds the remains of **King Lunalilo**, who ruled for less than two years after his election in 1872. Feeling slighted that his mother's body had not been removed from the churchyard to the royal mausoleum (see p.78), he chose to be buried here instead. The rest of the graves in the **cemetery** around the back form a potted history of Hawaii's nineteenth-century missionary elite, with an abundance of Castles and Cookes, Alexanders and Baldwins, and the only president of the Republic, Sanford B. Dole.

THE MISSION HOUSES

Map 5, K5. 553 S King St; Tues–Sat 9am–4pm; adults $6, under-19s $2; ℗531-0481.

Hawaii's first Christian missionaries are recalled by the partly reconstructed **Mission Houses**, behind Kawaiaha'o Church. Standing cheek by jowl on S King Street, these three nine-teenth-century buildings commemorate the pioneers of the Sandwich Islands Mission, who arrived from Boston in 1820.

The oldest edifice, the two-story **Frame House**, was shipped in whole from New England in 1821. Reluctant to let outsiders build permanent structures, the king only allowed it to go up with the words "when you go away, take everything with you". Local fears that its cellar held weapons for use in a planned takeover of the islands were allayed when Kamehameha's principal adviser, Kalanimoku, built a house with a larger cellar across the street. The house, whose tiny windows were entirely unsuited to the heat of Honolulu, was home to four missionary families. A kitchen had to be added because cooking outdoors attracted too much attention from the islanders, for whom it was *kapu* (forbidden) for women to prepare food.

One of the missionaries' first acts, in 1823, was to set up the **Print House**, which produced the first Hawaiian-language Bible – *Ka Palapala Hemolele*. The current building – not the original, but its 1841 replacement – holds a replica of its imported Ramage printing press, whose limitations were among the reasons that to this day the Hawaiian alphabet only has twelve letters.

The largest of the three buildings, the **Chamberlain House**, started life in 1831 as the mission storehouse. As the missionary families became increasingly embroiled in the economy of the islands, that role turned it into the commercial headquarters of Castle and Cooke, one of the original "Big Five" (see p.230).

HONOLULU ACADEMY OF ARTS

Map 5, N1. 900 S Beretania St; Tues–Sat 10am–4.30pm, Sun 1–5pm; tours Tues–Sat 11am, Sun 1pm; free first Wed of month, otherwise $5, under-13s free; ℂ532-8700. The #2 bus from Waikīkī stops outside.

Honolulu residents take great pride in the stunning fine art on display at the **Academy of Arts**. Few tourists find their way here – half a mile east of the Capitol – but two or three hours wandering the galleries of this elegant former private home, with its open courtyards and fountains, is time well spent.

The bulk of the Academy's superb collection of **paintings** adorns the **Mediterranean Court** to the right of the entrance. Highlights include Van Gogh's *Wheat Field*, Gauguin's *Two Nudes on a Tahitian Beach* and one of Monet's *Water Lilies*. Other pieces date from the Italian Renaissance, with *Two Apostles* by Carlo Crivelli, as well as engravings by Rembrandt and Dürer; more recent canvases include lesser works by Picasso, Léger, Braque, Matisse and Tanguy. Of American artists, Winslow Homer is represented by a landscape of the English fishing village of Cullercoats, and Thomas Moran by his *Grand Canyon of the Yellowstone*.

Although most of them have more historic value than artistic merit, the Academy also holds some fascinating **depictions of Hawaii** by visiting artists, including a pencil sketch of Waikīkī drawn in 1838. The much-reproduced portrait of *Kamehameha in Red Vest*, painted by the Russian Louis Choris in 1816, shows the redoubtable monarch in his later years, and there are several dramatic renditions of the changing face of the volcano at Kīlauea. John Webber, who accompanied Cook to Hawaii in 1779, contributes a pen and watercolor sketch of the village of "Kowrooa" (Ka'awaloa), nestling beneath the palms of Kealakekua Bay, where Cook died. Tucked away in the contemporary collection, you'll find Georgia O'Keeffe's vivid, stylized studies of Maui's 'Īao Valley and Hāna coast.

....

The Academy's courtyard café serves lunch Tues–Sat 11.30am–2pm (reservations on ℗532-8734), and tea Tues–Sun 2–4pm.

....

To the left of the entrance, the centerpiece of the **Asian Court** is a 1993 bequest of 2000 pieces of ancient **Chinese** art. Among these magnificent artifacts are beautiful ceramics, four-thousand-year-old jade blades, green Zhou bronzes, and a column from a two-thousand-year-old Han tomb that looks like an Easter Island statue. There then follows a cornucopia of works from all over the world: Buddhist and Shinto deities, plus miniature *netsuke* (buckles) from Japan; Tibetan *thangkas* (religious images), Indian carvings ranging from Rajasthani sandstone screens to a stone Chola statue of Krishna; Mayan effigies and Indonesian stick figures; Melanesian masks incorporating such elements as boars' tusks and cobwebs; and pottery from the *pueblos* of Arizona and New Mexico. There are also a few ancient Hawaiian artifacts, though better ones are on show at the Bishop Museum (see p.82).

Chinatown

J ust five minutes' walk west of downtown Honolulu along Hotel Street, the fading green clapboard store-fronts of **Chinatown** seem like another world. Traditionally the city's red-light district, the narrow streets leading down to the Nu'uanu Stream are still characterized by pool halls, massage parlors and tawdry bars. However, there's far more to Chinatown than sleaze. Cosmopolitan, atmospheric and historic in equal proportions, it's the only part of the city that's genuinely fun to explore on your own. It's also changing fast, blending futuristic elements in with its relics of the past to create a hybrid of old and new, East and West.

TheBus #2 and #20 run from Waikīkī to N Hotel Street, on the edge of Chinatown.

EXPLORING CHINATOWN

Of Chinatown's two main axes, North Hotel and Maunakea streets, **Hotel Street** best lives up to the area's low-life reputation, with drunken sailors lurching between the *Club Hubba Hubba Topless-Bottomless* and assorted sawdust-floored bars.

The actual intersection of Hotel and Maunakea is dominated by the ornate façade of **Wo Fat's**, topped by a pagoda-

The Chinese in Hawaii

Strangely enough, there was a Hawaiian in China before there were any Chinese in Hawaii – Kai'ana, a chief from Kauai, was briefly abandoned in Canton in 1787 by a British fur-trader he had thought was taking him to Europe. Within three years, however, Chinese seamen were starting to jump ship to seek their fortunes in the land they knew as Tan Hueng Shan, "the Sandalwood Mountains". Trading vessels regularly crossed the Pacific between China and Hawaii, and Cantonese merchants and entrepreneurs became a familiar sight in Honolulu. Even the granite that paved the streets of what became Chinatown was brought over from China as ballast in ships.

Some of Hawaii's earliest Chinese settlers were sugar boilers, and the islands' first sugar mill was set up by a Chinese immigrant on Lanai in 1802. American capital proved itself more than a match for any individual Chinese endeavor, however, and Chinese only began to arrive in Hawaii in sizeable numbers when the sugar plantations started to import laborers in 1852. Workers were usually indentured for five years, so by 1857 Chinese were leaving the plantations, and using their small savings to finance their own businesses. At first, the majority were on Kauai, where they began to turn neglected Hawaiian farmlands into rice paddies, even using water buffalo shipped over from China.

In time, however, the Chinese settled increasingly in Honolulu, where "friendly societies" would help new arrivals find their feet. Inevitably, many of these were renegades and outlaws, ranging from gang members to political dissidents. **Sun Yat Sen**, for example, who became the first President of the Republic of China when the Manchu Dynasty was overthrown in 1911, was educated at 'Iolani School.

By the 1860s there were more Chinese than whites in Hawaii. With the native Hawaiian population shrinking, the pro-American establishment in Honolulu felt threatened. Accordingly, their maneuverings ensured that, while white residents could vote for the national legislature, Asians were excluded, and induced the plantations to switch their recruiting policies and focus on other parts of the globe.

At the end of the nineteenth century, Chinatown was at its zenith. Its crowded lanes held more than 7000 people, including Japanese and Hawaiians as well as Chinese. When bubonic plague was detected in December 1899, however, city authorities decided to prevent its spread by systematic **burning**. The first few controlled burns were effective, but on January 20, 1900, a small fire started at Beretania and Nu'uanu rapidly turned into a major conflagration. The flames destroyed Kaumakapili Church as well as a 38-acre swathe that reached to within a few yards of the waterfront. Police cordons prevented the quarantined residents from leaving during the fire, while any already outside were unable to return to salvage possessions. White-owned newspapers were soon rhapsodizing about the opportunity to expand downtown Honolulu, convincing the Chinese community, which never received adequate compensation, that the destruction was at the very least welcome and at worst deliberate.

Nonetheless, Chinatown was rebuilt, and the fact that almost all its surviving structures date from that rebuilding gives it an appealing architectural harmony. Chinatown has since 1974 been declared a preservation district, and it still remains Honolulu's liveliest, most characterful quarter, albeit much more commercial than it is residential. Most local Chinese, like the rest of the city's inhabitants, live in outlying suburbs.

THE CHINESE IN HAWAII

style green tiled roof. A hundred years old, *Wo Fat's* is Chinatown's longest-standing restaurant. Its main rival as the leading local landmark is the Art Deco **Hawaii Theater**, further east at 1130 Bethel St, which reopened after extensive restoration in 1996. Guided tours of the theater ($5) take place on the first Monday of each month, at 10am and 2pm, but a far better way to appreciate the gorgeous interior is by attending one of its varied program of (mostly one-off) performances; call ✆528-0506 for more details.

Many of Chinatown's old walled courtyards have been converted into open malls, but the businesses within remain much the same. Apothecaries and herbalists weigh out dried leaves in front of endless arrays of bottles, shelves and wooden cabinets, while fridges in hole-in-the-wall stores burst with *leis*, and food smells waft from backstreet bakeries.

....

To join an organized walking tour of Chinatown, call either the Chinese Chamber of Commerce (Tues 9.30am; $5; ✆533-3831), or the Hawaii Heritage Center (Fri 9.30am; $4; ✆521-2749).

....

If you get hungry, call in at *Char Hung Sut*, on North Pauahi at Smith (daily except Tues 5.30am–3pm) for freshly made dim sum, or browse through the oriental food specialities at **Oahu Market**, on N King and Kekaulike. This traditional market was scheduled for demolition in 1988, but the traders banded together to buy it. The fastest-selling item seems to be *ahi* (yellow-fin tuna), used for making sashimi or *poke*, but it's also just the place if you're looking for a pig's snout or a salmon's head.

The best selection of fast food in Chinatown is at the newer **Maunakea Marketplace**, a couple of blocks north and entered via either Hotel or Maunakea streets. Once you enter the main building, beneath the watchful gaze of the statue of Confucius in its central plaza, the temperature is likely to be sweltering, but the choice of cuisines is amazing, and it's all available at the lowest prices in Honolulu. The plaza itself is surrounded by a wide assortment of souvenir and trinket stores, with Chinese calendar scrolls and miniature statuettes among the specialties.

Some of the best Chinatown restaurants are listed on p.173.

Chinatown is bordered to the west by the **Nu'uanu Stream**, flowing down to Honolulu Harbor. **River Street**, which runs alongside, becomes an attractive, restaurant-filled pedestrian mall between Beretania and Kukui streets. At the port end stands a *lei*-swaddled statue of **Sun Yat Sen** (see p.56), while over Kukui Street at the opposite end is the tiny Lum Hai So Tong **Taoist temple**. Most of the interior of the block next to the mall is occupied by the **Chinatown Cultural Plaza**, filled with slightly tacky souvenir stores and conventional businesses that cater to the Chinese community.

Across the stream, a block south beyond the Izumo Taisha **Shinto shrine**, erected by local Japanese citizens in 1923, retired citizens of Chinatown unwind in **'A'Ala Triangle Park**. The **railroad station** here was used by the Oahu Railway until it went broke in 1947; it's now owned by the Hawaii Railway Society (see p.126).

Foster Botanic Garden

Map 5, B–C1. Daily 9am–4pm; adults $5, under-13s $1.

At the top end of River Street, and entered via a short driveway that leads off North Vineyard Boulevard beside the Kuan Yin **Buddhist temple**, is the twenty-acre **Foster Botanic Garden**. Established in the middle of the nineteenth century as a sanctuary for Hawaiian plants and a

FOSTER BOTANIC GARDEN

testing ground for foreign imports, it has become one of Honolulu's best-loved city parks. Different sections cover spices such as vanilla and pepper, herbs, flowering orchids and tropical trees from around the world. As well as sausage trees from Mozambique, the latter collection includes a *bo* (or *peepal*) tree supposedly descended from the *bo* tree at Bodh Gaya in north India where the Buddha achieved enlightenment.

Waterfront Honolulu

A lthough the ocean is just a few yards from central Honolulu, pedestrians have to negotiate the fearsome traffic of **Nimitz Highway** to reach it. Only one small segment of the waterfront is worth attempting to stroll along – the stretch that runs for a couple of hundred yards east of the venerable **Aloha Tower**. Until 1857, this area was covered by the waves; then the city **fort**, which had previously stood at Fort and Queen streets, was torn down, and the rubble used to fill in a fifteen-acre expanse of the sea floor. Now, as well as watching the comings and goings of **Honolulu Harbor**, you can join a sunset dinner cruise or similar expedition from the piers nearby, or learn something of the port's history in the **Hawaii Maritime Center**.

In the heart of the city, the sea is still turquoise, and clean enough to support conspicuous populations of bright tropical fish, but the shoreline is consistently concrete. To find a **beach**, head west to **Sand Island** or, preferably, east to **Ala Moana**, home to the city's largest beach park as well as a huge shopping mall.

CHAPTER 4 ● WATERFRONT HONOLULU |

61

ALOHA TOWER

Map 5, E9. Observation deck Sun–Thurs 9am–9pm, Fri & Sat 9am–10pm; free.

The **Aloha Tower**, on Pier 9 of Honolulu Harbor, was built in 1926 to serve as a control center for the port's traffic and a landmark for arriving cruise passengers. At 184ft high, it was then the tallest building in Honolulu; with its four giant clock-faces, each surmounted by the word "ALOHA", it was also the most photographed. Seventy years of skyscraper construction have made it seem progressively smaller and smaller, but the tower has recently returned to prominence as the centerpiece of the **Aloha Tower Marketplace** shopping mall.

....

Both TheBus #2, and the Aloha Tower Trolley, run from Waikīkī to the Aloha Tower; see p.16.

....

The stores and restaurants tend to be expensive and predictable (see p.203 and 176), geared more towards day-trippers from Waikīkī than residents, while the tower itself feels a little stranded and incongruous; as the placard at its base puts it, "Aloha Tower now stands alone for the first time in its history". However, with the mall walkways ending right at the dockside, this is a surprisingly enjoyable place to get a sense of the ongoing life of the port. Cargo vessels from all over the world tie up alongside, and there's always something going on out in the water.

Taking a free trip up to the tenth-floor **Observation Deck** of the Aloha Tower is also worthwhile. Balconies on each of its four sides, originally used as lookouts by harbor pilots, give views that are little short of ugly – freeways, airport runways and grimy harbor installations – but make an excellent orientation to the city. Looking towards Diamond

Head – which may well be obscured by haze – the twin stereo speakers of the Waterfront Towers condominiums loom above the black glass of Restaurant Row (see p.176), while Pearl Harbor sprawls to the west, and the green mountains soar inland.

HAWAII MARITIME CENTER

Map 5, F9. Daily 8.30am–5pm; adults $7.50, under-18s $4.50; ☏536-6373.

A short walk east of the Aloha Marketplace, the **Hawaii Maritime Center**, at Pier 7, illustrates Hawaii's seafaring past in riveting detail.

You may prefer to explore the modern museum building – known as the King Kalākaua Boathouse – at your own pace, rather than follow the audio-cassette tour, but in any case, begin on the second floor. Displays here trace the voyages of **Captain Cook**, who sailed the world in small flat-bottomed boats originally designed for trips along the English coast, and named "Whitby Cats" after his home port. A crude copper plaque left by an English ship at the site of Cook's death – and seen there by Mark Twain in 1866, as noted in his book, *Roughing It* – stands alongside a cannonball found nearby.

The **whaling** industry is then recalled by exhibits such as huge iron try-pots, scrimshaw carved by nineteenth-century seamen on ivory smoothed with sharkskin "sand-paper", and a large painting of whalers at anchor at Lahaina. In the center of the gallery hangs the skeleton of a humpback whale beached on the uninhabited island of Kahoolawe in 1986.

Posters, timetables, menus and reconstructed interiors cover the growth of **tourism** and the heyday of cruise ships and passenger ferries – Hawaii's last inter-island steamer, the *Humu'ula*, ceased regular runs in 1952.

HAWAII MARITIME CENTER

Having examined plans and photos showing the development of Honolulu Harbor, you can see the whole thing yourself by climbing the 81 steps up the museum's observation tower.

On the first floor, the emphasis is on the **Polynesians**. A full-sized, double-hulled canoe has been cut in half, and framed in cross section behind clear plastic to show the equipment and cargo carried by the first voyagers. There's also a wall of huge historic **surfboards** – and some smaller *pāipus*, the ancient equivalent of today's boogie boards – together with a brief history of the sport. Its modern popularity stems from the international successes of Olympic champion Duke Kahanamoku during the early 1900s, who features prominently in photos of Waikīkī's first surfing clubs.

For many, however, the **chief attractions** of the Maritime Center are the two distinguished vessels moored on the adjacent dock. The *Falls of Clyde*, floating to the right of the entrance, is the only four-masted, full-rigged sailing ship left in the world. Built of wrought iron in Glasgow in 1876, it's also the world's only sail-powered oil tanker; after years of ferrying sugar and passengers between California and Hawaii, it was converted to carry petroleum in 1907.

When it's not sailing to Tahiti, New Zealand or the far reaches of the South Pacific, the replica Polynesian sailing canoe *Hōkūleʻa* is moored at the end of the pier. Its long-distance voyages, designed to rediscover the routes and methods used by Hawaii's first human inhabitants, have inspired a huge revival of interest in traditional methods of navigation, and parties of eager schoolchildren flock here for close-up inspections. During its frequent absences, visitors have to content themselves with "navigating" an enjoyable computer simulation of the *Hōkūleʻa*.

THE WESTERN WATERFRONT: SAND ISLAND

Honolulu Harbor, which, west of the Aloha Tower, is inaccessible to casual viewing, is a relatively narrow deep-water channel shielded from the open ocean by the bulk of **Sand Island**. The seaward side of the island is a state park, where the plentiful supply of restrooms, showers and pavilions does little to alleviate the impression of being trapped in an industrial wasteland. There's a certain amount of sandy beach, and locals come to hang out and fish, but it's hard to see why any tourist would drive five miles to get here. If you insist on doing so, follow Nimitz Highway almost as far as the airport, and then loop back along Sand Island Access Road.

EAST TO WAIKĪKĪ: ALA MOANA

East of the Aloha Tower and Maritime Center, **Ala Moana Boulevard** runs along the shoreline towards Waikīkī. Along the way it passes a few more of Honolulu's main **shopping malls** – the Ward Warehouse, the Ward Center and the pick of the bunch, the Ala Moana Center. Year after year, the stores here seem to increase both in quality and quantity, and for an ever-greater proportion of visitors to Honolulu, the Ala Moana district constitutes their only foray into the city proper. For more details, see the *Shopping* chapter, on p.198 onwards.

The first spot where you can enter the ocean in this stretch is the unenticingly but appropriately-named **Point Panic**. Serious board- and body-surfers swear by its powerful waves, but a lack of sand, an abundance of sharks, and the fact that the surf hammers straight into a stone wall, combine to ensure that few visitors are tempted to join them.

ALA MOANA BEACH COUNTY PARK

Though tourists tend not to realize it, the long green lawns across Ala Moana Boulevard from the malls flank a superb **beach** – the long white-sand strand preserved as the **Ala Moana Beach County Park**. This is where Honolulu city-dwellers come, in preference to Waikīkī, to enjoy excellent facilities and, especially during working hours, a relative absence of crowds. Like most of the beaches in Waikīkī, it's artificial, having been constructed during the 1930s on the site of a garbage dump; the name "Ala Moana," meaning "path to the sea", is a postwar coinage. Inshore swimming is generally safe and good, and there's some potential for snorkeling around the reef; just watch out for the steep drop-off, only a few yards out at low tide, that marks the former course of a boat channel.

At its eastern end, Ala Moana Beach curves out and around a long promontory. Known as **Magic Island** or **'Aina Moana**, this too is artificial. It was one of the most ambitious elements of the state's plans to expand tourism in the early 1960s, the idea being to reclaim an "island" of shallow coral reef, connect it to the mainland, and build luxury hotels on it. The hotels never materialized, so the vast sums of money involved have instead resulted in the creation of a tranquil park that's ideal for sunset strolls. Surfers come here too, and the swimming is on a par with the rest of the park, though few people make the effort to walk out as far as the little crescent lagoon at its tip.

Tantalus, Makiki Heights and Mānoa Valley

T he more time you spend in Honolulu, the more your eyes are likely to stray towards the mysterious mountains that soar just a short distance inland, and the valleys that lie between them. Many former wilderness areas have been colonized by residential developments over the years, but there are still plenty of stretches of pristine rainforest within easy reach of downtown, waiting to be explored along a comprehensive network of spectacular **hiking trails**. In addition, the few roads that wind through the hills also hold some notable city landmarks, including Punchbowl cemetery and the Contemporary Arts Museum.

Tantalus and Makiki Valley

For a quick escape into Honolulu's hilly hinterland, there's no better choice of route than **Tantalus** and **Round Top** drives. This eight-mile road climbs up one flanking ridge of **Makiki Valley** and then wriggles back down the other, changing its name from Tantalus Drive in the west to Round Top Drive in the east. Along the way you'll get plenty of views of Honolulu and Waikīkī, but the real attraction is the dense rainforest that cloaks the hillside, often meeting overhead to turn the road into a tunnel. It's a slow drive, which in places narrows to just a single lane of traffic, but a spellbinding one.

To join Tantalus Drive from downtown, follow signs for the **Punchbowl cemetery** until you reach the right turn onto Pūowaina Drive, and head straight on instead. Coming from Waikīkī, take Makiki Street up from Wilder Avenue, which runs parallel to and just north of H-1 west of the University. It's also possible to miss out the bulk of the circuit by taking **Makiki Heights Drive**, which passes the stimulating **Contemporary Museum** as well as trail-heads for some superb mountain **hikes**.

PUNCHBOWL: NATIONAL MEMORIAL CEMETERY

Map 2, F3. March–Sept daily 8am–6.30pm, Oct–Feb daily 8am–5.30pm; TheBus #15 from downtown Honolulu.

The extinct volcanic caldera known as Punchbowl, perched above downtown Honolulu, makes an emotive setting for the **National Memorial Cemetery of the Pacific**. To ancient Hawaiians, this was Pūowaina, the hill of human sacrifices; somewhere within its high encircling walls stood a sacrificial temple. It's now possible to drive right into the crater – having first spiraled around the base of the cone to meet up with Pūowaina Drive from the back – and park in one of the many small bays dotted around the perimeter road.

Beneath the lawns that carpet the bowl-shaped interior, far removed from the noise of the city, almost 25,000 victims of US Pacific wars, including Vietnam, now lie buried. Famous names include the Hawaiian astronaut Ellison Onizuka, killed when the *Challenger* shuttle exploded, but no graves are singled out for special attention. Instead, each gravestone, marked perhaps with a bouquet of ginger and heliconia, is recessed into the grass, with space left for their families or still-living veterans to join those laid to rest.

At the opposite end to the entrance rises the imposing marble staircase of the **Honolulu Memorial**, where ten "Courts of the Missing" commemorate a further 28,778 service personnel listed as missing in action. It culminates in a thirty-foot marble relief of the prow of a naval ship, bearing the words sent by President Lincoln to Mrs Bixby, whose five sons were killed in the Civil War: "The solemn pride that must be yours to have laid so costly a sacrifice upon the altar of freedom". As with all such US memorials, a "graphic record" of the conflicts is provided, so incongruous colored maps of the war in the Pacific cover the walls to either side.

Only when you climb the footpath to the top of the crater rim, and find yourself looking straight down Punchbowl Street to the Capitol, do you appreciate how close this all is to downtown Honolulu. During World War II, before the creation of the cemetery, this ridge held heavy artillery trained out to sea.

CONTEMPORARY MUSEUM

Map 6, A7. 2411 Makiki Heights Drive; Tues–Sat 10am–4pm, Sun noon–4pm; $5, free Thurs, under-15s free; ©526-1322. TheBus #15 from downtown Honolulu.

Just above Makiki Heights Drive and a short distance east of its intersection with Mott-Smith Drive, a grand 1920s country estate houses the lovely **Contemporary Museum**. Tastefully landscaped with ornamental Oriental gardens that offer a superb overview of Honolulu – and are packed with playful sculptures – this hosts changing exhibitions of up-to-the-minute fine art. Few last more than eight weeks, but each is installed with lavish attention to detail, and the effect is consistently magnificent. A separate pavilion highlights a permanent display of the sets created by David Hockney for the Metropolitan Opera's production of Ravel's *L'Enfant et les Sortilèges*; a recording of the work plays constantly. Excellent lunches, with daily specials priced at $10–12, are available at the on-site *Contemporary Café* (Tues–Sat 11am–3pm, Sun noon–3pm).

MAKIKI VALLEY TRAILS

Honolulu's finest **hiking trails** wind their way across and around the slopes of **Makiki Valley**. The network is most easily accessed via a short spur road that leads inland from a hairpin bend in Makiki Heights Drive, roughly half a mile east of the Contemporary Museum, or half a mile west of the intersection with Makiki Street. Follow the dead-end road to park just beyond the ramshackle green trailers of the **Hawaii Nature Center** (a volunteer educational group that works mainly with schoolchildren). If you haven't already picked up trail maps from the state office downtown (see p.154), they may have some at the center.

....

**The Hawaii Nature Center organizes guided hikes,
open to all, at weekends – call ℗955-0100 for details.**

....

The best loop trip from this point begins by following the **Maunalaha Trail**, which starts across the Kanealole Stream beyond the center's restrooms. From the banana grove here, you swiftly switchback on to the ridge for a long straight climb, often stepping from one exposed tree root to the next. Despite being in the shade most of the way, it's a grueling haul. Looking back through the deep green woods, you'll glimpse the towers of downtown Honolulu and then of Waikīkī. At first you can see the valleys to either side of the ridge, but before long only Mānoa Valley to the east is visible. After roughly three-quarters of a mile, you come to a **four-way intersection** at the top of the hill.

Continuing straight ahead from here for around three miles connects you via the Moleka and Mānoa Cliff trails to the Nu'uanu Valley Lookout, described on p.73; turn left and you're on the Makiki Valley Trail, detailed below. Turning right on to the **'Ualaka'a Trail**, however, adds an enjoyable if muddy half-mile to the loop trip (making it a total of three miles in all). Plunging into the forest, the level path soon passes some extraordinary banyans, perched on the steep slopes with their many trunks, which have engulfed older trees. Having rounded the ridge, where a magnificent avenue of Cook pines marches along the crest in parallel rows, an arm-span apart, you curve back to cross Round Top Drive twice. In between the two crossings, take the short spur trail that leads left and up to the highest point on the hike. A clearing here perfectly frames Diamond Head against the ocean, with Waikīkī to the right and the gleaming silver dome of the sports stadium at the University of Hawaii straight below. Once you rejoin the main trail on the far side

MAKIKI VALLEY TRAILS

of Round Top Drive – it starts fifty yards to the right – a brief woodland walk returns you to the four-way junction.

The next stretch, on the **Makiki Valley Trail**, is the most gorgeous of the lot. A gentle descent angled along the steep valley wall, it heads inland to cross Moleka Stream at Herring Springs, amid a profusion of tiny bright flowers. Climbing away again you're treated to further ravishing views of the high valley, bursting with bright gingers and fruit trees. Birds are audible all around, and dangling lianas festoon the path. Take **Kanealole Trail**, which cuts away to the left shortly before this trail meets Tantalus Drive, and you'll drop back down through endless guava trees to your starting point at the Nature Center.

TANTALUS TRAILS

Tantalus Drive is at its highest just below the 2013-foot pinnacle of **Tantalus** itself, near the point, halfway between the two intersections with Makiki Heights Drive, where it changes its name to Round Top Drive. Two roadside parking lots here stand close to the trailhead for the three-quarter-mile **Puʻu ʻŌhiʻa Trail**. The initial climb up through the eucalyptus trees to the summit is steep enough to require the aid of a wooden staircase, which comes out after a few hundred yards onto a little-used paved track. Follow this to the right until you reach a fenced-off electrical substation, then cut down the footpath to the left, which leads through a dense grove of bamboo before veering right to join the **Mānoa Cliff Trail**. By now you'll have seen the vastness of Nuʻuanu Valley extending away to your left; heading left brings you, in a couple of hundred yards, to the **Pauoa Flats Trail**. As that in turn heads for three quarters of a mile into the valley, it's met first by the Nuʻuanu Trail from the west, and then by the Aihualama Trail from Mānoa Falls (see p.75) from the east.

The Pauoa Flats Trail officially ends at a vantage point poised high above Nu'uanu Valley, though for even more dramatic views you can double back slightly and climb the knife-edge ridge to your left. It's obvious from here how Nu'uanu Valley cuts right through the heart of Oahu, but you can't quite see the abrupt *pali* at its eastern end that traditionally made reaching the windward shore so perilous (see p.76). Down below the lookout, the **Nu'uanu Reservoir** is an artificial lake that's kept stocked with crayfish and catfish; fishing is only permitted on three weekends in the year.

PU'U 'UALAKA'A PARK

Map 6, C7.

The best single view along Round Top Drive comes at **Pu'u 'Ualaka'a Park**, on the western flank of Mānoa Valley. There's not much of a park here, though there's a sheltered hilltop picnic pavilion at the first of its two parking lots. Continue to the second lot, however, where a paved walkway leads to a railed-off viewing area right at the end of the ridge, and you'll be rewarded with a panorama of the entire southern coast of Oahu. The twin craters of Diamond Head to the left and Punchbowl to the right most readily draw the eye, but looking away to the west you can see beyond the airport and Pearl Harbor and all the way to Barber's Point. Pools of glittering glass in the parking lot attest to the many break-ins up here, so don't spend too long away from your vehicle.

The small summit that separates the two lots is Round Top itself. The Hawaiians called it *'Ualaka'a*, or "rolling sweet potato", because Kamehameha the Great decreed the planting of sweet potatoes here, which when dug up rolled down the hillside.

Mānoa Valley

Mānoa Valley may lie just a couple of miles from Waikīkī – directly inland, to the north – but it's light years away from the commercial hustle of the city. Behind the **University of Hawaii** – a Mecca for students from around the Pacific, but of no great appeal for casual visitors – lies a quiet residential suburb that peters out as it narrows into the mountains, to culminate in a spectacular tropical **waterfall**.

UNIVERSITY OF HAWAII

Map 2, H4.

The main campus of the **University of Hawaii** sprawls along University Avenue in Mānoa, bounded on its southern side by Hwy-1, Honolulu's major east–west freeway. The University has recently undergone massive budget cuts, and has found itself forced to choose between providing a full spectrum of courses or concentrating on its specialties of geology, marine studies, astronomy and other Pacific-related fields. As only a tiny proportion of students live on campus, there are fewer stores, restaurants and clubs in the vicinity than you might expect. The **Campus Center**, set a little way back from University Avenue, is the place to head for general information and orientation. **Hemenway Hall** alongside holds the inexpensive *Mānoa Garden* café, as well as a movie theater, and its noticeboards carry details of short-term courses open to visitors.

LYON ARBORETUM

Map 6, G4. Mon–Sat 9am–3pm; $1 donation. TheBus #5 from Ala Moana.

To drive to the uppermost reaches of Mānoa Valley, continue

along University Avenue beyond the campus, cross East Mānoa Road on to Oahu Avenue, and then turn right on to Manoa Road itself. Immediately you'll see the silver stream of Mānoa Falls amid the trees at the head of the valley. Mānoa Road comes to a halt just beyond the **Lyon Arboretum**, which belongs to the University and preserves Hawaiian and imported trees in a reasonable approximation of their native environment. Several short trails crisscross beneath the canopy.

MĀNOA FALLS

Map 6, G2.

The half-hour trail to **Mānoa Falls** follows straight on from the point where it becomes impossible for Mānoa Road to squeeze any further back into the valley. Parking at the end of the road should be no problem, though, as ever, it's unwise to leave valuables in your car – and be sure not to set off without mosquito repellent. Having passed over a footbridge and through a soggy meadow, the trail soon starts to climb beside one of the two main tributaries of Mānoa Stream. After scrambling from root to protruding root, over intertwined banyans and bamboos, you come out at the soaring high falls, where the flat, mossy cliff face is at enough of an angle that the water flows rather than falls into the small pool at its base.

Many hikers cool off in the pool before attempting the more demanding **Aihualama Trail**, which switchbacks away west of the falls. After something over a mile, it comes out on top of the ridge, amid a thick cluster of bamboo, to connect with the Makiki network of trails half a mile short of the Nu'uanu Lookout (see p.73).

MĀNOA FALLS

The Pali and Likelike highways

I n ancient times, the **Koʻolau Mountains** constituted an impassable obstacle between the Honolulu area and windward Oahu. Early tourists to Hawaii would make a point of riding up to the 3000-foot ridge at the top of the Nuʻuanu Valley, but there was no way to get down the far side – as was grimly attested by the skeletons strewn at the bottom, the remains of warriors driven over the cliffs in a mighty battle in 1795.

These days, three separate roads cross the mountains, the long-suffering **Pali** and **Likelike Highways** having been joined in December 1997 by the **Hwy-3** freeway. Thirty-seven years in the making, thanks to an interminable series of disputes over its environmental and archeological impact, Hwy-3 was originally intended for military use, as a direct link between Pearl Harbor and the Marine Corps base at Kāneʻohe. With the end of the Cold War, that role ceased to be a high priority, and critics charged that Hwy-3 was a fast-track route "from nowhere to nowhere." However, in the last four decades, windward communities such as **Kailua** and **Kāneʻohe** (see p.101 and p.103) have become home to an ever-higher proportion of Honolulu's work-force, and Hwy-3 has considerably eased the strain for commuters using the two older roads.

> **The Hawaiian word *pali* simply means "cliff";
> Likelike, which is pronounced *leek-e-leek-e*, is named
> after the younger sister of Queen Lili'uokalani.**

The opening of Hwy-3 has little significance for tourists, on the other hand, as the Pali and Likelike highways hold far more potential for sightseeing. Both can still get hideously congested at peak times, but the Pali Highway in particular is an exhilarating drive, whether you head straight for the clifftop **Nu'uanu Pali Lookout**, or call in at the various **royal sites** on the way up.

The Pali Highway

Christian missionaries hacked a crude footpath into the sheer windward cliffs beyond Nu'uanu Valley during the first half of the nineteenth-century, but not until 1898 did the first proper trans-Koolau road open to traffic. Its original route, which included sections poised above the abyss on wooden trestles, was finally superceded with the completion of a tunnel through the mountains in 1961. High-speed traffic thunders along the **Pali Highway** day and night, but it remains an attractive drive nonetheless, and at several points along the way it's possible to detour onto delightfully peaceful stretches of its former route, now known as **Nu'uanu Pali Drive**.

To reach the Pali Highway from downtown Honolulu, either drive straight up **Bishop Street**, which becomes Pali

Highway as soon as it cross the Hwy-1 freeway, or take **Nu'uanu Avenue**, which connects with the highway a mile or so further up.

ROYAL MAUSOLEUM

Map 2, F2. Mon–Fri 8am–4.30pm; free.

The Gothic-influenced **Royal Mausoleum** is located very near the top of Nu'uanu Avenue, shortly before it joins the Pali Highway. It would be very easy to miss – there's no HVB sign, so watch out on the right as soon as you've passed the Japanese cemetery – and frankly it's not worth losing any sleep if you do.

The drab, gray mausoleum itself, built in 1865 to replace the overcrowded Kamehameha family tomb at 'Iolani Palace, stands at the end of a short oval driveway ringed with lumpy palm trees. It's now simply a chapel, as the bodies it held for its first forty years or so were later moved to various sarcophagi dotted around the lawns. Kamehameha the Great was buried in secret on the Big Island, but most of his closest family, as Christians, now lie here. Along with his widow Ka'ahumanu, Kamehamehas II to V are in the pink granite tomb to the left, while the separate Kalākaua dynasty were reinterred in the gilded vault beneath the central black column. Incidentally, this spot is said to be the precise site where the Nu'uanu Valley battle began in 1795.

QUEEN EMMA SUMMER PALACE

Map 2, F1. Daily 9am–4pm; adults $4, children 12–15 $1, under-12s 50¢.

A couple of miles up the Pali Highway, just over half a mile after its intersection with Nu'uanu Avenue, a former royal retreat stands on the brow of a small hill to the right of the road. The **Queen Emma Summer Palace** made a welcome escape from the heat of Honolulu for the former Emma Rooke, who married King Kamehameha IV in 1856, was queen consort until 1863, and lived here until her death in 1885. It's now run as a somewhat cloying shrine to Emma by the Daughters of Hawaii, a group composed of descendants of missionary families.

Behind its entrance stairway, framed with six Doric pillars, the single-story white frame house is surprisingly small. Guided tours lead at a snail's pace through rooms lined with royal souvenirs; only the splendidly grumpy Princess Ruth relieves the monotony of the official portraits. Among touching memorabilia of the young Prince Albert Edward – Queen Emma's only child, who died at the age of four – are his beautiful *koa*-wood crib, carved to resemble a canoe rocked by the waves, and a fireman's outfit he once wore in a parade. Gifts from Queen Victoria – after whose husband the boy was named – make up a large proportion of the items on show. Both Victoria and Emma were widowed – Emma was still only 27 when her husband died a year after their son – and they carried on exchanging presents for the rest of their lives.

NU'UANU PALI DRIVE

Half a mile up the Pali Highway beyond Queen Emma's palace, an inconspicuous right turn leads onto **Nu'uanu Pali Drive**. Other than having to drive slower, you lose nothing by taking this detour into succulent rainforest, which curves back to meet the highway two miles up. There are no specific stops en route, but the density of the overhanging tropical canopy, lit with flashes of color, is irresistible.

NUʻUANU PALI STATE PARK

Map 1, K7. Daily 4am–8pm; free.

Back on the highway, it's now just a mile until the next right turn – confusingly, it too is Nuʻuanu Pali Drive – which leads in a few hundred yards to **Nuʻuanu Pali State Park**. Miss this, and you'll miss a staggering overview of the cliffs of windward Oahu; the highway goes into a tunnel at this point, and emerges much lower down the hillside. At the edge of a small parking lot, the railed viewing area of the **Nuʻuanu Pali Lookout** turns out to be perched near the top of a magnificent pleated curtain of green velvet, plunging more than a thousand feet. Straight ahead lie the sprawling coastal communities of **Kailua** and **Kāneʻohe**, separated by the Mōkapu Peninsula, but your eye is likely to be drawn to the north, where the mighty *pali* seems to stretch away forever, with a waterfall in every fold.

It was over this fearsome drop that the defeated warriors of Oahu were driven in 1795 (see opposite); placards at the overlook explain the course of the battle and point out assorted landmarks. Notches higher up the ridge are said to have been cut to provide fortified positions for the defenders, an estimated four hundred of whose skulls were found down below when the Pali Highway was built a century later. The stairs that lead down to the right enable you to join the highway's original route (abandoned when it was upgraded to take automobiles) as it edges its way above the precipice. It's blocked off about a mile along, but walking to the end makes a good, if windy, mountain hike.

As you leave the parking lot, it would seem obvious, if you're heading across the island, to turn right. In fact, however, you have to drive back down to rejoin the highway where you left it. To the right, Nuʻuanu Pali Drive crosses over the tunnel and meets the highway's other carriageway on the far side, to drop back into Honolulu.

The Battle of Nuʻuanu Valley

For early foreign visitors, the ride to the top of Nuʻuanu Pali was an essential part of a Hawaiian itinerary. As their horses struggled up, native guides would recount tales of the epic Battle of Nuʻuanu Valley in 1795, in which Kamehameha the Great (from the Big Island) defeated Kalanikūpule and conquered the island of Oahu.

No two versions completely agree, but according to James Macrae, who accompanied Lord Byron to Hawaii in 1825 – soon enough afterwards to meet some of the participants – Kamehameha's army landed at Honolulu to find Kalanikūpule waiting for them in Nuʻuanu Valley. Kamehameha sent men along the tops of the ridges to either side, and advanced towards Kalanikūpule in the center himself. By this time, his entourage included Europeans and, crucially, a few European guns. Isaac Davis, who five years previously had been the sole survivor of a Hawaiian raid on a small boat at Kawaihae on the Big Island, positioned himself at the front of the attack.

Before the usual ritual of challenges and counter-challenges could even begin, Davis killed Kalanikūpule's leading general with a single lucky shot. The soldiers of Oahu turned and ran, pursued all the way to the head of the valley. When they reached the top, where the thousand-foot Nuʻuanu Pali precipice drops away on the far side, they had no choice and hurled themselves to their deaths.

Likelike Highway

You're most likely to use the Pali Highway to get to windward Oahu from Honolulu, but the **Likelike Highway**, which was completed in 1961, provides a less spectacular alternative. Starting roughly two miles to the west, it runs through residential Kalihi Valley and then passes through its own tunnel to emerge just above Kāneʻohe. There's no great reason to cross the island this way – the traffic is unlikely to be any easier – but you'll have to drive a short stretch of Likelike Highway to visit Honolulu's best museum, the **Bishop Museum**.

BISHOP MUSEUM

Map 2, E1. 1525 Bernice St; daily 9am–5pm; adults $14.95, under-18s and seniors $11.95; prices include the planetarium.
Planetarium shows take place daily at 11am & 2pm, plus Fri & Sat at 7pm; admission to those alone costs $4.50; ☏847-3511.
The best museum of **Hawaiian history**, **anthropology** and **natural history** – and the world's finest collection of the arts of the Pacific – is located in an otherwise obscure district of Honolulu, two miles northwest of downtown.

The **Bishop Museum** was founded in 1889 by Charles Reed Bishop, to preserve the heirlooms left by his wife Princess Bernice Pauahi, the last direct descendant of Kamehameha the Great. Spread across three principal buildings on a 12-acre hillside estate, it sets out to demonstrate the reality of Polynesian culture, as opposed to the fakery of Waikīkī.

TheBus #2 from Waikīkī stops on Kapalama Street, two blocks east of the Bishop Museum. If you're driving, take the first exit on the right as you head up Likelike Highway

The first section you come to, beyond the ticket hall – Hawaii's only **planetarium** – has a practical relevance to the current "Hawaiian Renaissance". Master navigator Nainoa Thompson of the *Hōkūleʻa* used the virtual sky here to reinvent traditional Polynesian navigational techniques, as used in the voyages mentioned on p.64. Visitors can make their own observations of the real night sky after the evening planetarium shows on Fridays and Saturdays.

The huge main building of the museum houses the bulk of its historic displays. To the right of the entrance, the **Hawaiian Hall** consists of a large ground-level room overlooked by two tiers of wood-paneled balconies. Suspended in the central well is the skeleton of a sperm whale, half clad in papier-mâché skin. Among the priceless ancient artifacts down below are carved stone and wooden images of gods, including what may be at least one of the legendary "poisonwood gods" from Molokai, which were said to possess such powerful magic that only Kamehameha the Great could handle them, and Kamehameha's own personal image of the war god Kūkā'ilimoku, found in a cave in Kona on the Big Island. You'll also see *koa* platters and calabashes, and multicolored feather *leis* and capes.

A scale model of the Big Island's Waha'ula *heiau*, built in 1903 using stones from the site, now serves as a valuable record of an important piece of Hawaiian history. The original – thought to have been founded thirty generations ago by the warrior-priest Pā'ao from Tahiti – was recently overrun by lava from the Kīlauea volcano. Nearby stands a sharkskin drum that was once used to announce human sacrifices in a similar *luakini* temple on the seaward slopes of Diamond Head – the only such drum known to have survived the overthrow of the *kapu* system. There's also a full-sized *hale,* or traditional hut, brought here from Hā'ena on Kauai. Standing as usual on a platform of smooth stones, it's windowless, and thatched with *pili* grass.

On the lower of the Hawaiian Hall's balconies, you'll find weapons, such as swords embedded with sharks' teeth, plus exhibitions on the nineteenth-century distribution of land known as the Great Mahele (see p.229), whaling, and the creation and dying of *tapa* (the bark-cloth also known as

BISHOP MUSEUM

kapa). The higher balcony is devoted to the contributions of Hawaii's immigrants, with costumes and artifacts from such countries as Germany, Spain, Portugal, Puerto Rico, the Philippines, Japan, Korea and China.

The **Polynesian Hall**, above the entrance in the same building, emphasizes the full diversity of Polynesia. After the breaking of the *kapu* (see p.228), the Hawaiians themselves set about destroying the relics of their ancient religion; most other Polynesian cultures have preserved far more of their heritage. Stunning exhibits here include woven-grass masks and dance costumes from Vanikoro; modeled skulls and figures from Vanuato; stark white and red sorcery charms from Papua New Guinea; and stick charts used by Pacific navigators. The Maoris of New Zealand are represented by the facade of a storehouse, carved in high relief with human figures and inlaid with abalone-shell eyes.

On the top floor, the **Hall of Hawaiian Natural History** explains the origin of the Hawaiian islands with a large-scale relief model of the entire chain, then covers the development of life, from the first chance arrivals to recently-introduced pests. The new **Castle Building** next door houses top-quality temporary exhibitions.

The Bishop Museum holds an excellent bookstore, Shop Pacifica, and *Woody's Snack Bar* (daily 9am–4pm). On the first Sunday of every month, known as **Family Sunday**, Hawaii residents are allowed in free and the lawns play host to food stalls, *hula* performances and all sorts of other activities.

Pearl Harbor

ncient Hawaiians knew the vast inlet of **Pearl Harbor**, reaching deep into the heart of Oahu, as *Wai Momi*, "water of pearl", on account of its pearl-bearing oysters. Their canoes had no need of deep-water anchorages, but Westerners came to realize that dredging its entrance would turn it into the finest harbor in the Pacific. With its strategic potential, the desire to control Pearl Harbor played a large role in the eventual annexation of Hawaii by the United States. The US first received permission to develop installations here in 1887, in return for granting Hawaiian sugar duty-free access to US markets, and construction of the naval base commenced in 1908.

To this day, the 12,600 acre Pearl Harbor Naval Complex is the headquarters from which the US Pacific Fleet patrols 102 million square miles of ocean. The entire fleet consists of 265 ships, 1900 aircraft and 268,000 personnel, while Pearl Harbor itself is the home port for twenty surface vessels and twenty nuclear submarines.

Except for the offshore **Arizona Memorial**, commemorating the surprise **Japanese attack** with which Pearl Harbor remains synonymous, almost the whole area is off-limits to civilians.

The Attack on Pearl Harbor

As the winter of **1941** approached, with German soldiers occupying most of Europe and moving into Soviet Russia, and Japanese forces advancing through Southeast Asia, the United States remained outside the global conflict. However, negotiations to halt Japanese progress had stalled, and on November 27 the US government sent secret "war warnings" to its military units throughout the world. The version received by the commanding general in Hawaii read: "Japanese future action unpredictable but hostile action possible at any moment. If hostilities cannot, repeat cannot, be avoided the United States desires that Japan commit the first overt act."

A few days earlier, a Japanese attack fleet, with six aircraft carriers among its 33 vessels, had sailed from northern Japan. By maintaining strict radio silence, it dodged American surveillance. The conventional wisdom was that it must be heading towards the Philippines, site of the furthest-flung US base in the Pacific, and a detachment of B-17 "Flying Fortress" aircraft was sent from Hawaii to bolster the islands' defences. In fact, however, Hawaii itself, where **Pearl Harbor** had since the previous spring been the headquarters of the US Pacific Fleet, was the target. The Japanese fleet sailed there along an icy, rarely-used northerly course, keeping well clear of usual shipping lanes. The Japanese did not expect to achieve complete surprise, and were prepared to engage the US fleet in battle if they met them on the open sea, but reconnaissance flights from Pearl Harbor only covered the likeliest angle of attack, from the southwest, and the Japanese approach was not detected. By the early morning of December 7, the fleet was in position 230 miles northwest of Oahu.

The first wave of the attack, consisting of 183 aircraft, was launched at 6am. As the planes passed over the western

Wai'anae mountains, they were picked up by radar screens at a nearby tracking station. When the operators called Honolulu with the news that a large group of aircraft had been spotted, they were told "Well, don't worry about it," in the belief that these were replacement B-17s arriving from the mainland. Meanwhile, the cloud cover had lifted to give the attackers a perfect view of Pearl Harbor, where seven of the US fleet's nine battleships lay at anchor along "Battleship Row." At 7.53am, Commander Mitsuo Fuchida sent the code word "*Tora! Tora! Tora!*" (Tiger! Tiger! Tiger!) to his flagship, the *Akagai*, signalling that a surprise attack was under way.

Within two hours the US Navy lost eighteen warships: eight battleships, three light cruisers, three destroyers and four auxiliary craft. In addition to 87 Navy planes, simultaneous attacks on other bases on Oahu destroyed 77 Air Force planes and damaged 128 more. Following recent warnings, the planes were parked wingtip-to-wingtip on the airfields. This was supposed to make them easier to protect against sabotage by Japanese agents among the *nisei* (Hawaiian residents of Japanese ancestry); instead it left them utterly exposed to aerial attack. During the onslaught, the expected squadron of B-17s arrived from California; unarmed, several were shot down.

In total, 2400 US military personnel were killed, and 1178 wounded. The Japanese lost 29 aircraft, plus five midget submarines that had sneaked into Pearl Harbor during the previous night in the hope of torpedoing damaged ships. Ten hours later, Japanese aircraft did indeed attack Clark Airfield in the Philippines, and there too they destroyed large numbers of aircraft on the ground. The next day, declaring the United States to be at war with Japan, President Franklin D. Roosevelt condemned the "dastardly" Pearl Harbor attack as "a day that will live in infamy".

The official postwar **inquiry** into "the greatest military and naval disaster in our nation's history" set out to explain why the attack was possible, let alone successful. Answering the issue of the fleet being based in Hawaii, instead of the relative safety of the US West Coast, the inquiry explained that not fortifying Pearl Harbor would have signalled a lack of will to resist Japanese expansion in the Pacific. As to whether the fleet's vulnerability had invited the attack, Japanese plans were drawn up expecting a much larger fleet at Pearl Harbor, and they were disappointed to find that both US aircraft carriers were out of port. The fact that the Japanese withdrew from Hawaii almost immediately, instead of destroying port installations such as the vast oil tanks, and thereby crippling US Navy operations for years – or even by invading the islands – suggests that they overestimated US defences.

No hard evidence has been produced to support **revisionist assertions** that Roosevelt knew the attack was coming, but allowed it to happen because he wanted an excuse to join the war, or that the British knew, and they deliberately failed to warn the Americans for the same reason. It makes no sense, if Roosevelt did know, that he didn't at least alert US defences a few hours in advance, when an unprovoked Japanese attack was imminent.

Mistakes were certainly made. Among the most glaring was the fact that Navy authorities were never told of intercepted messages from Tokyo in which the Japanese consulate in Honolulu was asked to divide the moorings in Pearl Harbor into five separate areas, and specify which ships were anchored in each section. Each side's post-attack reactions were as follows: the Japanese commander, reporting to his superiors a fortnight later, wrote that "good luck, together with negligence on the part of the arrogant enemy, enabled us to launch a successful surprise attack." Admiral Husband E. Kimmel, in charge of the US Pacific Fleet, was asked informally why he had left the ships exposed in Pearl Harbor, and replied, "I never thought those little yellow sons-of-bitches could pull off such an attack, so far from Japan."

THE ATTACK ON PEARL HARBOR

In the long run, the Japanese decision to provoke the US into all-out **war in the Pacific** proved suicidal. What's more, most of the vessels damaged and even sunk at Pearl Harbor eventually returned to active service. Only the *Arizona* and the *Utah* could not be salvaged, while the *Oklahoma* sank once again, 500 miles off the Big Island. By contrast, just two of the Japanese ships that were involved survived the war; four of the anti-aircraft carriers were sunk during the Battle of Midway. In 1945, the *West Virginia*, risen from the waters of Pearl Harbor, was in Tokyo Bay to witness the Japanese surrender.

ARIZONA MEMORIAL

Map 1, G7. Daily 7.30am–5pm; tours 8am–3pm; free; ℂ422-0561.
Almost half the victims of the December 1941 Japanese attack on Pearl Harbor were aboard the battleship **USS Arizona**. Hit by an armor-piercing shell that detonated its magazine and lifted its bow twenty feet out of the water, it sank within nine minutes. Of its crew of 1514 – who had earned the right to sleep in late that Sunday morning by coming second in a military band competition – 1177 were killed.

The *Arizona* still lies submerged where it came to rest, out in the waters of the harbor along "Battleship Row", next to Ford Island. Its wreck is spanned (though not touched) by the curving white **Arizona Memorial**, maintained by the National Park Service in honor of all the victims of the attack; small boats ferry a stream of visitors out from the mainland.

The **visitor center** for the memorial is located six miles west of Honolulu, just over a mile after Kamehameha Highway cuts off to the left of Hwy-1. It takes up to an hour to drive across town from Waikīkī. In addition to TheBus #20, overpriced commercial tours run direct from Waikīkī for around $20. On arrival, pick up a numbered ticket for the free memorial tour; in peak season, it can be two or three

> **TheBus #20 takes just over one hour to reach Pearl Harbor from Waikīkī.**

hours before you're called to board the ferry. Many people try to beat the crowds by arriving early, but if anything your chances of a short wait may be better in the afternoon.

Perhaps because so many of the 1.5 million annual visitors are Japanese, the displays in the visitor center are surprisingly even-handed, calling the attack "a daring gamble" by Admiral Yamamoto to knock out the US fleet and give the Japanese time to conquer Southeast Asia. Until the planned new museum is completed, which will trace the build-up, the attack itself, and the course of the war in the Pacific, the best place to get a sense of what happened is in the water-front **garden** outside. From here, you see the low and undramatic mountain ridges that ring Pearl Harbor, together with the gap down the center of the island through which the first planes arrived. Captioned photographs clearly illustrate the disposition of the ships moored along "Battleship Row" on the fateful morning, as well as their eventual fate. Survivors of the attack are often on hand to tell their stories.

When your number finally comes up, you're first shown a twenty-minute film that pays tribute to "one of the most brilliantly planned and executed attacks in naval history." A pained female voice narrates the course of the attack, over footage of Japanese planes taking off from their aircraft carriers.

> **The USS Arizona memorial was partly financed by Elvis Presley's 1961 Honolulu concert, his first show after leaving the Army.**

Crisp-uniformed Navy personnel then usher you on to open-sided boats, which they steer for ten minutes across a tiny fraction of the naval base. At the memorial, whose

ARIZONA MEMORIAL

white marble walls are inscribed with the names of the dead, you disembark for the twenty minutes until the next boat arrives. The outline of the *Arizona* is still discernible in the clear blue waters, and here and there rusty metal spurs poke from the water. All those who died when the *Arizona* went down remain entombed in the wreckage, occasionally joined by veteran survivors who choose to be buried here.

....

The decommissioned *USS Missouri* will open soon as a commercial attraction in Pearl Harbor, serving as an interactive "Combat Engagement Center" where visitors can relive epic naval battles.

....

USS Bowfin Submarine Museum and Park

Map 1, G7. Daily 8am–5pm; sub and museum adults $8, under-13s $3; museum only, adults $4, under-13s $2.

Alongside the *Arizona* visitor center, the **USS Bowfin Submarine Museum and Park** makes a feasible alternative if you have a couple of hours to wait before your ferry. Its main focus, the claustrophobic *Bowfin* itself, is a still-floating, 83-man submarine that survived World War II unscathed, having sunk 44 enemy vessels. Once you've explored it on a self-guided audio tour – complete with a first-person account of one of the *Bowfin's* most hair-raising missions, narrated by the captain in charge – you can learn more about the whole story of twentieth-century submarines in the adjoining museum.

The park outside, to which access is free, holds various missiles and torpedoes, including the Japanese naval equivalent of a *kamikaze* airplane, a *kaiten*. Such manned, single-seater torpedoes were designed for suicide attacks on larger ships; only one, piloted by its inventor, ever succeeded in sinking a US Navy ship.

USS BOWFIN SUBMARINE MUSEUM AND PARK

The rest of Oahu

I f all you see of Oahu is Waikīkī and Honolulu, you may never get a real sense of the island's beauty, or of how it must have looked before the arrival of foreigners. By using the myriad routes offered by **TheBus**, as detailed on p.15, it's a small enough island that you can visit anywhere as a day-trip from the capital. With a car, one day is sufficient for a thorough exploration of Oahu. What you can't do, however, is make a complete circuit along the coast; the northwestern tip of the island, Ka'ena Point, is only accessible on foot.

The most popular short excursion from Honolulu is down to the **southeast** corner of Oahu, where the superb snorkeling waters of **Hanauma Bay** are sheltered in an extinct volcanic caldera. If you want to spend a full day touring, however, a more manageable route sets off directly inland from Honolulu, climbing across the dramatic Ko'olau Mountains. The green cliffs of the **windward coast** on the far side are awe-inspiring, lined with safe, secluded beaches and indented with remote time-forgotten valleys. Towns such as **Kailua**, **Kāne'ohe** and **Lā'ie** may be far from exciting, but you're unlikely to tire of the sheer beauty of the shoreline drive – so long as you time your forays to miss the peak-hour traffic jams.

Driving the full length of the windward coast brings you out at the eastern end of the **North Shore**, the world's

premier **surfing** destination. Mere mortals can only marvel
at the winter waves here; for anyone other than experts,
entering the water at that time is almost suicidal. However,
Waimea, **Sunset** and **'Ehukai** beaches are compelling
spectacles, little **Hale'iwa** makes a refreshing contrast to
Waikīkī, and in summer you may manage to find a safe spot
for a swim. From Hale'iwa, a much shorter drive across the
agricultural plains of **central Oahu** can get you back to
your hotel within an hour.

Although the **west** (or **leeward**) **coast** of Oahu also
holds some fine beaches – including the prime surf spot of
Mākaha – it remains very much off the beaten track.
There's just one route in and out of this side of the island,
and the locals are happy to keep it that way.

···

**Hotels and restaurants all over Oahu are reviewed in
chapters 9 and 10 respectively.**

···

Southeast Oahu

The high crest of the Ko'olau Mountains curves away to the
east beyond Honolulu, providing Oahu with its elongated
southeastern promontory. The built-up coastal strip is
squeezed ever more tightly between the hills and the ocean,
but not until you reach **Koko Head**, eight miles out from
Waikīkī and eleven from downtown, do you really feel you've
left the city behind. Thereafter, however, the shoreline is so
magnificent – punctuated by towering volcanoes, sheltered
lagoons and great beaches – that there have been serious pro-
posals to designate the entire area as a state park, under the
Hawaiian name of **Ka Iwi**, and devote it to eco-tourism.

KĀHALA AND HAWAII KAI

Hwy-1 ends at the Kāhala Mall, just beyond Diamond Head, to become Hwy-72, or **Kalaniana'ole Highway**. Both **Kāhala** itself, and **Hawaii Kai** further along, are upmarket residential communities that have little to attract visitors, and no desire to encourage them. Hawaii Kai spreads back inland to either side of the large Kuapā Pond, an ancient fishpond that has been remodeled to create the Koko Marina; the one reason to stop is to eat at *Roy's* gourmet restaurant (see p.180). None of the beaches along this stretch merits a pause.

HANAUMA BAY

Map 7, C8. Daily, for day-use only, except Wed mornings before noon; admission is $3 for adults, free for under-13s; parking costs an additional $1.

Beautiful **Hanauma Bay** is barely half a mile beyond Hawaii Kai, just across the volcanic ridge of Koko Head. So curved as to be almost round, the bay was created when part of yet another volcano – southeast Oahu is one long chain of volcanic cones – collapsed to let in the sea.

This spellbinding spot, where a thin strip of palms and sand nestles beneath a green cliff, has long been famous as Oahu's best place to **snorkel**. Unfortunately, however, the sheer quantity of Waikīkī-based beach-lovers who come here poses a constant threat to the fragile underwater environment. Since the 1960s, Hanauma Bay has been a Marine Life Conservation District, and organized tour parties are now banned, but all the inshore coral reef has died. Though the sea still holds enough brightly colored fish to satisfy visitors, they're sustained these days by handouts of fish food; the minute coral creatures that should underpin the food chain have gone.

Visiting Hanauma Bay

Cars and buses alike have to stop at the **parking lot** just off the highway; parking is limited, so arrive early. A few stalls up here sell sodas and T-shirts. The beach is five minutes' walk away, down a gently winding road used only by a regular open-sided "trolly" (75¢).

As you walk down, the ridge rises like a rich green curtain ahead of you, but the vegetation on the more exposed northeast side of the bay, off to your left, is generally dry and faded. From here you can see patches of reef in the turquoise water, standing out against the sandy seabed, and swarms of fish too are clearly visible. The largest gap in the reef, at the parking lot end of the bay, is known as the **Keyhole**.

You reach the beach at its sheltered central pavilion, where a **snack bar** sells drinks, sandwiches, and hot dogs. A kiosk alongside **rents out snorkels** until 4.30pm daily. A regular mask and fins costs $6, and you have to leave some form of deposit: rental car keys, but not hotel keys, are accepted. This is also the place to buy approved **fish food**; you're not allowed to bring your own.

Even if the crowds spoil the romance a little, it's worth spending a few hours at Hanauma Bay whether or not you go in the water. The crisp green lawns along the foot of the *pali*, dotted with banyan trees, are ideal for picnics. At either end of the beach, you can walk along the rocky ledge that rings the old crater walls, just above sea level, though there is a real risk of being swept off by the waves. Just before the open ocean, at the far northeastern limit of the bay, the indelicately-named **Toilet Bowl** is a natural hole in the lava that repeatedly fills with gushing sea water and then gurgles dry. On the western limit of the bay, there's the similar **Witch's Brew**, which fills and empties like a whirlpool. You may see people jumping into these pools, but that doesn't mean it's safe to do so.

> **TheBus #22 ("The Beach Bus") from Waikīkī runs by Hanauma Bay every forty minutes.**

Snorkeling at Hanauma is a bit like snorkeling in an aquarium; although you'll see a lot of fish, it can all feel rather tame. The water is so shallow near the shore that it's hard to stay off the reef, but it's essential to try – walking on the coral kills the reef, and can cause cuts that take weeks to heal. Reasonable swimmers who want to see living coral, and bigger fish, can swim out to the deeper waters beyond the inner reef. However, the currents through the reef are notoriously strong, and the one that sweeps across the mouth of the bay is known as the "Molokai Express", because it's capable of sucking you all the way to Oahu's easterly neighbor.

KOKO HEAD AND KOKO CRATER

Right after the highway turnoff for Hanauma Bay, a dirt road climbs straight along the bare ridge above the beach. It's not always open to hikers but, if it is, it affords great views of the 642-foot summit of **Koko Head**, fifteen minutes' walk away. From the summit you can see back to Diamond Head, and walk down a footpath to peek into the southern end of Hanauma Bay.

Koko Head Regional Park, which covers Koko Head and Hanauma Bay, extends another couple of miles northeast to take in **Koko Crater**. The youngest of southeastern Oahu's volcanic cones, this is considerably higher than Koko Head, and makes a very impressive spectacle. Like its neighbor, it is topped by a double crater. The road up its far side – reached from Hawaii Kai, or by doubling back further along the coastal highway – comes to a dead end at Koko Crater Stables. Alongside you'll find the barely developed

Botanic Garden (daily 9am–4pm; free), where a twenty-minute stroll is rewarded by a grove of sweet-smelling, heavy-blossomed plumeria trees. The crater's rim, however, is inaccessible to hikers.

HĀLONA BLOWHOLE

A couple of miles beyond Hanauma Bay, where Kalaniana'ole Highway squeezes between Koko Crater and the ocean, a roadside parking lot enables drivers – and a *lot* of tour buses – to stop off for a look at the **Hālona Blowhole**. The coastline consists of layer upon layer of flat lava, each sheet set back from the one underneath to form a stairway up from the sea. Here, the waves have carved out a cave below the visible top layer, and as each new wave rushes in it's forced out through a small hole to create a waterspout up to fifty feet high. The hole itself does not go straight down, but is stepped; if you fall in, it's almost impossible to get out.

Little **Hālona Cove**, to the right of the Blowhole overlook and sheltered by tall cliffs, holds enough sand to make a welcome private beach, if you're lucky enough to get it to yourself. Only swimming within the cove itself is safe, and even then only in summer.

SANDY BEACH

Avoiding the crowds is not at all the point at **Sandy Beach**, half a mile further on as the shoreline flattens out between Koko Crater and Makapu'u Head. Kids from both sides of Oahu meet up here for the best **body-surfing** and **boogie-boarding** in Hawaii; it's also one of the few places where the waves remain high enough in summer to tempt pro surfers. Tourists who try to join in soon find that riding surf of this size takes skill and experience; Sandy Beach is notorious for serious injuries. If you just want to watch, settle down in the broad sands southwest of the central lava spit; swimming is never safe at Sandy Beach, and beyond the spit it's all but suicidal.

MAKAPU'U POINT

The rising bulk of Oahu's easternmost point, **Makapu'u Head**, pushes Hwy-72 away from the coastline as it swings round to run back up the island's windward flank. Shortly before it finishes climbing up the last low incline of the Ko'olau Ridge, there's just about room to park beside the road at **Makapu'u State Wayside**.

A dirt road here snakes off to the right, soon curving south towards the hillock of Pu'u O Kīpahulu. An hourlong hike (there and back) wends around the hill, and back north along the coastal cliffs to **Makapu'u Point**. From the viewing platform at the end, you can look straight down the cliffs to the Makapu'u lighthouse below, out to Molokai on the horizon, back to Koko Head and up along the spine of eastern Oahu.

Rounding Makapu'u Point on the highway – especially if you manage to stop at the small official **lookout** at the top – is equally memorable. The coastal *pali* suddenly soars away to your left, while straight out to sea a couple of tiny islands stand out in misty silhouette. The larger of the two, Mānana, is also known as **Rabbit Island**, thanks to its population of wild rabbits. They share their home only with seabirds – both Mānana and its neighbor, Kāohikaipu or Turtle Island, are bird sanctuaries, and off-limits to humans.

Makapu'u Beach County Park

Few drivers who miss the lookout can resist stopping to drink in the views as they descend from Makapu'u Point.

The first proper parking lot, however, is down below, at **Makapuʻu Beach County Park**. In summer, this is a broad and attractive strip of sand; in winter, pounded by heavy surf, it's a rocky straggle. Swimming is rarely safe even at the best of times – ask the lifeguards if you're in doubt. Like Sandy Beach, however, it's a greatly loved **body-surfing** and **boogie-boarding** site and, with the same propensity to lure unwary tourists into the water, it boasts a similarly dismal record of fatalities.

Sea Life Park

Map 7, F5. Mon–Thurs & Sat 9.30am–5pm, Fri 9.30am–10pm; adults $19.95, seniors $15.95, ages 4–12 $9.95. Call ©259-7933 for details of free shuttle buses from Waikīkī. TheBus #22 ends its route here.

Immediately opposite the Makapuʻu Beach parking lot stands the entrance to the expensive but popular **Sea Life Park**, which tends to hold greater appeal for children than for their parents. Along with the predictable dolphin and porpoise shows, which feature human co-stars dressed up as pirates and princesses, there's a giant Reef Tank, a penguin enclosure, and a hospital for injured monk seals. The park also raises rare green sea turtles for release into the ocean, and has even bred a **wholphin** – half-whale, half-dolphin. With a couple of snack bars, where live entertainment is provided by unidentifiable costumed characters who have yet to secure their own TV series, plus a bar run by the *Gordon Biersch Brewery*, it's all too possible to find yourself spending an entire day here.

WAIMĀNALO

WAIMĀNALO, four miles on from Makapuʻu, holds one of the highest proportions of native Hawaiians of any town on Oahu, and has become a stronghold for advocates of Hawaiian sovereignty. The main drag, lined with fast-food joints, is far from picturesque, but as long as you take care not to intrude, you can get a real glimpse of old-time Hawaii by exploring the back roads. The small family-run farms and nurseries along Waikupanaha Street in particular, which runs inland along the base of the *pali*, are utterly rural and verdant.

The most compelling reason to come to Waimānalo, however, is its **beach**. At over three miles long, it's the longest stretch of sand on Oahu, and the setting, with high promontories to either end and a green cradle of cliffs behind, is superb. The most accessible place to park, and also the safest swimming spot, is **Waimānalo Beach County Park** at its southern end, but wherever you start you're likely to feel tempted to stroll a long way along the endless sands.

Around a mile further north, where the fir trees backing the beach grow thicker again beyond a residential district, you come to **Waimānalo Bay State Recreation Area**. The waves here are a little rougher, but it feels even more secluded, and you can **camp** for up to five days with a permit from the state parks office in Honolulu (closed Wed & Thurs; see p.154).

Further on still, access to pristine **Bellows Field Beach Park** – ideal for lazy swimmers and novice body-surfers – is controlled by the adjoining air force base. The public is only allowed in between noon on Friday and 8am on Monday. This time it's the county parks office (see p.154) that runs the **campground**, also open weekends only.

Windward Oahu

Less than ten miles separate downtown Honolulu from Oahu's spectacular **windward coast**. Climb inland along either the **Pali Highway**, the **Likelike Highway**, or the new **Hwy-3**, and at the knife-edge crest of the Ko'olau

Mountains you're confronted by amazing views of the serrated *pali* that sweeps from northwest to southeast. As often as not, the abrupt transition from west to east is marked by the arrival of **rain** – it has, after all, been raining on this side of the island for several million years, cutting away at the cliffs to create a long, sheer wall.

The mountain highways drop down to the twin residential communities of **Kailua** and **Kāne'ohe**, both of minimal appeal to visitors. On a day's tour of Oahu you'd probably do better to avoid them altogether, and head straight off north on **Hwy-83**. This clings to the coastline all the way up to Oahu's northernmost tip, sandwiched between a ravishing belt of well-watered farmland and tree-covered slopes, and a tempting fringe of golden sand. On most Hawaiian islands, the windward shore is too exposed to be safe for swimming, but here a protective coral reef makes bathing possible at a long succession of narrow, little-used **beaches**. Oahu is also exceptional in having a chain of picturesque little **islets** just offshore; you're unlikely to set foot on any of them, but they provide a lovely backdrop.

Though driving through such luscious scenery is a real joy, there are few specific reasons to stop. The **Byōdō-In Temple** provides a great photo opportunity, while further north the **Polynesian Cultural Center** attracts a million visitors each year; otherwise you might want to spend an hour or two hiking in the backcountry, somewhere like **Kahana Valley** or **Hau'ula**.

KAILUA

The shorefront town of **KAILUA** stretches along Kailua Bay roughly four miles down from the Nu'uanu Pali lookout, and four miles north from Waimānolo. Now little more than an exclusive suburb of Honolulu, it was once a favorite dwelling place for the chiefs of Oahu, surrounded by wetlands and rich soil ideal for growing *taro*. Exploring the little side-streets that lead off Kalāheo Avenue as it parallels the bay may fuel your fantasies of relocating to Hawaii, but inquiring about real-estate prices will soon put paid to that dream, and any time you have here is best spent on the **beach**.

Kailua Beach County Park, which fills the colossal main curve of the bay, is utterly gorgeous, and makes an ideal family swimming spot year-round. The soft wide sands slope down into turquoise waters much used by **windsurfers**; windsurfing equipment, as well as **kayaks**, can be rented from vans and stalls along the park approach road, or on the beach itself. Just be sure to keep away from the polluted area around the Ka'elepulu Canal.

Head north from here, and you'll soon reach **Kailua Beach**, where the waves hit a little harder, so there's less sand, but swimming conditions are generally safe. Walking south on the other hand, beyond Alāla Point, swiftly brings you to the similar but less crowded **Lanikai Beach**.

Lanikai consists of just a few short streets of priceless homes, all but cut off from the rest of Kailua by Ka'iwa Ridge. The coastal road beyond the beach park becomes a one-way loop immediately south of the ridge, forcing you to turn slightly inland on A'alapapa Road. Take the second right onto Ka'elepulu Street and park near the gate of the Mid-Pacific Country Club. Here you'll see the **Ka'iwa Ridge Trail** leading away to the left. Just a few minutes' steep climbing is rewarded with superb views up and down the coast and out to the tiny islands in the bay.

Almost the only vestige of Kailua's past is **Ulupo Heiau**, an ancient temple once used for human sacrifice. This long, low platform of rounded lava boulders looks out across the Kawainui Marsh from a hillock to the left of Kailua Road. To get there, take Uluo'a Road, the first left after Kailua Road breaks away from Kalaniana'ole Highway, and then turn right.

As for Kailua itself, the only area that feels much like a genuine community lies around the intersection of Kailua and Ku'ulei roads, a few hundred yards inland from the beach park. Here you'll find assorted neighborhood stores as well as the **Kailua Shopping Center** mall.

THE MŌKAPU PENINSULA

Kailua's northern limit is defined by Oneawa Ridge, stretching towards the ocean and culminating in the **Mōkapu Peninsula**. More of an island than a peninsula, joined to the rest of Oahu by two slender causeways, Mōkapu is entirely taken up by a Marine base, and no public access is permitted. It was to connect the base with Pearl Harbor that Hwy-3, the new trans-Ko'olau highway, was originally commissioned. Archeologists have found the extensive sand dunes along Mōkapu's northern shore to be the richest ancient burial site in all Hawaii.

KĀNE'OHE

Slightly smaller than Kailua, and boasting a far less robust economy, as well as considerably fewer amenities for visitors, **KĀNE'OHE** is seldom seen as an exciting destination in its own right. That's largely because none of its silty beaches are suited for swimming. However, seven-mile **Kāne'ohe Bay**, reaching northwards from the Mōkapu peninsula, is the largest bay in Hawaii and, once you're outside the main built-up strip, one of the most beautiful. If you want to join the local pleasure-boaters out on the calm waters of the bay, take a one-hour **cruise** from He'eia Kea Pier on the glass-bottomed *Coral Queen* (Mon–Sat 10am, 11am, noon & 1.30pm; adults $7.50, under-13s $3.50; ℂ235-2888).

He'eia State Park, on the headland immediately before the pier, is a landscaped area set aside largely for its views of the adjoining **He'eia Fishpond**. Ancient Hawaiians built the low curving stone walls that enclose this saltwater lagoon; it's now once more being used to raise mullet. What little you see from the park probably won't hold your attention long, however. Tiny **Coconut Island**, out to sea, is used for marine research by the University of Hawaii, but is better known from the credits sequence of *Gilligan's Island*.

Inland, Kāne'ohe holds several attractive public **gardens**. Among the quietest and most relaxing is the nature reserve of **Ho'omaluhia Botanical Garden** (daily 9am–4pm; free), at the top of Luluku Road, which loops back into the hills off Kamehameha Highway between Pali and Likelike highways. Several short trails lead swiftly into the wilderness.

For a more commercial display of flowers, fruits and orchids, head instead for **Senator Fong's Plantation**, near Kahalu'u in northern Kāne'ohe (daily 9am–4pm; adults $10, children $5), where trams whisk visitors along the paved walkways. The smaller, free **Ha'ikū Gardens**, just off Hwy-83 at the entrance to glorious **Ha'ikū Valley**, is a nice little lily pond designed to lure diners into the on-site *Chart House* steakhouse (✆247-6671).

Byōdō-In Temple

A clearly marked side-road *mauka* of Hwy-83 (Kahekili Highway) just beyond central Kāne'ohe leads to the inter-denominational cemetery known as the **Valley of the Temples** (daily 8.30am–4.30pm; adults $2, under-12s $1). Several religions have chapels and monuments here, but casual visitors are always drawn to the Buddhist **Byōdō-In Temple**, built in the 1960s to celebrate a hundred years of Japanese immigration to Hawaii. This unexpected replica of a 900-year-old temple at Uji in Japan looks absolutely stunning, its red pagodas standing out from the trees at the base of the awesome *pali*.

Having parked outside the temple gates, you cross an arching footbridge to stroll through the peaceful gardens. A fishpond here is so full of orange, black and white carp that they squeeze each other out of the water in their frenzy for fish food. Before you reach the main pavilion, you're encouraged to use a suspended battering ram to ring a three-ton brass bell; you'll probably have heard it echoing through the valley as you arrive. Once inside, you're confronted by a nine-foot meditating Buddha made of gilded, lacquered wood.

KUALOA PARK AND MOKOLI'I

At **Ka'alaea**, a mile north of the Byōdō-In Temple, Kahekili Highway joins Kamehameha Highway on its way up from He'eia State Park, and the two then run on together as Kamehameha Highway. Looking inland, the tumbling waterfalls at the heads of Waihe'e and Waiāhole valleys are superb, but the next point worthy of a halt is at the northern tip of Kāne'ohe Bay.

From the crisp green lawns of **Kualoa Point**, out on the headland, you can look through a gap-toothed straggle of windswept coconut palms to conical **Mokoli'i Island**. To ancient Hawaiians, this picturesque little outcrop was the tail of a dragon; its more banal modern nickname is "Chinaman's Hat". At low tide, you can wade out to it along the reef – the water should never rise more than waist high, and reef shoes are an absolute must – to find a tiny hidden beach on its northern side. Otherwise, content yourself with a swim from the thin shelf of sand at Kualoa Park.

Kualoa Ranch

Map 1, J4. For full details, including rates and schedules for specific activities, call ©237-7321.

Roughly 200 yards north of Kualoa Park, a driveway *mauka* of the highway (left as you head north) leads into the expansive grounds of **Kualoa Ranch**. Until recently a conventional cattle ranch, this now plays host to flocks of Japanese tourists instead. Individual travelers are welcome to sign up for any of a wide range of activities – such as horse-riding, bicycling, helicopter rides, para-sailing and snorkeling, as well as a "Haunted House" in a natural cave at the foot of the *pali* – but the place is dominated by large groups of honeymooners.

Ka'a'awa

Several more good beaches lie immediately north of Kāne'ohe Bay. There's no danger of failing to spot them; in places the highway runs within a dozen feet of the ocean. So long as the surf isn't obviously high, it's generally safe to park by the road at any of the consecutive **Kanenelu**, **Kalae'ō'io**, and **Ka'a'awa** beaches, and head straight into the water. Only **Swanzy Beach County Park**, a little further along, really demands caution, on account of its unpredictable currents. It became a beach park thanks to a rich Kailua resident of the 1920s, who donated this land to the state on condition that they didn't create any other public parks nearer her home.

Just beyond Swanzy, by which time the beach has often narrowed away to nothing, you'll probably have trouble recognizing the rock formation known as the **Crouching Lion**. That this is one of windward Oahu's best-known landmarks is largely thanks to the *Crouching Lion Inn*, reviewed on p.182.

KAHANA VALLEY

The whole of the deeply indented **Kahana Valley**, tucked in behind a high serrated *pali* around the corner from the Crouching Lion, is a state park. The basic economic unit of ancient Hawaii was the *ahupua'a*, a wedge of land reaching from the mountain peaks down to the ocean; Kahana is now the only *ahupua'a* to be entirely owned by the state. Still farmed by thirty native Hawaiian families, it aims to be a "living park", though what that means has never quite been settled. In theory, the residents educate visitors in Hawaiian traditions, but while traditional crops are still grown they don't dress up or pretend to *be* ancient Hawaiians. There's a friendly, helpful **visitor center** (©237-8858) a little way back from the highway as it curves around Kahana Bay, but most people who call in have come simply to **hike**. Be sure to bring waterproof clothing if you plan to join them.

Kahana trails

The easiest of Kahana Valley's attractive **trails** starts by following the dirt road that heads to the right in front of the visitor center. After passing a few houses, it heads out into a lush meadow scattered with fruit trees, and then veers left at a far-from-obvious junction to climb into the woods. It soon reaches a clearing where you can gaze across the valley to the high walls on the far side, and watch as it recedes away inland. Not far beyond, a few weather-worn stones mark the site of the **Kapa'ele'ele Ko'a** fishing shrine. A steep climb then leads up to **Keaniani Kilo**, a vantage point from which keen-eyed Hawaiians would watch for schools of fish, and signal canoes waiting below to set off in pursuit. There's nothing here now, but it's a lovely spot. The trail drops down to the highway, and you can make your way back along the beach.

To take the **Nakoa Trail**, which heads for the back of the valley, you should once again leave your car at the visitor center. Assuming that it hasn't been raining – in which case the valley streams will be too high to cross – keep walking along the main valley road for a mile or so before a gate bars the way. The trail then rambles up and around the valley walls for roughly four miles, with some great views and plenty of mosquitoes for company. For a shorter adventure, simply head left at the start and you'll soon come to an idyllic little swimming hole in **Kahana Stream**.

Kahana Bay

The beach at **Kahana Bay**, straight across from the park entrance, hangs on to an ample spread of fine sand all year round, and is very safe for swimming. It's possible to **camp** in the woods that line its central section; free permits are issued by the park visitor center, or the state parks office in Honolulu (see p.154).

HAU'ULA AND PUNALU'U

Beyond Kahana, the highway continues to cling to every curve of the coastline, and traffic moves slowly. Maps show **HAU'ULA** and **PUNALU'U** as distinct towns, but on the ground it's hard to tell where one ends and the next begins: both are quiet little local communities that barely reach a hundred yards back from the shore.

Of the half-dozen named beaches in this stretch, **Punalu'u Beach Park**, the furthest south, is the best for swimming, so long as you keep away from the mouth of Wai'ono Stream. The strip of sand is so thin here that the coconut palms rooted in the lawns behind it manage to curve out over the waves. **Hau'ula Beach Park**, a few miles along, is equally sheltered, but only snorkelers derive much pleasure from swimming out over the rocks.

Sacred Falls State Park

A very inconspicuous parking lot, *mauka* of the highway a mile past Punalu'u, is the trailhead for **Sacred Falls**. Two miles up from here – half through flat and featureless fields, and half hacking through the undergrowth beside Kalanui Stream – the **Kaliuwa'a Falls** plummet eighty feet from a green crevice in the hillside.

This area is a state park, but that doesn't mean the trail is easy or even safe – in fact it's often closed to the public, as the latest landslide is cleared up, or when flash floods threaten. Several hikers have been killed by falling rocks over the years, and there was a notorious incident when a tourist group was held up at gunpoint.

Hau'ula trails

Three exhilarating but muddy trails enable hikers to explore **Ma'akua Gulch**, behind central Hau'ula. To reach them, park at the *mauka* end of Hau'ula Homestead Road, which starts opposite the northern limit of Hau'ula Beach Park. Having walked a hundred yards up the track (officially Ma'akua Road) from here, you'll see a small driveway on the left, with a mailbox-style check-in station to write down your details before you set off.

The best short hike, the **Hau'ula Loop Trail**, branches off to the right just beyond the entrance gate. In something under two hours, with a few stretches of steep climbing, it carries you up and over the high ridge to the north, through sweet smelling forests of ironwood and pine. As well as ocean views, you get amazing panoramas of neighboring Kaipapa'u Valley, reaching far inland and looking as though no human has ever entered it.

The similar but more overgrown **Ma'akua Ridge Trail** twists its own circuit around the southern wall of the Gulch, while the **Ma'akua Gulch Trail** follows the central stream back towards the mountains. As the gulch narrows, you have to hike more and more in the stream bed, which can be dangerous after rain. Otherwise, it's a good opportunity to see the luscious blossoms for which Hau'ula – meaning "red *hau* trees" – is named.

LĀ'IE

The town of **LĀ'IE**, three miles on from Hau'ula, owes its neat, prim appearance to the fact that it was founded by Mormons in 1864, and remains dominated by the Latter-Day Saints to this day. This was the second major Mormon settlement in Hawaii; the first, on Lanai, was abandoned when church elders discovered that its President, William Gibson, had registered all its lands in his own name. Gibson went on to be Prime Minister of Hawaii, while his congregation moved to Oahu. Lā'ie now holds an imposing **Mormon Temple**, built in 1919 as the first such temple outside the continental United States – the temple itself is not open to the public, though a separate visitor center is (daily 9am–9pm) – and a branch of the Mormon-run **Brigham Young University**, but is best-known to visitors for a less obviously Mormon enterprise, the **Polynesian Cultural Center**.

Mormon colleges tend not to spawn lively alternative scenes, and Lā'ie is no exception. Local students do at least get to body-surf the heavy waves at **Pounders Beach** at the south end of town, but don't join in if you lack their know-how. **Kokololio Beach** just south of that is an attractive curve of sand where swimming is only safe in summer, while **Lā'ie Beach** in the center of town is prone to strong currents. The two-part **Mālaekahana Bay State Recreation Area** further north provides the best recreational swimming, and also makes an excellent place to camp, with a free state permit picked up in Honolulu (see p.154). At low tide, it's possible to wade out to **Goat Island**, a bird sanctuary that has a beautiful protected beach on its north shore.

The Polynesian Cultural Center

Map 8, G4. Mon–Sat 12.30–9pm; adults $27, children $16. Extra
charges for lū'au and IMAX movie show. For reservations, call
©293-3333. Two hours from Ala Moana on TheBus #52.

An incredible one million customers per year pay to visit
Lā'ie's **Polynesian Cultural Center**. Part entertainment
(with joke-telling guides and displays of fire-walking) and
part educational (with step-by-step demonstrations of traditional crafts), it's a haphazard mixture of real and bogus
Polynesia. Kids tend to love it, while adults think of it
either as uproarious kitsch, or insulting.

Daytime visits consist of touring seven themed "villages" – by tram, on foot or in a canoe – to learn about
seven Polynesian groups. Unless you time your visit to
each village to coincide with the daily schedule of pre-
sentations, there's very little to see, so if you're going to
come at all be prepared to spend at least half a day in
total. As well as Hawaii, you'll find Tahiti and the
Marquesas, plus the further-flung cultures of Fiji, Tonga,
Samoa and the Maori. Most of the staff are students from
the adjoining University, who don't necessarily come
from the relevant parts of the Pacific – some of the
milder-mannered Mormons have a hard time looking
suitably ferocious when they're pretending to be Maori
warriors, for example. It's also worth bearing in mind
that the information they give you is laced with Mormon
theology; thus the Polynesians are said to be descended
from one of the lost tribes of Israel, who migrated from
Central America under the leadership of a certain
Hagoth. Come in the evening, pay extra, and you can eat
bad lū'au food and watch a banal program of amateurish
song-and-dance routines.

KAHUKU

KAHUKU, a couple of miles on from Lāʻie, may look run-down by comparison, but is considerably more atmospheric. Though the plantation it served went out of business in 1971, the rusting hulk of the **Kahuku Sugar Mill** still overshadows this small town. Assorted outbuildings now house a half-hearted shopping mall. Unidentified lumps of machinery are dotted around the courtyard, painted in peeling pastel blues and yellows. Most of the old mill workings remain in place; some parts are color-coded according to their former function, as you'll see while exploring inside on the metal walkways.

Behind the sugar mill are a few dirt lanes holding tin-roofed plantation homes. The long **beach** beyond is not suitable for swimming, but stretches a full five miles up to Turtle Bay if you fancy a solitary, bracing hike.

Beyond Kahuku, the highway veers away from the shore to run alongside the **Amorient Aquafarms**. Fresh shrimp from this series of ponds can be bought from trucks and vans stationed along the highway nearby. The Walsh Farms complex of small, brightly-painted shacks at the far end sells fresh fruit and an entertaining mixture of antiques and junk.

TURTLE BAY

Just before Kamehameha Highway rejoins the ocean on the North Shore, an obvious spur road leads *makai* past some expensive condos and private homes, to end at **Turtle Bay**. Here photogenic beaches lie to either side of **Kuilima Point** – long, wave-raked Turtle Bay to the west, and the sheltered artificial lagoon of Kuilima Cove to the east – but you'd only choose to come here if you were staying at the luxury **hotel** on the point, reviewed on p.152.

Central Oahu

Thanks to the island's butterfly-like shape, the quickest route from Honolulu to the North Shore lies across the flat agricultural heartland of **central Oahu**. Cradled between the mountains, the **Leilehua Plateau** was created when lava from the Ko'olau eruptions lapped against the older Wai'anae Range. Sugar cane and pineapples raised in its rich soil were the foundation of the Hawaiian economy until less than fifty years ago. As commercial farming has dwindled, however, the area has become neglected and dejected. More people than ever live in towns such as **Waipahu** and **Wahiawa** – many of them personnel from the military bases tucked into the hillsides – but there's very little here to interest tourists. If you plan to drive around Oahu in a single day, you'd do better to press straight on to Hale'iwa (see p.117).

'AIEA AND PEARL CITY

Whichever road you follow, you have to drive a long way **west of Honolulu** before reaching open countryside. Hwy-1, the main "interstate", curves past the airport and Pearl Harbor, while Hwy-78 sticks closer to the Ko'olau foothills, but they eventually crisscross each other to run through the nondescript communities of **'AIEA** and **PEARL CITY**. Restaurants where commuters can grab a quick meal loom on all sides, but neither town has a center worth stopping for.

Keaīwa Heiau State Park

Only hilltop **Keaīwa Heiau State Park**, in suburban **'Aiea Heights** above 'Aiea proper, merits a detour from the highway, and even that appeals more to local residents than to outsiders. The road up heads right from the second stop light after the 'Aiea Stadium turnoff on Hwy-78, and then twists for almost three miles through a sleepy residential area.

Keaīwa Heiau, whose ruined walls are on the left as soon as you enter the park, was a center where healers, such as Keaīwa – "the mysterious" – himself, practised herbal medicine, using plants cultivated in the surrounding gardens. Lots of *ti* plants, together with a few larger *kukui* trees, still grow within the otherwise well-maintained precinct, which also holds a little shrine and a central ring of stones that encloses a small lawn. This layout is largely conjectural, however, as the *heiau* was severely damaged during the sugar-plantation era.

There are no views from the *heiau*, but a mile-long **loop road** circles the ridge beyond, where the ironwood forest is punctuated with meadows and picnic areas looking out over Pearl Harbor. Halfway around, the **'Aiea Loop Trail** traces a five-mile circuit through the woods, offering views of the interior valleys as well as Honolulu. The highlight is the wreckage of a World War II cargo plane that crashed into a remote gully.

Camping at the park's cool, secluded campground (closed Wed and Thurs) is free, with a state permit.

WAIPAHU

Just beyond Pearl City, both Hwy-2 and Kamehameha Highway branch away to head north across the central plateau. Only a mile or so west, however, the small town of **WAIPAHU** holds one of Hawaii's best historical **museums**, an evocative memorial to the early days of immigration. It's also home to the unexpectedly upmarket **Waikele Center** shopping mall, with a giant Borders bookstore, and lots of discount "factory outlets".

Body surfing, Sandy Beach, Oahu

Waikīkī Beach and Diamond Head

Waikīkī seen from the sea

VW Beetle and wind-surfing board

Surf mural and palm trees, Waikīkī

Hanauma Bay, Oahu

Sunset Beach, North Shore, Oahu

Kodak Hula Show, Waikīkī

Hawaii's Plantation Village

Map 1, F7. Mon–Fri 9am–4.30pm, Sat 10am–4.30pm; guided tours only, hourly until 3pm; adults $5, under-18s & seniors $3; ©667-0110.

Hawaii's Plantation Village is located a mile south of Hwy-1 in Waipahu, just below the sugar mill to which it owes its existence. It's a loving non-profit re-creation of the living conditions of the almost 400,000 agricultural laborers who migrated to Hawaii between 1852 and 1946, and were largely responsible for spawning the ethnic blend of the modern state.

Enthusiastic guides lead visitors around a small museum, and then through a "time tunnel" onto the former plantation estate. Simple houses – some always stood on this site, others have been brought in – contain personal possessions, illustrating both how much the migrants brought with them, and how different groups mingled to create a common Hawaiian identity. Cumulatively, the domestic details – pots, pans, buckets, family photographs, even the tiny boxing gloves used to train Filipino fighting cocks – make you feel the occupants have merely stepped out for a minute. The most moving artifacts are the *bangos*, the numbered metal badges that helped the *lunas* (whip-cracking Caucasian plantation supervisors) to distinguish each worker from the next. Goods could be obtained in the company store by showing your *bango*, with the cost deducted from your next pay packet.

WAHIAWA

All routes across central Oahu – whether you take Hwy-2 or Kamehameha Highway from Pearl City, or the more scenic **Kunia Road** though the fields from Waipahu – have to pass through the large town of **WAHIAWA** in the heart of the island. The main drag holds the dismal array of bars, fast-food outlets and gun stores that you'd expect to find this close to the **Schofield Barracks**, Oahu's largest military base (which by all accounts is actually very pretty, if you can get through the gates).

A couple of mildly diverting sites lie just outside the town. The **Wahiawā Botanical Gardens** (daily 9am–4pm; free), a mile east, is a reasonably attractive enclave of tropical trees and flowers, but nothing special by Hawaiian standards. To the north, on Whitmore Avenue off Kamehameha Highway, what look like faintly marked reddish-brown lava boulders in a pineapple field actually constitute an archeological site known as **Kukaniloko**, or the **Birthing Stones**. Tradition had it that any chief hoping to rule Oahu should be born here.

Dole Plantation

Map 1, F4. Daily 9am–5.30pm; free.

The single-story building of the **Dole Plantation** stands east of Kamehameha Highway a mile north of Wahiawā. Though the large number of cars and tour buses parked outside might lead you to expect something more interesting, the plantation is basically a large covered mall-cum-marketplace, which sells the usual assortment of tacky souvenirs and craft items, as well as fresh pineapples and pineapple products such as juices and frozen "whips". Outside, they've recently opened what's claimed to be the world's largest **maze**, composed of Hawaiian plants, but it will take a few more years' growth for it to become genuinely taxing. Visitors can also wander around the back into a small display garden of pineapple species, and read a perfunctory history of the Dole family business.

The North Shore

Although the **surfing beaches** of Oahu's **North Shore** are famous the world over, the area as a whole is barely equipped for tourists. **Waimea**, **Sunset** and **'Ehukai** beach parks are all laid-back roadside stretches of sand, where you can usually find a quiet spot to yourself. In summer, the tame waves may leave you wondering what all the fuss is about; see them at full tilt in the winter, between October and April, and you'll have no doubts.

If you plan to do some surfing – and this is no place for casual amateurs – then you'd do best to base yourself in **Pūpūkea** (see p.121). Otherwise, you can see all there is to see in an easy day-trip from Waikīkī, with a pause to shop and snack in **Hale'iwa**.

HALE'IWA

The main town on the North Shore stands at the point where Kamehameha Highway reaches the ocean, 24 miles north of Honolulu. For most visitors, **HALE'IWA** (pronounced "*ha-lay-eve-a*") comes as a pleasant surprise. Despite the fact that tourists have been coming here ever since the opening of a train line from Honolulu in 1899, it's one of the very few communities on Oahu whose roots have not been obscured by a century of rebuilding and development.

Since the 1960s, Hale'iwa has become a mecca for **surfers** from all over the world. Many of the originals, lured here from California by the movie *Endless Summer*, seem to have remained not only in Hawaii, but also in the 1960s. The town is bursting with half-hippie businesses, such as surf shops, tie-dye stores, organic restaurants and galleries of ethnic knick-knacks. Add those to a scattering of upfront tourist traps, and local stores and diners, and you've got an intriguing, energetic blend that entices many travelers to stay for months.

....

Cafés and restaurants in Hale'iwa are reviewed on p.182.

....

That said, there's precious little to see in Hale'iwa. Its main street, **Kamehameha Avenue**, runs for a mile from the Paukauila Stream to the Anahulu River, well back from the ocean, passing a cluster of gas stations and then a succession of low-rise malls. In the largest of these, the **North Shore Marketplace**, Strong Current is the most interesting of the **surf shops**, for devotees and idle browsers alike. As well as selling nine-foot boards for anything from $500 up to $2500 (no rentals), it's crammed with historic boards, books, memorabilia and videos.

Only as you approach the river do you finally come to the heart of Hale'iwa, a short stretch of old-fashioned boardwalk lined with false-front wooden buildings. One of these houses Matsumoto's, a Japanese grocery store renowned for its heavenly **shave ice** – the Hawaiian equivalent of a sno-cone, a mush of ice saturated with flavored syrup.

Beyond that, narrow Rainbow Bridge crosses Anahulu River, with great views upstream towards the green slopes of the Anahulu Valley. Traffic congestion led to the opening in 1995 of the Hale'iwa Bypass. Now that tourists circling Oahu can avoid Hale'iwa altogether, the town is having to work a little harder to lure them in – hence the highway signs that plead "Don't Bypass Hale'iwa". Even so, the decrease in business should ensure that the delightfully rural back-roads that lead away from Kamehameha Avenue, such as **Pa'ala'a Road**, will remain unspoiled for many years to come.

The small bay at the rivermouth is **Waialua Bay**, with Hale'iwa Harbor sheltered by a breakwater on its southwestern side. Southwest of the harbor, **Hale'iwa Ali'i**

Hale'iwa Equipment Rental

The best known **surf outfitter** in Hale'iwa is Surf'n'Sea, to the left of the highway immediately across Rainbow Bridge (62-595 Kamehameha Hwy; ©637-9887 or 1-800/899-SURF). As well as renting surfboards ($5 per hour, $24 per day), bodyboards ($4/$20), windsurfing boards ($12/$40) and snorkel equipment ($6.50 half-day, $9.50 all day), they organize dive trips (1 tank $65, 2 tanks $90), provide lessons in surfing and windsurfing ($65 for two hours, $150 all day), and sell new and used boards and souvenirs.

Raging Isle, in the North Shore Marketplace (©637-7700), also sells surfboards and rents mountain bikes ($20 half-day, $35 full day).

Beach Park is a favorite place for local kids to learn to surf – there are even **free surfing lessons** on weekend mornings in winter – but inexperienced outsiders who have a go are taking their lives in their hands. Just to reach the waves, you have to pick your way across a tricky shallow coral reef, while once you're out there you're at the mercy of strong cross-currents. Swimming at **Hale'iwa Beach Park**, on the northeast shore of the bay, is much safer.

WAIMEA BAY

Long **Kawailoa Beach** stretches for almost five miles northeast of Hale'iwa, interrupted repeatedly by rocky reef and swept by fierce currents. Driving along the highway, however, the first glimpse you get of the ocean comes as you crest a small promontory to look down on **Waimea Bay**.

Waimea Bay is the most famous **surfing** spot in the world, thanks to what are generally believed to be the biggest rideable waves on the planet. During the summer, it's often calm as a lake, but in winter the break off its craggy headlands can remain over twenty feet high for days at a time. Anywhere else, even the waves right on the beach would count as monsters, and lethal rip currents tear along the shoreline. While entering the ocean at Waimea in winter is extremely dangerous for anyone other than expert surfers, the beautiful sands of **Waimea Bay Beach County Park** are usually crowded with swimmers, snorkelers and boogie-boarders in summer, and with awestruck spectators in winter.

Until a huge flood in 1894, Waimea River flowed freely into the sea, and the valley behind was densely populated. Most of its farms and homes were destroyed, however, and the mouth of the river is now blocked by a sandbar that forms part of the beach park.

Waimea Falls Park

Map 8, D4. Daily 10am–5.30pm; adults $19.95, ages 6–12 $8.95, ages 4–5 $3.95.

All of Waimea Valley inland of the highway bridge is now occupied by the commercially-run **Waimea Falls Park**. The tame but reasonably sensitive exploitation of this beautiful valley makes a good introduction to Hawaii and its natural history for first-time visitors; it's considerably higher-minded than the Polynesian Cultural Center (see p.111), though the emphasis on plants rather than people means that if you're hoping to be entertained you may leave disappointed.

The valley's most prominent historical relic is the restored *Hale O Lono* or "House of Lono", an ancient *heiau* whose three stone terraces rise next to the main gate; in fact you could take a look without entering the park. If you pay to go in, once past the entrance complex of gift stores and snack bars you can wander stream-side walkways that lead through botanical gardens planted with native flowers and healing herbs, as well as aviaries and the fenced-off ruins of further *heiaus* and ancient burial sites.

In the **kauhale kahiko**, a mock-Hawaiian village of thatched huts, costumed guides display Polynesian crafts. Beyond a *hula* demonstration area, almost a mile up from the gates, the path reaches the double **Waimea Falls** at the head of the valley. Cliff divers regularly leap sixty feet into the pool below.

In addition to the basic walking tour, the park organizes various other activities. As Waimea Adventure Tours (©638-8511 for reservations), it conducts valley tours in individual off-road buggies (1hr $35, 2hr 30min $75), on mountain bikes (a van ride to the head of the valley so you can freewheel back down costs $60) or in kayaks ($35 for a 1hr guided tour, or $15 per hour).

PŪPŪKEA

Immediately beyond Waimea Bay, Kamehameha Highway starts to cruise beside a succession of magnificent surfing beaches. Driving demands patience; at the best of times, vehicles pull off without warning, while during major competitions traffic slows to a standstill.

Pūpūkea Beach County Park, which, like Hanauma Bay (see p.94), is a Marine Life Conservation District, stretches for well over a mile from the mouth of Waimea Bay. At its western end, the Three Tables surf break is named after three flat-topped chunks of reef, where plenty of unwary swimmers have come to grief, while **Shark's Cove** to the east, riddled with submarine caves, is a popular site for snorkelers and scuba divers in summer.

Bumper stickers all over Oahu carry the slogan "Save the North Shore", a reference to the planned Lihi Lani real-estate development on the cliffs above **PŪPŪKEA**. For the moment, Pūpūkea is a low-key community composed largely of international surf-bums, with a few stores and no restaurants. It offers by far the best **accommodation** along the North Shore, however, in the shape of the *Backpacker's Vacation Inn* (see p.152).

Pu'u O Mahuka Heiau State Monument

For a superb view of Waimea Valley and the bay, head up to the **Pu'u O Mahuka Heiau**, perched on the eastern bluff above the mouth of the river. As Oahu's largest temple of human sacrifice, this was once home to a terrifying brotherhood of *pahupu* ("cut-in-two") warrior-priests, who tattooed half their bodies completely black. To reach it, turn off the highway at the Foodland supermarket, a few hundred yards beyond the bay. Climb the hill on twisting Pūpūkea Road, then turn right onto a narrow track that skirts the cliff-edge for just under a mile.

The parking lot at the end stands alongside the higher of the temple's two tiers. The meadow that from here appears to lie just beyond the *heiau* is in fact on the far side of the deep cleft of Waimea Valley. **Trails** lead around and partly through the old stone walls, within which the outlines of several subsidiary structures can be discerned; most were originally paved with water-worn stones carried up from Waimea Bay. The main "altar" at the *mauka* end is usually covered with wrapped offerings, and probably bears little resemblance to its original configuration. From the little loop path around the java plum trees nearby, you can see right along the North Shore to Ka'ena Point in the western distance.

Kaunala trail

Beyond the *heiau* turnoff, Pūpūkea Road heads inland for another two miles, to end at the gates of a Boy Scout Camp. From here, the five-mile **Kaunala Trail**, open on weekends only, runs along the thickly wooded crest of a high mountain ridge. As well as views of the deep and inaccessible gorges to either side, if the clouds clear you'll eventually get to see Oahu's highest peak, 4020-foot **Mount Ka'ala**, far across the central plains.

SUNSET BEACH

With its wide shelf of yellow sand, lined by palm trees, **Sunset Beach**, northeast of Pūpūkea, is perhaps the most picture-perfect beach on Oahu. Only occasional gaps between the oceanfront homes allow access, but once there you're free to wander for two blissful miles of paradise-island coastline. Unless you come on a calm and current-free summer's day (ask the lifeguards), it's essential to stay well away from the water; the "Sunset Rip" can drag even beachcombers out to sea.

In winter, when the waves are stupendous, Sunset Beach fills with photographers in search of the definitive surfing shot, while reckless pro surfers perform magazine-cover stunts out on the water. Each of the breaks here has its own name, the most famous being the **Banzai Pipeline**, where the goal is to let yourself be fired like a bullet through the tubular break and yet manage to avoid being slammed down onto the shallow, razor-sharp reef at the end. To watch the action, walk a few hundred yards west (left) from **'Ehukai Beach County Park**, where a small patch of lawn separates the beach from the road.

Sunset Beach, a mile past 'Ehukai, was where North Shore surfing first took off in the early 1950s, and remains the venue for many contests. The break known as **Backyards** is renowned as especially lethal, though it's a popular playground for windsurfers. **Kaunala Beach** beyond that, home to the **Velzyland** break, is the last surf spot before the highway curves away towards Turtle Bay (see p.112) and the Windward Coast. Velzyland offers reliable rather than colossal waves, but riding them with any degree of safety requires immense precision.

Breck's On The Beach Hostel, a little way north of Sunset Beach, is reviewed on p.153.

WEST FROM HALE'IWA: WAIALUA AND MOKULE'IA

The coast of northern Oahu to the **west of Hale'iwa** lacks suitable surfing beaches, and is so rarely visited that most people don't really count it as part of the North Shore at all.

The area's principal landmark is the **Waialua Sugar Mill**, gently rusting away at the foot of the Wai'anae mountains. A moderately interesting driving tour leads down the back roads of the village of **Waialua**, and along oceanfront Crozier Drive to even smaller **Mokulē'ia**. From here, you'll have attractive views of Hale'iwa in the distance, but with not much to do, you might as well go straight to Hale'iwa itself.

KA'ENA POINT

The westernmost promontory of Oahu, **Ka'ena Point** is only accessible on foot or mountain bike; it's not possible to drive all the way around from the North Shore to the Leeward Shore. As Farrington Highway runs west of Waialua and Mokulē'ia, the landscape grows progressively drier, and the road eventually grinds to a halt a couple of miles beyond Dillingham Airfield.

On the far side of the gate, you can follow either a bumpy, dusty dirt road beside the steadily dwindling Wai'anae Ridge, or a sandy track that straggles up and down across the coastal rocks. The only sign of life is likely to be the odd local fisherman, perched on the spits of black lava reaching into the foaming ocean.

After roughly an hour of hot hiking, the ridge vanishes altogether, and you squeeze between boulders to enter the **Ka'ena Point Natural Area Reserve**. This flat and extremely windswept expanse of gentle sand dunes, knitted together with creeping ivy-like *naupaka*, is used as a nesting site in winter by Laysan **albatrosses**. At the very tip, below a rudimentary lighthouse – a slender white pole topped by flashing beacons – tiny beaches cut into the headland. Winter waves here reach over fifty feet high, the highest recorded anywhere in the world. That's way beyond the abilities of any surfer, though humpback whales often come in close to the shore.

From Ka'ena Point, you can see the mountains curving away down the leeward coast, as well as the white "golfball" of a military early-warning system up on the hills. Just out to sea is a rock known as **Pōhaku O Kaua'i** ("the rock of Kauai"); in Hawaiian legend, this is a piece of Kauai, which became stuck to Oahu when the demi-god Maui attempted to haul all the islands together.

The Leeward Coast

....

TheBus #51 from the Ala Moana Center runs up the Wai'anae Coast as far as Mākaha.

....

The **west** or **leeward coast** of Oahu, cut off from the rest of the island behind the Wai'anae mountains, is only accessible via the **Farrington Highway** that skirts the southern end of the ridge. Customarily dismissed as "arid", it may not be covered by tropical vegetation, but the **scenery** is still spectacular. As elsewhere on Oahu, the mountains are pierced by high green valleys – almost all of them inaccessible to casual visitors – while fine beaches such as Mākaha Beach Park line the shore.

However, the traditionally minded inhabitants of towns such as **Nānākuli** are not disposed to welcome the encroachment of hotels and golf courses, and visitors tend to be treated with a degree of suspicion. The further north you go, the stronger the military presence becomes, with soldiers in camouflage lurking in the hillsides. It's not possible to drive all the way up to Ka'ena Point.

THE SOUTHWEST CORNER

The strip development that characterizes both sides of Hwy-1 from Honolulu to Waipahu finally comes to an end as you enter the **southwest** corner of Oahu. Ambitious plans to turn this region into a tourist center to rival Waikīkī have so far come to nothing, and the only town is the former plantation settlement of **'Ewa**.

'Ewa

A couple of miles south of Farrington Highway along Fort Weaver Road, **'EWA** is a picturesque little hamlet of wooden sugar-plantation homes, arranged around a well-kept village green. Other than snapping a few photos along the back lanes, the only reason to come here is to take a **train excursion** with the Hawaii Railway Society, based just west of town along Renton Road. Their souvenir store and museum is open all week (Mon–Sat 9am–3pm, Sun 10am–3pm; free), but only on Sunday afternoons (at 12.30pm and 2.30pm) does the restored *Waialua #6* locomotive set out on its ninety-minute return trip (adults $8, seniors and under-13s $5; ✆681-5461) to the Ko Olina

Resort (see below). On the second Sunday of each month, by reservation only, you can have a private narrated tour in a luxury parlor car ($15).

'Ewa Beach Park, three miles south of the village, is an attractive oceanfront park popular with sailors from the nearby base. It has plenty of sand, and views across to Diamond Head, but the water tends to be too murky for swimming, and there's an awful lot of seaweed around.

Ko Olina Resort

During the 1980s, a great deal of money was poured into landscaping the **Ko Olina Resort**, just north of **Barbers Point** at the southwest tip of the island. Four successive artificial lagoons were blasted into the coastline, each a perfect semi-circle and equipped with its own crescent of white sand. Work also began on creating a marina for luxury yachts at the Barbers Point Harbor. However, of the projected residential estates, condo blocks, shopping centers and hotels, only the *Ihilani Resort*, reviewed on p.153, has so far materialized. Its one neighbor, the relentlessly tacky *Paradise Cove lū'au* site (see p.157), is something of a poor relation.

NĀNĀKULI

Farrington Highway reaches the Wai'anae Coast at **Kahe Point Beach Park**, near the section known as "Tracks" because of the adjacent railroad tracks. As well as being a small but pretty strip of sand, this is Oahu's most popular year-round **surfing** site. The waves offshore remain high (but not overpoweringly so) even in summer, and break much closer to the shore than usual. Since the bay itself is relatively sheltered, swimming usually only becomes dangerous in the depths of winter.

A couple of miles further on, **NĀNĀKULI** is the southernmost of a string of small coastal towns. Local legends explain its name as meaning either "look at knee" or "pretend to be deaf"; the population is largely Hawaiian, and there's little attempt to cater to outsiders. **Nānākuli Beach Park**, which runs alongside the highway all through town, is another good summer swimming beach, while **Zablan Beach** at its southern end is much used by scuba divers. The beach immediately north of Nānākuli is called **Ulehawa** or "filthy penis", after a particularly unsavory ancient chief.

WAI'ANAE

WAI'ANAE, five miles up the coast, centers on curving **Pōka'ī Bay**. Thanks to the breakwaters constructed to protect the boat harbor at its northern end, the main sandy beach here is the only one on the Leeward Coast where swimming can be guaranteed safe all year round. An irresistible backdrop is provided by the high-walled valley behind.

Beyond a flourishing coconut grove at the tip of the flat spit of land that marks the southern end of Pōka'ī Bay stand the ruined walls of **Kū'īlioloa Heiau**. Unusual in being virtually surrounded by water, this three-tiered structure is said to commemorate Wai'anai as the place where the first coconut tree was planted in Hawaiian soil.

MĀKAHA

MĀKAHA, or "savage", the last of the leeward towns, was once the hideout of a dreaded band of outlaws. Now famous for the savagery of its **waves**, it began to attract surfers in the early 1950s. Before World War II, virtually all Oahu surfing was concentrated in Waikīkī. When changes in the ocean conditions there, and the development of new techniques and equipment, led surfers to start looking elsewhere,

Mākaha was the first place they hit on. The waves at its northern end are said to be the largest consistently reliable surf in Hawaii, and several major surfing contests are still held at **Mākaha Beach Park** each year. In summer, when sand piles up in mighty drifts, it's often possible to swim here in safety, and Mākaha retains enough of it to remain a beautiful crescent beach even in winter. You'll probably notice what look like hotels along the oceanfront nearby, but they're all long-term condo rentals intended for local families.

Kāne'āki Heiau

Map 1, C5. Tues–Sun 10am–2pm; free.

A couple of miles back from the ocean in Mākaha Valley, beyond the defunct *Sheraton Mākaha Resort*, a private driveway leads to **Kāne'āki Heiau**. The most thoroughly restored ancient temple in Hawaii, it was excavated by Bishop Museum archeologists in 1970, and can now be visited with permission from the security guards at the gate; you'll have to leave a drivers' license or passport as security. Its principal platform of weathered, lichen-covered stones is topped once more by authentic thatched structures such as the *anu'u* or "oracle tower", as well as carved images of the gods. The *heiau* originated as an agricultural temple to the god Lono in the fifteenth century. Two hundred years later, it was converted into a *luakini*, where human sacrifices were dedicated to the god Kū.

THE ROAD TO KA'ENA POINT

Beyond Mākaha, the highway traces a long, slow curve up the coast to Yokohama Bay. Barely populated, and splendidly bleak, this region attracts very few visitors other than a handful of daredevil surfers prepared to risk its sharks, currents and mighty waves.

KĀNE'ĀKI HEIAU, THE ROAD TO KA'ENA POINT |

Looking inland, the rolling green slopes of **Mākua Valley** also conceal dangerous secrets. Used by the Air Force for bombing practice during and after World War II, the valley is still barred to the public due to the possible presence of unexploded war toys. Gaping **Kāneana Cave** to the south is too vandalized to be worth investigating.

Not even the sturdiest four-wheel-drive vehicle could negotiate the dirt road that continues from the end of the highway. In any case, the dunes beyond were designated as the **Ka'ena Point Natural Area Reserve** to help repair damage done by military jeeps and motorbikes. However, an exposed one-hour hike along the route of the old railroad tracks will bring you to the very tip of the island. The walk is substantially similar to the corresponding trail along the North Shore, described on p.124.

LISTINGS

Accommodation

Virtually all the **accommodation** available in the city of Honolulu, and on the entire island of Oahu for that matter, is confined to **Waikīkī**, which holds an extraordinary concentration of hotels in all price ranges. Unless you're happy to spend hundreds of dollars per night for world-class luxury, however, Waikīkī rooms are far from exciting. Most are in anonymous tower blocks, charging at least $100 for a standard en-suite double room, with another $50 for an ocean view, and $50 more again if they're right on the seafront. Few have any sort of personal touch – the gay *Hotel Honolulu*, the opulent *Halekūlani* and the *New Otani Kaimana Beach Hotel* are exceptions – and there are few B&Bs.

The very cheapest option is a $12–20 dorm bed in one of Waikīkī's half dozen **hostels**, all of which are geared heavily towards young international backpackers. However, so long as you don't mind missing out on a sea view, or having to walk a few minutes to the beach, it's normally possible to find an adequate hotel room for around $50 per night. Note that the Hawaiian word *lānai* is universally used to mean "balcony".

The telephone area code for all Hawaii is ©808.

Except at the very top hotels there's little point choosing a hotel with a **swimming pool** – most are squeezed on to rooftop terraces, overlooked by thousands of rooms in the surrounding high-rises and attracting all the dirt and fumes of the city.

To get your first-choice hotel in peak season, be sure to **reserve** well in advance. That said, even if you arrive in Hawaii with nowhere to stay, it's seldom hard to find a room at short notice. In the baggage claim area at Honolulu Airport, you'll find a notice board listing discounted rates in assorted Waikīkī hotels, together with courtesy phones to make your reservation.

As for possibilities away from Waikīkī, **Honolulu** proper offers a small selection of hotels and B&Bs aimed primarily at business travelers, and a couple more hostels, while the rest of the island holds very few alternatives. The only hotels **elsewhere on Oahu** are the *Hilton* and *Ihilani* resorts, at the far northeast and southwest corners respectively, while the bargain *Backpackers Vacation Inn* and *Breck's On The Beach Hostel* cater for the surf crowd on the North

Accommodation Price Codes

All the accommodation prices listed here have been graded with the symbols below, which refer to the quoted rates for a double room in high season (December to March), not including state taxes of 10.17 percent. In low season, Waikīkī hotels in categories ④, ⑤ and ⑥ tend to drop their rates by $10 to $20 per night, and some have intermediate summer rates in July and August.

① up to $30	④ $75–100	⑦ $170–225
② $30–50	⑤ $100–130	⑧ $225–300
③ $50–75	⑥ $130–170	⑨ over $300

Shore. Other than a few tiny B&Bs in Kailua and Kāneʻohe on the windward coast, that's about it.

There are no **campgrounds** in Waikīkī, and camping at Honolulu's only site, in Sand Island State Park (see p.65), is not recommended. Other Oahu campgrounds are reviewed on p.154.

WAIKĪKĪ HOSTELS

Hawaiian Seaside Hostel

Map 3, D2. 419 E Seaside Ave, Waikīkī HI 96815; ✆924-3306, fax 923 2110.

Basic, unofficial hostel, for international travelers with passports and onward flight tickets only (US citizens included), a few blocks from the beach in a quiet area of central Waikīkī. $13 dorms and some private doubles; no curfew, free breakfasts, $4 dinners, and Internet access. ①–②.

Hostelling International Waikīkī

Map 3, G4. 2417 Prince Edward St, Waikīkī HI 96815; ✆926-8313, fax 922-3798.

Official but informal youth hostel in the heart of Waikīkī, a couple of minutes from the beach. Office open 24 hours; no curfew. Dorm beds are $16, and everything, especially the four $40 double rooms, should be reserved in advance. ①–②.

Interclub Waikīkī Hostel and Hotel

Map 3, G4. 2413 Kūhiō Ave, Waikīkī HI 96815; ✆924-2636, fax 922-3993.

Incongruous, light-blue, motel-style address, tucked in among the high-rises a block from the ocean in central Waikīkī. Staff and guests tend to be laid-back, friendly and very young in this private hostel offering inexpensive breakfasts and $4 dinners, free use of snorkels, boogie boards and surfboards, courtesy phone at the airport, and car-rental discounts. There are $15 beds in mixed and women-only dorms, and a few basic $45 private en-suite rooms. ①–②.

Island Hostel

Map 4, E3. Hawaiian Colony Building, 1946 Ala Moana Blvd, Waikīkī HI 96815; ✆ & fax 924-8748.

Unofficial, good-value hostel, a little way back from the *Hilton Hawaiian Village,* in western Waikīkī. Not quite in the thick of things, but a good base. No curfew, dorm beds $15, doubles with kitchenette and TV $45. ①–②.

Polynesian Hostel Beach Club

Map 4, I4. 2584 Lemon Rd, Waikīkī HI 96815; ✆922-1340, fax 923-4146; email *dbhawaii@lava.net*.

Former motel converted into clean, private, air-conditioned hostel, a block from the sea at the Diamond Head end of Waikīkī. All rooms have en-suite bathrooms; some hold four $15 bunk beds, while others serve as good-value private doubles. Free snorkels and boogie boards are available, and meals are served in the communal area some nights. ①–②.

Waikīkī Beachside Hostel

Map 4, I4. 2556 Lemon Rd, Waikīkī HI 96815; ✆923-9566, fax 923-7525; email *hotelcondo@aol.com*.

Motel near the park in eastern Waikīkī that has been rather perfunctorily rejigged as a private hostel, and looks a lot smarter from the outside than it does once you go in; $17.50 dorm beds, plus double rooms and also two-room suites that aren't a bad deal if you're traveling as a group. An additional night's rent is taken as a deposit. ①–③.

HONOLULU YMCAS AND HOSTELS

Central Branch YMCA

Map 2, F5. 401 Atkinson Drive, Honolulu HI 96814;
℃941-3344, fax 941-8821.

Set in attractive grounds opposite Ala Moana shopping mall, a
few minutes by bus from either Waikīkī or downtown, and
offering plain single rooms for men only, plus some nicer en-
suite doubles available to women too. Guests choose between
the on-site swimming pool and the nearby beach. ②.

Fernhurst YWCA

Map 2, G4. 1566 Wilder Ave, Honolulu HI 96822;
℃941-2231, fax 949-0266.

Women-only lodging, not far west of the University and quite
a way from the ocean. Double rooms share a bathroom with
one other room; some can be rented by single travelers. The
$25 per-person rate includes simple buffet breakfasts and din-
ners from Mon–Sat; a $30 membership is compulsory for stays
of four nights or more. ①–②.

Honolulu International AYH Hostel

Map 2, G4. 2323-A Seaview Ave, Honolulu HI 96822;
℃946-0591, fax 946-5904.

Youth hostel in college residence, a couple of miles from
Waikīkī, across from the University of Hawaii in Mānoa.
There's no direct bus from the airport: change at Ala Moana on
to TheBus #6 or #18 as far as Metcalfe Street/University
Avenue, one block south of the hostel. Office hours 8am–noon
& 4pm–midnight; no curfew. Dorm beds are $12.50 for
AYH/IYHA members, $15.50 for non-members, and there's a
three-night maximum stay for non-members. ①.

Nu'uanu YMCA

Map 5, E2. 1441 Pali Hwy, Honolulu HI 96813;
✆536-3556, fax 533-1286.

Men-only single rooms for $30 per night, in a well-equipped new block that's just up from downtown and easily accessible by bus. ②.

WAIKĪKĪ HOTELS: BUDGET

Aloha Punawai

Map 3, A5. 305 Saratoga Rd, Waikīkī HI 96815;
✆923-5211, fax 622-4688.

Miniature hotel, opposite the post office, whose assorted studios and apartments – with and without air-conditioning – are furnished in a crisp, vaguely Japanese style. All units have kitchens, bathrooms, balconies and TV. ③.

The Breakers

Map 3, A5. 250 Beach Walk, Waikīkī HI 96815;
✆923-3181 or 1-800/426-0494, fax 923-7174.

Small, intimate hotel on the western edge of central Waikīkī, offering two-person studio apartments and four-person garden suites; all have kitchenettes and TV, and there's a bar and grill beside the flower-surrounded pool. ④–⑥.

Hale Pua Nui

Map 3, A6. 228 Beach Walk, Waikīkī HI 96815;
✆923-9693, fax 923-9678.

Small, clean motel-like hotel, which is among the best deals in central Waikīkī. The studio apartments are not exactly luxurious, but all have two twin beds, kitchenettes, cable TV and free local calls. Reserve well ahead. ③.

Hawaii Polo Inn

Map 2, F5. 1696 Ala Moana Blvd, Waikīkī HI 96815; ℂ949-0061 or
1-800/669-7719, fax 923-4906; reserve through *Marc Resorts*,
ℂ 922-5900 or 1-800/535-0085, fax 922-2421 or 1-800/633-5085;
email *marc@aloha.net*; Web site *www.marcresorts.com*.
Newly-converted traditional hotel at the western edge of
Waikīkī, just across the canal from the Ala Moana Center.
Good weekly rates for rooms and suites. ⑤.

Hotel Honolulu

Map 3, A3. 376 Kaiʻolu St, Waikīkī HI 96815; ℂ926-2766 or
1-800/426-2766, fax 922-3326; email *HotelHNL@lava.net*.
The only hotel in the state specifically to cater for gays and les-
bians, offering studios and one-bedroom suites, in what's left of
Waikīkī's gay district. Each suite in the main building is styled to
a theme such as Santa Fe, English or Rangoon, while the lobby
is crammed with tropical vegetation. Even the smaller studios in
the *Bamboo Lanai* building have kitchenettes, but the noise from
the club behind continues until 1.30am. There's a $40 sunset
dinner cruise with entertainment every Wed. ④–⑤.

Imperial of Waikīkī

Map 3, B7. 205 Lewers St, Waikīkī HI 96815;
ℂ923-1027 or 1-800/347-2682, fax 923-7848.
Studio rooms and one- or two-bedroom balcony suites in a
tower block set slightly back from the beach, just south of
Kalākaua Avenue. A bit hemmed in by the oceanfront giants,
but not bad for groups traveling together. The best views are
from the terrace around the 27th-floor pool. ④–⑥.

Kai Aloha

Map 3, A5. 235 Saratoga Rd, Waikīkī HI 96815;
ℂ923-6723, fax 922-7592.
Tiny, very central hotel. *Lānai* studios plus apartments sleeping
up to four, all with kitchenettes, bathrooms, TV and air-con. ③.

Malihini Hotel

Map 3, A6. 217 Saratoga Rd, Waikīkī HI 96815; ©923-9644.
Plain, thirty-unit hotel close to the beach, offering double- or
twin-bedded studios with and without air-conditioning, plus
larger one-bedroom apartments. Three-day minimum stay
Dec–April. ②–④.

Royal Grove

Map 3, H4. 151 Uluniu Ave, Waikīkī HI 96815;
©923-7691, fax 922-7508.
Small-scale, family-run hotel with a personal touch in central
Waikīkī. The facilities improve the more you're prepared to
pay, but even the most basic rooms are of a reliable standard.
There's also a courtyard pool, making the *Royal Grove* one of
Waikīkī's best bets for budget travelers. Special weekly rates
apply April–Nov only. ②–④.

Waikīkī Gateway Hotel

Map 4, F3. 2070 Kalākaua Ave, Waikīkī HI 96815;
©921-3202 or 1-800/247-1903, fax 923-2541.
High-rise hotel on the western side of central Waikīkī, budget-
oriented by local standards. Free continental breakfast on 16th-
floor *lānai*. The highly-rated lobby restaurant, *Nick's Fishmarket*,
is reviewed on p.170. ④–⑤.

Waikīkī Hana

Map 3, H5. 2424 Koa Ave, Waikīkī HI 96815;
©926-8841 or 1-800/367-5004, fax 924-3770.
Small and central Waikīkī hotel, situated one block from the
sea, behind the *Hyatt Regency*. Some tiny motel-style rooms,
some larger ones with sea views plus kitchenettes, and a few
classier suites. Your choice of sixth night free or a free rental car
for your whole stay. ③–⑤.

Waikīkī Prince

Map 3, H5. 2431 Prince Edward St, Waikīkī HI 96815; ©922-1544, fax 924-3712.

Slightly drab but perfectly adequate and very central budget hotel. All rooms offer air-conditioning, en-suite baths and basic cooking facilities, but no phones. Office open 9am–6pm only, seventh night free. **③**.

Most mid-priced Waikīkī hotels work out much cheaper if booked as part of a package; see p.3.

WAIKĪKĪ HOTELS: MID-RANGE

Aston Coral Reef Hotel

Map 3, E4. 2299 Kūhiō Ave, Waikīkī HI 96815; ©922-1262 or 1-800/922-7866, fax 922-8785.

Relatively inexpensive but still classy hotel, a couple of blocks back from the beach near the International Marketplace. The extra-large rooms sleep three or four people, while room rates drop by $25 from April to Christmas. **⑤**.

Aston Pacific Monarch

Map 3, H4. 2427 Kūhio Ave, Waikīkī HI 96815; ©923-9805 or 1-800/922-7866, fax 924-3220.

Tall condo block in the heart of Waikīkī, holding small studios with kitchenettes, plus larger four-person suites with full kitchens and balconies. **⑥–⑦**.

Aston Waikīkī Beachside Hotel

Map 3, H6. 2452 Kalākaua Ave, Waikīkī HI 96815; ©931-2100 or 1-800/922-7866, fax 931-2129.

An elegant oceanfront option, with a marble lobby, and pan-eled chinoiserie in the bathrooms. Avoid the cheapest rooms,

Outrigger Hotels

The **Outrigger** chain of hotels runs twenty hotels in Waikīkī, with a total of more than 7500 rooms. The buildings themselves, and the rooms within them, are very similar. All are clean and well-maintained, with standard upmarket hotel furnishings. Although specific room rates largely depend on whether you get an ocean view, and how near you are to the beach, there is also a hierarchy within the chain, with the *Waikīkī on the Beach*, the *Reef on the Beach* and the *Prince Kūhiō* considered deluxe properties.

A high proportion of Outrigger guests are on all-inclusive vacation packages. If you contact Outrigger direct – reservations are handled centrally, at the numbers opposite – be aware that all the hotels offer one free night to guests who stay six nights or more, and ask about room-and-car deals. In addition, most Outrigger rooms (but not suites) are $10–20 cheaper per night in spring (April to mid-June) and fall (mid-Aug to mid-Dec); in the lower price ranges, there are also small reductions in summer.

Hotel:

Ala Wai Towers, 1700 Ala Moana Blvd (Map 4, D3)	④–⑤
Coral Seas, 250 Lewers St (Map 3, B5)	④–⑥
East, 150 Kaʻiulani Ave (Map 3, F4)	⑤–⑦
Edgewater, 2168 Kālia Rd (Map 3, A7)	④–⑥
Hobron, 343 Hobron Lane (Map 4, D3)	④–⑥
Islander Waikīkī, 270 Lewers St (Map 3, B5)	⑤–⑦
Maile Sky Court, 2058 Kūhiō Ave (Map 4, F3)	④–⑦
Malia, 2211 Kūhiō Ave (Map 3, C3)	⑤–⑥
Prince Kūhiō, 2500 Kūhiō Ave (Map 3, I4)	⑥–⑨
Reef Lanais, 225 Saratoga Rd (Map 3, A6)	⑤–⑥
Reef on the Beach, 2169 Kālia Rd (Map 3, A7)	⑥–⑨

Reef Towers, 227 Lewers St (Map 3, B5)	⑤–⑥
Royal Islander, 2330 Kālia Rd (Map 3, A7)	④–⑥
Surf, 2280 Kūhiō Ave (Map 3, D3)	④–⑤
Village, 240 Lewers St (Map 3, B6)	⑤–⑥
Waikīkī on the Beach, 2335 Kalākaua Ave (Map 3, E6)	⑦–⑨
Waikīkī Surf, 2200 Kūhiō Ave (Map 3, B3)	④–⑥
Waikīkī Surf East, 422 Royal Hawaiian Ave (Map 3, C2)	⑤–⑥
Waikīkī Tower, 200 Lewers St (Map 3, B7)	⑤–⑥
West, 2330 Kūhiō Ave (Map 3, F3)	⑤–⑥

Reservation numbers	Toll-free phone	Toll-free fax
US & Canada	☎1-800/688-7444	1-800/622-4852
Australia	☎1-800/124 171	1-800/124 173
New Zealand	☎0800/440 852	0800/440 854
UK & Ireland	☎0800/894015	0800/894014

however: glibly promoted as "inside cabins", they have no windows. There's no restaurant, but a continental breakfast is included, and guests can charge meals at the *Hyatt Regency* to their accounts. ⑦–⑧.

Aston Waikīkī Circle Hotel

Map 3, H6. 2464 Kalākaua Ave, Waikīkī HI 96815; ☎923-1571 or 1-800/922-7866, fax 926-8024.
Round, off-white tower, dwarfed by its surroundings but one of the cheapest options along the oceanfront. Each of its thirteen circular floors is divided into eight identical rooms, with prices varying according to how much sea you can see. The hotel is the base for Aloha Express Tours; see p.206. ⑤.

Note that almost all Waikīkī hotels charge guests around $6–10 per night to park in their garages.

WAIKĪKĪ HOTELS: MID-RANGE

Hawaiian Regent

Map 4, H4. 2552 Kalākaua Ave, Waikīkī HI 96815; ✆922-6611 or
1-800/367-5370, fax 921-5222; email *hwnrgnt@aloha.net*.

Large and characterless tower-block hotel opposite the widest
section of Waikīkī Beach, at the Diamond Head end of central
Waikīkī. Two swimming pools, the *Acqua* Latin nightclub (see
p.188), and all the facilities, but not as special as the rates might
lead you to expect. ⑥–⑧.

Hawaiian Waikīkī Beach Hotel

Map 4, I4. 2570 Kalākaua Ave, Waikīkī HI 96815; ✆922-2511 or
1-800/877-7666, fax 923-3656.

A 25-story behemoth at the Diamond Head end of Waikīkī,
notable for its above-average nightly entertainment (see p.186).
Rooms further back from the ocean – especially in the separate
Mauka Tower – are considerably better value than those overlooking the beach. ⑥–⑧.

Hawaiiana Hotel

Map 3, A4. 260 Beach Walk, Waikīkī HI 96815; ✆923-3811, fax
923-9678; reserve through Marc Resorts, ✆ 922-5900 or 1-800/535-
0085, fax 922-2421; email *marc@aloha.net*; Web site
www.marcresorts.com.

Pleasant low-rise family motel close to the heart of Waikīkī.
Rooms – all with kitchenettes, but equipped to varying
degrees of luxury – are arranged around two pools. ⑥–⑧

New Otani Kaimana Beach Hotel

Map 2, G7. 2863 Kalākaua Ave, Waikīkī HI 96815; ✆923-1555 or
1-800/421-8795, fax 922-9404; email *webmaster@kaimana.com*;
Web site *www.kaimana.com*.

Intimate, Japanese-owned, Japanese-toned hotel on quiet and
secluded Sans Souci Beach (see p.35), a half-mile east of the bustle of central Waikīkī, and boasting lovely backdrops of Diamond
Head. The *Hau Tree Lanai* restaurant is reviewed on p.169. ⑤–⑨.

Pacific Beach Hotel

Map 3, I6. 2490 Kalākaua Ave, Waikīkī HI 96815; ℂ922-1233 or 1-800/367-6060, fax 922-8061.

The *Pacific Beach* boasts 830 rooms in two separate towers, at the Diamond Head end of Kalākaua Avenue. The high central tower contains the Oceanarium – a three-story fish tank focus for diners in the *Neptune* and *Oceanarium* (see p.165) restaurants. ⑦–⑧.

Queen Kapiʻolani

Map 4, I4. 150 Kapahulu Ave, Waikīkī HI 96815; ℂ922-1941 or 1-800/533-6970, fax 922-2694.

One of Waikīkī's older high-rises, overlooking Kapiʻolani Park at the east end of town. Relatively good value, as long as you don't get one of the handful of undersized rooms. ⑤–⑧.

Sheraton Princess Kaʻiulani

Map 3, F5. 120 Kaʻiulani Ave, Waikīkī HI 96815; ℂ922-5811 or 1-800/782-9488, fax 923-9912.

Tower-block hotel, not quite on the seafront but big enough to command wide views of ocean and mountains. A spacious and attractive garden surrounds the tiny street-level pool. ⑦–⑨.

Waikīkī Beachcomber

Map 3, D5. 2300 Kalākaua Ave, Waikīkī HI 96815; ℂ922-4646 or 1-800/622-4646, fax 923-4889; email *beach@dps.net*.

Identical rooms, with the usual comforts and private balconies, in a gleaming and central white tower block, just a short walk from the beach. Prices depend on the view. ⑥–⑧.

Waikīkī Joy

Map 3, B4. 320 Lewers St, Waikīkī HI 96815; ℂ923-2300 or 1-800/922-7866, fax 924-4010.

Friendly, small-scale hotel. Marble decor throughout, from the airy garden lobby through the well-appointed rooms – all of which contain jacuzzis. ⑥–⑧.

WAIKĪKĪ HOTELS: MID-RANGE

145

Waikīkī Parc

Map 3, C7. 2233 Helumoa Rd, Waikīkī HI 96815; ℮921-7272 or 1-800/422-0450, fax 923-1336.

Modern high-rise set slightly back from the beach, operated by the same management as the *Halekūlani* opposite, and offering a taste of the same luxury at more affordable prices. Conventional top-of-the-line rooms, plus two good restaurants: *Kacho* (see p.170) and the *Parc Café* (see p.171). ⑥–⑧.

Waikīkī Royal Suites

Map 3, B5. 255 Beach Walk, Waikīkī HI 96815; ℮926-5641; reserve through Marc Resorts, ℮ 922-5900 or 1-800/535-0085; fax 922-2421 or 1-800/633-5085; email *marc@aloha.net*; Web site *www.marcresorts.com*.

Plush all-suite property in the heart of Waikīkī. The building itself is not all that large, which gives it a friendly atmosphere, but each individual suite, complete with living room and *lānai*, offers extensive living space for families. ⑦.

> **Waikīkī hotels and restaurants are shown on maps 3 and 4**

WAIKĪKĪ HOTELS: EXPENSIVE

Halekūlani

Map 3, C7. 2199 Kālia Rd, Waikīkī HI 96815; ℮923-2311 or 1-800/367-2343, fax 926-8004; Web site *www.halekulani.com*.

Stunning oceanfront hotel, in prime location for views along the beach to Diamond Head, but aloof from the Waikīkī bustle. Probably the most luxurious option in the area, and home to the highly-rated *La Mer* restaurant (see p.170). The open-air *House Without a Key* bar (see p.187) is perfect for sunset cocktails. ⑧–⑨.

Hilton Hawaiian Village

Map 4, E4. 2005 Kālia Rd, Waikīkī HI 96815; ℰ949-4321 or
1-800/221-2424, fax 947-7897.

The biggest hotel in Hawaii, with over 2500 rooms, the *Hilton*
is a scaled down version of all of Waikīkī, holding almost a
hundred of the exact same stores and restaurants you'd find out
on the streets. The center of Waikīkī is a 15min walk away, and
the beach here is as good as any stretch in town (see p.33), so
there's little incentive to leave the hotel grounds – which is of
course the point. If you like this kind of self-contained resort,
however, there are better ones on the other islands. ⑦–⑨.

Hyatt Regency Waikīkī

Map 3, G6. 2424 Kalākaua Ave, Waikīkī HI 96815; ℰ923-1234 or
1-800/233-1234, fax 923-7839.

Two enormous towers across the road from central Waikīkī
Beach, engulfing a central atrium equipped with cascading
waterfalls and tropical vegetation. Also holds a sixty-store shopping mall, a bar and nightclub, 1230 "oversized" rooms and five
restaurants, of which three, *Ciao Mein*, *The Colony* and *The
Texas Rock'n'Roll Sushi Bar*, are reviewed on pp.168–171. ⑦–⑨.

The Royal Hawaiian

Map 3, D7. 2490 Kalākaua Ave, Waikīkī HI 96815; ℰ922-7311 or
1-800/782-9488, fax 931-7840.

The 1920s "Pink Palace" (see p.39), now owned by Sheraton,
remains one of Waikīkī's best-loved landmarks. The original
building still commands a great expanse of beach, and looks over
the terrace gardens to the sea, but is now flanked by a less atmospheric tower block holding the most expensive suites. ⑧–⑨.

**Our humble price category ⑨ barely does justice to
Waikīkī's top hotels, which can charge as much as
$4000 per night for their swishest suites.**

Sheraton Moana Surfrider

Map 3, F6. 2365 Kalākaua Ave, Waikīkī HI 96815; ℂ922-3111 or 1-800/782-9488, fax 923-0308.

Waikīkī's oldest hotel, built at the end of the nineteenth century (see p.38). Despite extensive restoration, the "Colonial" architectural style of the original building – now the focus of the Banyan wing – remains intact, though these days it's flanked by two huge towers. The main lobby, with its wooden walls and old-time atmosphere, is a delight. ⑧–⑨.

Sheraton Waikīkī Hotel

Map 3, C7. 2255 Kalākaua Ave, Waikīkī HI 96815; ℂ922-4422 or 1-800/782-9488, fax 923-8785.

Ultra-modern, 1852-room skyscraper on Waikīkī Beach, with beachside gardens and pool. The rooms are deluxe, but can't compete with the thrill of the high-speed, glass-sided, ocean-view elevators. ⑦–⑨.

HONOLULU HOTELS

Ala Moana Hotel

Map 2, F5. 410 Atkinson Drive, Honolulu HI 96814; ℂ955-4811 or 1-800/367-6025, fax 944-2974.

Set in a tower block directly above the Ala Moana Center, this hotel's uninspiring and overpriced rooms are primarily aimed at business visitors and shopaholics, though the beach across the road is as good as any in Waikīkī (see p.66). ⑤–⑦.

Executive Center Hotel

Map 5, F5. 1088 Bishop St, Honolulu HI 96813; ℂ539-3000 or 1-800/949-EXEC, fax 523-1088.

All-suite downtown hotel, on top of a skyscraper and geared to business travelers, but with prices that compare well with similar standard Waikīkī hotels. ⑤–⑦.

Airport Accommodation

If you find yourself stuck at **Honolulu Airport** and desperate for sleep, the ideal solution is right there in the main lobby. The *Honolulu Airport Mini Hotel* (©836-3044, fax 834-8985; ②) – also known as *Sleep & Shower* – offers tiny but clean private rooms, for single occupancy only, at $30 for eight hours, or $17.50 for two hours, including shower.

Nearby on N Nimitz Highway, and served by complementary shuttle buses, there's a *Best Western Plaza* (no 3253; ©836-3636 or 1-800/800-4683, fax 833-2349; ④) and a *Holiday Inn* (no 3401; ©836-0661 or 1-800/800-3477, fax 833-1738; ⑤).

Nakamura Hotel
Map 2, F4. 1140 S King St, Honolulu HI 96814; ©593-9951.
Small and simple, old-style family hotel, more than a mile east of downtown, and half a mile back from Ala Moana mall. If you get the chance, stay in a non-air-conditioned mountain-view room, away from the noise of King Street. Guests must arrive before 9pm Mon–Sat, 8pm on Sun. ②.

Pagoda Hotel
Map 2, F4. 1525 Rycroft St, Honolulu HI 96814; ©941-6611 or 1-800/367-6060, fax 955-5067.
Roughly halfway between downtown Honolulu and Waikīkī, within easy walking distance of Ala Moana mall, and offering two pools and two restaurants. The *Pagoda* has conventional, comfortable hotel rooms plus one- and two-bedroom suites. ④.

HONOLULU B&BS

The Mango House
Map 2, F2. 2087 Iholena St at Judd, Honolulu HI 96817; ℂ595-6682 or 1-800/77-MANGO, fax 595-6682; email *mango@pixi.com*.
Small gay-friendly B&B in peaceful setting a mile north of downtown. The main house holds one en-suite guest room, and one which shares its bathroom with owners Tracey and Marga; the separate guest cottage has a fully-equipped kitchen. ④.

Mānoa Valley Inn
Map 2, F2. 2011 Vancouver Drive, Honolulu HI 96822; ℂ947-6019 or 1-800/634-5115, fax 946-6168; reserve through Marc Resorts, ℂ 922-5900 or 1-800/535-0085, fax 922-2421 or 1-800/633-5085; email *marc@aloha.net*; Web site *www.marcresorts.com*.
One of Honolulu's most relaxing options: a plush, antique-filled B&B inn, near the University in lush Mānoa Valley. Waikīkī feels a lot further away than the mile it really is. Eight rooms, some sharing bathrooms and some en-suite. As you linger over breakfast, sit in one of the wicker chairs on the back porch. ④–⑦.

For a selection of top-quality B&Bs on all the Hawaiian islands, contact Hawaii's Best Bed & Breakfasts, PO Box 563, Kamuela HI 96743; ℂ885-4550 or 1-800/262-9912, fax 885-0559; email *bestbnb@aloha.net*.

THE REST OF OAHU

KAILUA

Akamai B&B
Map 1, L7. 172 Ku'umele Place, Kailua HI 96734; ℂ261-2227 or 1-800/642-5366.

B&B half a mile back from Kailua Beach, where two small, well-equipped en-suite units, each with basic cooking facilities, share use of a pool and laundry room. ③.

Lanikai B&B
Map 1, L7. 1277 Mokulua Drive, Kailua HI 96734; ℂ261-1059 or 1-800/258-7895, fax 261-7355; email *hi4rent@aloha.net*.
Long-established B&B across from Lanikai Beach, which has a studio room facing the mountains and a larger seaview apartment. Three-night minimum stay. ③–④.

Sharon's Serenity
Map 1, L7. 127 Kakahiaka St, Kailua HI 96734; ℂ262-5621 or 1-800/914-2271.
Very comfortable B&B, alongside a golf course just back from Kailua Beach, where the two good-value guest bedrooms share use of a bathroom. Three-night minimum stay. ③.

KĀNE'OHE

Ali'i Bluffs B&B
Map 1, K6. 46-251 Iki'iki St, Kāne'ohe HI 96744; ℂ235-1124.
Two-room antique-furnished B&B on a suburban Kāne'ohe street, complete with pool, ocean view and en-suite facilities. Three-night minimum stay. ③.

Hula Kai Hale
Map 1, K6. 44-002 Hulakai Place, Kāne'ohe HI 96744; ℂ235-6754.
Delightful B&B overlooking Kāne'ohe Bay, in which the two guest rooms have en-suite bathrooms, kitchen facilities and access to a swimming pool. Three-night minimum stay. ③.

THE BEST OF OAHU |

Rodeway Inn

Map 8, G4. 55-109 Laniloa St, Lā'ie HI 96762; ℂ293-9282 or
1-800/526-4562, fax 293-8115.

Clean, new **motel** – anonymous and well away from the
ocean, but quite good value – less than a hundred yards north
of the Polynesian Cultural Center. Each room has its own *lānai*
overlooking the swimming pool. It shares its driveway with the
oddest *McDonalds* you ever saw, converted from a leftover section of the Polynesian Cultural Center and still featuring an
entrance carved to resemble a South Seas longhouse. ④.

Turtle Bay Hilton Golf and Tennis Resort

Map 8, E2. 57-091 Kamehameha Hwy, PO Box 187, Kahuku HI
96731; ℂ293-8811 or 1-800/221-2424, fax 293-9147.

Thousand-acre resort at the northeastern tip of Oahu, holding
almost five hundred ocean-view rooms, as well as two golf
courses, ten tennis courts and four restaurants. Handily positioned for the North Shore, but priced far beyond the pockets
of the surfing crowd, it feels oddly out of place in this remote
corner and, apart from children enthralled by the nearby
beaches, most guests seem to end up wondering what they're
doing here. The *Sea Tide Room* restaurant (daily 8.30am–2pm)
serves a lavish $27 brunch buffet, while dinner entrees such as
kiawe-smoked rack of lamb and fresh Maine lobster cost well
over $25 each at *The Cove* (Tues–Sat 6–9pm). ⑦–⑧.

Backpacker's Vacation Inn

Map 8, C3. 59-788 Kamehameha Hwy, Hale'iwa HI 96712;
ℂ638-7838, fax 638-7515.

The North Shore's best **accommodation** option, in tiny Pūpūkea (see p.121), was founded by Mark Foo, a daredevil Hawaiian surfer who died surfing in California in 1994. Its rambling main building, *mauka* of the highway, has dorm beds for $15 per night, and simple private double rooms sharing kitchen and bath for $50. Across the street in low oceanfront blocks, dorm beds cost $17 a night, and good-value studio apartments with great views start at $80. The *Plantation Village*, a hundred yards down the road, across from the sea and run by the same management, consists of nine restored plantation cabins, with dorm beds, private rooms and larger cabins at similar rates. All rates are discounted for stays of a week or longer, and there's a free twice-daily bus to Honolulu Airport. They also provide free snorkeling equipment and boogie boards, and arrange island tours, plus scuba diving in summer. ①–④.

Breck's On The Beach Hostel

Map 8, D2. 59-043 Huelo St, Hale'iwa HI 96712; ©638-7873; email *brecks@netsrvind.com*.

A similar operation to the *Backpacker's Inn*, a little way north of Sunset Beach. Dorm beds cost $12.50, while apartments of varying standards – some capable of sleeping four people – range from $45 to $70 per night. ①–④.

LEEWARD OAHU

Ihilani Resort and Spa

Map 1, D8. 92-1001 Olani St, Ko Olina Resort, Kapolei HI 96707; ©679-0079 or 1-800/626-4446. fax 679-0080.

The *Ihilani*, in the far southwest corner of Oahu, opened in 1993 as the island's closest approximation to the resorts elsewhere in the state. Owned by Japanese Airlines, it's an absolute idyll if you can afford it; its fifteen stories of state-of-the-art rooms are equipped with every high-tech device imaginable, from computerized lighting and air-conditioning systems to

THE REST OF OAHU

CD players and giant-screen TVs. The adjoining spa boasts thalassotherapy and sauna facilities, plus rooftop tennis courts and a top-quality golf course. The in-house restaurants are excellent – a meal at the least expensive, the poolside *Naupaka*, will set you back at least $50, though its delicate Pacific Rim fish dishes are well worth trying; alternatives include the formal *Azul* grill. ⑧–⑨.

CAMPING

Camping in both state and county parks on Oahu is free, with a permit from the relevant office. However, few sites are worth recommending, and none of those are especially convenient for Honolulu. Furthermore, all county and state campgrounds are closed on both Wednesday and Thursday nights, and you can't stay at any one site for more than five days in one month. The best options among the state parks are those at Keaīwa Heiau (see p.113), Mālaekahana Bay (p.110), Waimānolo Bay (p.99), and Kahana Bay (p.108); appealing county parks include Bellows Field Beach (p.100), and Kaiaka Beach Park, a mile out of Hale'iwa near the mouth of Kaiaka Bay.

The **state parks office** accepts postal applications seven to thirty days in advance, and is located in Room 310, 1151 Punchbowl St, Honolulu HI 96813 (Mon–Fri 8am–4pm; ✆587-0300). **County** permits can be obtained, in person only, from 650 S King St (Mon–Fri 7.45am–4pm; ✆523-4525), or from a subsidiary "City Hall" in the Ala Moana Center (Mon–Fri 9am–4pm, Sat 8am–4pm).

Eating

Thanks to two major factors, Honolulu and Waikīkī boast a **restaurant** scene to rival any in the world. First of all, there's Hawaii's **ethnic diversity**; national dishes and recipes brought from all over the world by nineteenth-century immigrants have subsequently mingled to create intriguing new flavors and specialties. Second, the presence of millions of **tourists**, eager to pay top rates for good food, means that Oahu holds more superb restaurants than its own population could ever sustain.

Almost all the hotels in **Waikīkī** have at least one on-site restaurant. As you'd expect, the standards in the major hotels are very high, but out on the streets the emphasis is on keeping the price low, rather than the quality high. Many of the better restaurants don't bother to open for lunch, but takeouts, fast-food chains and snack bars are everywhere you turn; the largest concentrations are along Kūhiō Avenue and, with more of a Japanese emphasis, on Kalākaua Avenue west of Lewers Street.

Other than **Chinatown**, no district of **Honolulu** holds a concentration of eating options to match those in Waikīkī. Several delectable alternatives are scattered throughout the city, however, and many of Honolulu's finest restaurants are now tucked away in tourist-free zones. If you don't want to interrupt a day's sightseeing by returning to Waikīkī to eat, the easiest solution is to head for one of the many malls, most of which hold a few formal restaurants, as well as plenty of fast-food takeouts.

Within the last ten years, chefs trained in both Eastern and Western traditions have returned to Hawaii to open restaurants that serve an exciting hybrid cuisine known variously as **Hawaii Regional**, **New Hawaiian**, or **Pacific Rim**. Drawing on fresh local ingredients and strong spices, they have placed Hawaii among the world's hottest culinary destinations. Roy Yamaguchi, of *Roy's* in Hawaii Kai, is generally credited as being the instigator of this movement; other practitioners include Alan Wong, Sam Choy, and Jean-Marie Josselin of *A Pacific Café*.

HONOLULU AND WAIKĪKĪ FAVORITES

Lūʻaus

All too many visitors to Hawaii – largely those reared on a steady diet of Elvis movies – arrive in the islands determined to attend a "traditional Hawaiian feast" or *lūʻau*. Local families do indeed celebrate holidays with beachside picnics they call *lūʻaus*, but the only *lūʻaus* a tourist can hope to attend are strictly commercial affairs. Besides pseudo-Polynesian entertainment, these always involve mass catering and canteen-style self-service. Though the food tends to be indifferent at best, they do provide the opportunity to sample such dishes as *kālua* pork, an entire pig wrapped in *ti* leaves and baked all day in an underground oven known as an *imu*; *poi*, a purple-gray paste produced by pounding the root of the *taro* plant; *poke*, which is raw fish, shellfish or octopus, marinated with soy and oriental seasonings; and *lomi-lomi*, made with raw salmon.

If you insist on going to a *lūʻau* while you're in Waikīkī, go to the *Royal Hawaiian Hotel*, on Monday at 6pm (℃923-7311). Their *lūʻau* costs over $70, but the food's not bad, the Waikīkī Beach setting is romantic, and you can get there and back easily.

The two biggest *lūʻaus* on Oahu, which you'll see advertised everywhere, are *Germaine's* (Tues–Sun; &949-6626) and *Paradise Cove* (nightly; ℃973-5828). What the adverts don't tell you is that they are both thirty miles from Waikīkī, in the far southwestern corner of the island. The price – reckon on $35 from an activity center – includes an hour-long bus trip each way (singalongs compulsory), and your reward at the end is the chance to spend hours looking at tacky overpriced souvenirs, eating indifferent food, drinking weak cocktails and watching third-rate entertainment.

LŪʻAUS

For inexpensive fare, Honolulu has an excellent selection of national fast-food chains, but typical budget restaurants, diners and takeout stands, serve "**local food**" – a blending of the US mainland along with Japan, China, Korea and the Philippines, all given a slight but definite Hawaiian twist.

Breakfast tends to be the standard combination of eggs, meat, pancakes, muffins or toast. At midday, the usual dish is the **plate lunch**, a molded tray holding meat and rice as well as potato or macaroni salad and costing from $5 to $8. **Bento** is the Japanese equivalent, with mixed meats and rice; in Filipino diners, you'll be offered *adobo*, which is pork or chicken stewed with garlic and vinegar. Korean barbecue, *kal bi* – prepared with sesame – is especially tasty, while **saimin** (pronounced *sigh-min* not *say-min*), a bowl of clear soup filled with noodles and other ingredients, has become something of a national dish. Finally, the carbohydrate-packed *loco moco* is a fried egg served on a hamburger with gravy and rice.

Food in general is often referred to as *kaukau*, and it's also worth knowing that *pūpūs* (pronounced *poo-poos*) is a general term for little snacks, the kind of finger food that is given away in early-evening happy hours.

WAIKĪKĪ – INEXPENSIVE

Caffe Pronto
Map 3, G5. King's Village Mall, 131 Ka'iulani Ave; ©923-0111.
Bright, cheerful takeout with small seating area, best appreciated in the morning for its fine coffees and assorted bagels and croissants. Later in the day it offers soup, salads and sandwiches. Daily 6.30am–11pm.

Waikīkī restaurants are keyed on maps 3 and 4.

China Garden
Map 3, E3. *Aston Coral Reef Hotel*, 2299 Kūhiō Ave; ©923-8383.
Inexpensive Chinese restaurant, with $6 lunch specials, and
one-plate dinners, with rice and soup, for $9. Entrees cost
$9–14; set meals for two or more are $14–18 per person. Daily
11am–10pm.

Eggs'n'Things
Map 4, E3. 1911B Kalākaua Ave; ©949-0820.
All-night diner drawing a big breakfast crowd for its bargain
omelets, waffles and crepes; $3 buys three pancakes or two
eggs. Daily 11pm–2pm.

Hawaii Seafood Paradise
Map 4, D3. 1830 Ala Moana Blvd; ©946-4514.
Almost three restaurants in one, not far from the *Hilton* at the
Ala Moana end of Waikīkī. At breakfast, the food is American
and very inexpensive. Chinese-style lunch specials cost around
$6, and only in the evening is it really a "seafood paradise",
with high-quality Chinese entrees such as crispy oysters and
steamed catfish priced at $10–15. Daily 6am–3am.

Internet C@fé
Map 4, I2. 550 Kapahulu Ave; ©735-JAVA
Spacious alternative coffee shop on the northeastern edge of
Waikīkī, not far below Diamond Head, with strong coffees,
superb cinnamon buns, Internet access at $7.50 per hour and
even all-night "psychic nights" (Mon, Thurs & Sat). Open
24hrs.

WAIKĪKĪ – INEXPENSIVE

....
As usual in Hawaii, the waiting staff in Waikīkī or
Honolulu restaurants expect tips of fifteen percent or
more of the total bill.
....

Java Java

Map 4, I1. 760 Kapahulu Ave; ⓒ732-2670.

Friendly coffee shop and snack bar just beyond Waikīkī, serving salads, smoothies, shakes and coffees, with live music and other performances nightly, usually at 8pm. Mon–Sat 9.30am–midnight, Sun 10am–midnight.

Leonard's Bakery

Map 4, I1. 933 Kapahulu Ave; ⓒ737-5591.

Long-standing Portuguese bakery on the northeastern fringes of Waikīkī, renowned for its delicious desserts and *malasadas*.

Moose McGillycuddy's

Map 3, B4. 310 Lewers St; ⓒ923-0751.

Nightclub and drinking venue, with booths in the bar downstairs, and a dining room on the second floor. Breakfasts start with $2 specials of two eggs and bacon. Later on you can get burgers and sandwiches for $6–8, snacks like quesadillas, wings or nachos for $5–8, or full dinners of fajitas, pasta, steak or chicken for $10–15. Youth Hostel Association members receive a fifteen percent discount on all entrees. Mon, Tues & Sun 7.30am–2am, Wed–Sat 7.30am–4am.

Perry's Smorgy

Map 3, G3. 2380 Kūhiō Ave; ⓒ926-0184.

Bland all-you-can-eat buffets, served indoors or in a nice little garden. Good for bulk, but always crowded, and hardly anything actually tastes nice. The $5 breakfast includes ham, beef, sausages, pancakes, pastries and juices; the $6 lunch consists of *mahi-mahi*, Southern fried chicken, garlic bread, rice, baked macaroni and desserts; and the $9 dinner features beef, shrimp, ribs, turkey and teriyaki chicken. (Note that there's another *Perry's* at the *Outrigger Coral Seas*, 250 Lewers St, Map 3, B6, but it's indoor-only and less appealing.) Mon–Sat 7–11am, 11.30am–2.30pm & 5–9pm, Sun 7–11am & 5–9pm.

WAIKĪKĪ – INEXPENSIVE

Popo's

Map 3, A3. 2112 Kalākaua Ave; ✆923-7355.

Garish, raucous Mexican place, with a large *lānai* beside a busy street, and indoor seating too. Inexpensive tacos, burritos, enchiladas and the like for $8.50–11, combos $9–12.50, and gallons of margaritas. Daily 11.30am–2.30pm & 5–9.30pm.

Ruffage Natural Foods

Map 3, H4. 2443 Kūhiō Ave; ✆922-2042.

Tiny wholefood grocery with a takeout counter and patio seating. Avocado and beansprout sandwiches, plus salads and vegetables with pasta or tofu, all cost under $10. The front part of the shop becomes an inexpensive sushi bar at night. Mon–Sat 9am–7pm.

WAIKĪKĪ MALL DINING

Waikīkī's most convenient **fast-food** option must be the International Food Court, in the **International Marketplace** on Kalākaua. Take-out counters with self-explanatory names – *Salveno's Pizza and Pasta, Yummy Korean B-B-Q, Bautista's Filipino Kitchen*, etc. – surround a sheltered area of tables, and there's often free musical entertainment of some kind. There's a similar, smaller food court beneath the **Waikīkī Shopping Plaza** at 2250 Kalākaua Ave, while *Starbucks* **coffee** outlets are located in the **Duty Free Shoppers** complex on Royal Hawaiian Avenue and the **Discovery Bay Center** at 1778 Ala Moana Blvd.

   If you want to cook for yourself, try the Food Pantry, a good-value 24-hour **supermarket** at the northwest corner of Kūhiō Avenue and Walina Street. Wholefood enthusiasts will probably prefer Down to Earth Natural Foods, a mile or so out of Waikīkī and near the University, at 2525 S King St (✆947-7678).

Shore Bird Beach Broiler

Map 3, A7. *Outrigger Reef on the Beach*, 2169 Kālia Rd; ✆922-2887.
Open-air hotel restaurant on the oceanfront serving breakfast
($7) and dinner ($13) buffets, with a communal grill on which
guests cook their own meat or fish. Excellent value, especially
if you use the $1-off coupons in the free magazines. Daily
7–11am & 4.30–10pm.

Tokyo Noodle House

Map 3, A4. 2113 Kalākaua Ave; ✆922-3479.
Clean, glass-fronted Japanese diner, offering large, tasty servings
of *ramen* noodle soups, fried noodles and rice dishes, all priced
at $6–7. Daily 11am–2am.

WAIKĪKĪ – MODERATE

Arancino

Map 3, B6. 255 Beach Walk; ✆923-5557.
Surprisingly authentic Italian trattoria – albeit decorated an
unlikely lurid orange – in central Waikīkī. The basic dinner
menu of $8 pasta and pizza is supplemented by tasty specials
such as a steamed mussel appetizer for $5.50, and a $14.50 lobster linguini, and there's always plenty of Chianti to go round.
Daily 11am–9.30pm.

Banyan Veranda

Map 3, F6. *Sheraton Moana Surfrider*, 2365 Kalākaua Ave; ✆922-3111.
Poolside hotel café on Waikīkī Beach. Breakfast is available
Mon–Sat 7–11am, with a continental buffet for $13 or a full
buffet for $20; Sunday brunch is 9am–1pm. Afternoon tea is
poured daily 3–5pm: $14.50 buys a plate of scones and pastries
and a pot of tea to be enjoyed as you listen to a Hawaiian gui-
tarist. There's an appetizer buffet for $10 (or $17 if you decline
to drink as well) nightly 6–10pm.

California Pizza Kitchen

Map 4, E3. 1910 Ala Moana Blvd; ☎955-5161.

Stylish-looking place in western Waikīkī, though the curved smoked-glass windows don't have much of a view. One-person pizzas ($10) – such as goat's cheese and bacon or Peking duck and wonton – are served in a high-tech, new-Asia sort of atmosphere, and they also have pasta with ginger and black-bean sauce ($12), and *foccacia* sandwiches ($7–8). Mon–Thurs 11.30am–10pm, Fri & Sat 11.30am–11pm, Sun noon–10pm.

Cheeseburger in Paradise

Map 3, I6. 2500 Kalākaua Ave; ☎923-3731.

The Waikīkī outlet of this successful Maui burger joint occupies a prime position facing the ocean, and shares its twin's retro 1950s South Seas/beachcomber style. The food, however, is uninspired: the $7 cheeseburgers are adequate, the $7–10 salads less so – and the service perfunctory. Daily 8am–midnight.

Duke's Canoe Club

Map 3, E6. *Outrigger Waikīkī on the Beach*, 2335 Kalākaua Ave; ☎922-2268.

Open-air beachfront restaurant/bar, named after legendary surfer Duke Kahanamoku, and boasting a great view of the waves. Good-value buffet breakfasts (until 11am) at $10 including cooked items, or $8 cold, are followed by fairly basic $10 lunch buffets. At night, there are full but unimaginative dinners, with a $10 salad bar and chicken, beef and fish entrees for $15–20. The bar stays open until midnight, and features live music. Daily 7am–10pm.

Golden Dragon

Map 4, E4. *Hilton Hawaiian Village*, 2005 Kālia Rd; ☎946-5336.

The smartest Chinese restaurant in Waikīkī, with garden seating overlooking a lagoon, and a tasteful indoor dining room. The food is good too, and the prices surprisingly low, with

WAIKĪKĪ – MODERATE

entrees such as lemon chicken and chow mein for under $15. Tues–Sun 6–9.30pm.

Hard Rock Café

Map 4, D2. 1837 Kapi'olani Blvd; ©955-7383.

Just across the Ala Wai Canal from Waikīkī, this is one of the earliest *Hard Rock Cafés*, here since 1971, and is usually jammed with memorabilia-hungry tourists. The food – ribs, burgers and so on – is predictable but not at all bad, and mostly costs under $10; the drinking and the music get progressively heavier as the night wears on. Mon–Thurs & Sun 11.30am–11pm, Fri & Sat 11.30am–11.30pm.

Jolly Roger

Map 3, G4.*Outrigger East*, 150 Ka'iulani Ave; ©923-2172.

Ordinary, safe, American steakhouse, with no views, but a big-screen sports bar attached. Breakfast starts daily at 6.30am; lunch (11am–4pm) features $5 burgers or soup, salad and sandwich for $7. For dinner, the usual steak, shrimp, rib, or chicken entrees cost $12–13, and you can combine any two for $14.50. Note that there's another, similar *Jolly Roger* at 2244 Kalākaua Ave (©923-1885). Daily 6.30am–1am.

Keo's Thai Cuisine

Map 4, I2. 625 Kapahulu Ave; ©737-8240.

Keo's, a mile northeast of Waikīkī, has long proclaimed itself to be Hawaii's best Thai restaurant, and its walls are festooned with photos of celebrities enticed by trademark dishes such as the "Evil Jungle Prince" curries, made with basil, coconut milk and red chili. The increasing worldwide familiarity of Thai cooking means that *Keo's* is no longer a novelty, and its menu may seem unexceptional, but the food tastes as good as ever, and with all entrees costing under $15, the prices are reasonable. There are several other *Keo's* branches in Honolulu, including one at the Ward Center (see p.203). Daily 5–11pm.

Lewers Street Fish Company

Map 3, B6. 247 Lewers St; ☎971-1000.

Basement fish restaurant below the *Outrigger Reef Towers*, where they make their own pasta – the linguini is good – and serve it especially with grilled or sautéed island fish. Most of the menu has a strong Italian twist, with dishes typically priced at around $20, but there's also *mahi mahi* fish'n'chips for $8. Selected specials cost $6 between 5pm and 6pm. Daily 5–10pm.

Oceanarium

Map 3, I6. *Pacific Beach Hotel*, 2490 Kalākaua Ave; ☎922-6111.

Minimally furnished restaurant with a big gimmick, which is more fun for kids than for adults – one wall of the dining room is a gigantic aquarium, so you're watched as you eat by 400 live fish, plus the occasional scuba diver. The day starts with a continental breakfast (6–11am) for $7.50 or a $9.50 buffet. Lunchtime noodles, burgers, salads or sandwiches all cost under $10, while the dinner menu features seafood pancakes for $24 or prime rib for $18.50, as well as surf'n'turf combos. Daily 6am–2pm & 5–10pm.

> **Waikīkī restaurants are keyed on maps 3 and 4.**

Peacock Room & Garden Lanai

Map 4, I4. Third Floor, *Queen Kapiʻolani Hotel*, 150 Kapahulu Ave; ☎922-1941.

Buffet-style restaurant in an old-fashioned Waikīkī hotel. The $11 breakfast buffet features fruit, eggs, meat and so on. Lunch and dinner both feature the same types of food: Mon–Wed it's Hawaiian à la carte; Thursday's Japanese buffet is $12 at lunch; and Fri–Sun there's a Hawaiian buffet, costing $11 at lunch. Dinner buffets cost $17, or $8 if you choose from the salad bar. Daily 6.30–10am, 11am–2pm & 5.30–9pm.

Planet Hollywood

Map 3, B4. 2155 Kalākaua Ave; ©924-7877.

Frenetic theme restaurant enlivened by faux zebra-skin and neon trimmings and cases of movie memorabilia (Hawaii-related where possible, so there's an abundance of discarded *Waterworld* costumes), but with very little substance – the food, be it $10 burgers and pizzas or $15 stir-fries, is glossy but mediocre. You may have to wait as much as an hour for a table – kill time by looking at Michael J Fox's high school yearbook, and reading house instructions on how to go about tipping. Daily 11am–2am.

Restaurant Suntory

Map 3, C5. Third Floor, Royal Hawaiian Shopping Center, Orchid Court, 2233 Kalākaua Ave; ©922-5511.

The *teppanyaki* menu, cooked at your table in this viewless Japanese restaurant, features squid or steak for around $16, and shrimp or scallop for more like $20, as well as mixed sashimi ($27); there's also a full sushi bar. Set meals cost from $55 to $100. Mon–Sat 11.30am–1.45pm & 6–9.45pm, Sun 6–9.45pm.

Seafood Village

Map 3, G5. 2424 Kalākaua Ave; ©971-1818.

Tasty Chinese food, below street level, beneath the *Hyatt Regency*. Dim sum trolleys do the rounds at lunchtime, when the menu is otherwise identical to that served at dinner, with seafood noodle soup for $10, and entrees such as stir-fried clams in black bean sauce for $16, a whole Peking duck for $21, and sashimi king clam for $28. Daily 11am–2pm & 5.30–10pm.

Singha Thai Cuisine

Map 4, E3. 1910 Ala Moana Blvd; ©941-2898.

Bright, modern place that serves delicious Thai food with a definite Hawaiian tinge. All sorts of fresh fish and scallop dishes, plus curries, hot and sour Tom Yum soups and Pad Thai (fried

Hawaiian Fish

Although the ancient Hawaiians were expert offshore fishermen, as well as being sophisticated fish farmers, the great majority of the **fish** eaten in Hawaii nowadays is imported. Local fishing is on too small a scale to meet the demand, and in any case many of the species that tourists expect to find on menus thrive in much cooler waters. Thus salmon and crab come from Alaska, and mussels from New Zealand, although Maine lobsters are now being farmed in the cold waters of the deep ocean off the Big Island.

However, if you feel like being adventurous, you should get plenty of opportunity to try some of the Pacific species caught nearby. If the list below still leaves you in the dark, personal recommendations include *opah*, which is chewy and salty like swordfish; the chunky *'ōpakapaka*, which because of its red color (associated with happiness) is often served on special occasions; the succulent white *ono* (which means "delicious" in Hawaiian); and the dark *'ahi*, the most popular choice for sashimi.

'ahi	yellow-fin tuna	*mano*	shark
a'u	swordfish or marlin	*moi*	thread fish
		onaga	red snapper
'ehu	red snapper	*ono*	mackerel or tuna-like fish
hāpu'upu'u	sea bass		
hebi	spear fish	*'ōpae*	shrimp
kākē	barracuda	*opah*	moonfish
kalekale	pink snapper	*'ōpakapaka*	pink snapper
kāmano	salmon	*pāpio*	pompano
kēmē	red goat fish	*uhu*	parrot fish
lehi	yellow snapper	*uku*	gray snapper
mahi mahi	dorado or dolphin fish	*ulua*	jack fish
		weke	goat fish

noodles); vegetables are organic, and salads available fat-free. Typical entrees cost $9–10 at lunchtime, and on average $4 more at dinner. Thai dancers perform nightly 7–9pm. Mon–Fri 11am–11pm, Sat & Sun 4–11pm.

Tanaka of Tokyo

Map 3, G5. Third Floor, King's Village, 131 Ka'iulani Ave; ©922-4233. Large, open Japanese place, serving *teppanyaki* cuisine sizzled at your table by chefs-cum-jugglers. You'll be squashed up with a bunch of strangers, but the food is good – a full steak meal costs $21–25, scallops and shrimps about the same, and there's a salmon special for $19 – and the experience is fun. Mon–Fri 11am–2pm & 6–10pm, Sat & Sun 6–10pm.

Texas Rock 'n' Roll Sushi Bar

Map 3, G5. *Hyatt Regency Hotel*, 2424 Kalākaua Ave; ©923-7655. A high-concept, postmodern restaurant/bar on the ground floor of the giant *Hyatt Regency*, the *Rock 'n' Roll Sushi Bar* is part Hawaiian *paniolo* cowboy, part Japanese, and part *Hard Rock Café*. The menu is truly bizarre, with "sushi" rolls of sea-weed-wrapped beef, duck and even BLT from as little as $1.50, plus more conventional sushi specialties for around $6, and straightforward barbecue beef, ribs and chicken for around $15. It all tastes surprisingly good. Daily 11.30am–2.30pm & 5.30–11pm.

WAIKĪKĪ – EXPENSIVE

Ciao Mein

Map 3, G5. *Hyatt Regency Waikīkī*, 2424 Kalākaua Ave; ©923-CIAO. Huge restaurant, serving an odd mixture of Chinese and Italian cuisine. Very few dishes actually combine the two, but the food is consistently good, with the Italian dishes the more sophisti-cated and less expensive. There's an excellent *foccacia* appetizer for under $5, and most pasta entrees cost $11–14; Chinese specialties include sizzling Mongolian beef ($14), black bean shrimp ($15.50) and steamed fish ($20), and there are vegetarian options, too. Set meals cost from $24 per person. Mon–Sat 6–10pm, Sun 10am–2pm & 6–10pm.

Hanohano Room

Map 3, C7. *Sheraton Waikīkī Hotel*, 2255 Kalākaua Ave; ✆922-4422. Glamorous restaurant, stacked thirty stories above Waikīkī, with nightly dancing to "contemporary jazz". Fixed-price menus range from $49 to $75; à la carte dishes average $35, whether you go for the rich array of meats with sauces, or for the broiled fresh fish. Mon–Sat 6–10.30pm, Sun 9am–2.30pm & 6–10.30pm.

Hau Tree Lanai

Map 2, G7. *New Otani Kaimana Beach Hotel*, 2863 Kalakaua Ave; ✆921-7066.
Intimate oceanfront restaurant, set beneath the shade of a magnificent spreading *hau* tree beside Sans Souci Beach, and perfect for romantic sunsets. Cuisine is mostly continental/ American, but with added Pacific Rim touches: choose from top-quality breakfasts (go for the $12 eggs Benedict), lunches ranging from sandwiches to *ahi* steaks for under $15, and full dinner menus at around $30, featuring fresh fish cooked to your specifications, lobster and duck's breast. Mon–Sat 7–11am, 11.30am–4pm & 5.30–9pm, Sun 7–11am, noon– 4pm & 5.30–9pm.

House Without a Key

Map 3, B7. *Halekūlani*, 2199 Kālia Rd; ✆923-2311.
Waikīkī's classiest venue for an open-air sunset cocktail (see p.187) is open all day, every day, for ample breakfast buffets ($20), light lunches (salads at $10–15), evening snacks and simple dinners (under $20). Daily 7.30am–10pm.

WAIKĪKĪ – EXPENSIVE

Kacho

Map 3, E6. *Waikīkī Parc*, 2233 Helumoa Rd; ©921-7272 ext 6045.
Superb Japanese restaurant, with typically understated decor.
The menu emphasizes Kyoto cuisine, with lots of raw and
pickled fish; look out for crab *sunomono* (in vinegar), and the
delicious, cod-like butterfish. Full dinners start at $30. Daily
6–10am, 11.30am–2pm, & 5.30–10pm.

La Mer

Map 3, B7. *Halekūlani*, 2199 Kālia Rd; ©923-2311.
If you're pushing the boat out, try this original and distinctively
Hawaiian restaurant specializing in imaginative twists on classic
French techniques. The highlight is seafood, with species such
as flaky *onaga* (red snapper) and *opah* (moonfish), and an amaz-
ing bouillabaisse. The full set menu starts at $85, individual
dishes $36–45. Formal dress required, reservations essential.
Open nightly from 6pm till late.

Matteo's

Map 3, D3. *Marine Surf Hotel*, 364 Seaside Ave; ©922-5551.
Dinner-only Italian restaurant, with added flavor drawn from
modern Southwest (chili, sundried tomato) and Hawaiian cuisine. Quite pricey and formal, but the food is well above average. Appetizers (around $10) are predominantly seafood; the
highlight is the spicy clams. Entrees start at $16 for ravioli, and
range through grilled fish and meats up to a $30 rack of lamb.
Daily 5.30–11pm.

Nick's Fishmarket

Map 4, F3. *Waikīkī Gateway Hotel*, 2070 Kalākaua Ave; ©955-6333.
Waikīkī's top fish restaurant, with dark leatherette seating, glittering glass and mirrors and a formal atmosphere. The cooking
is not especially innovative and the sauces are rich, but the
preparation is meticulous and the choice amazing. Appetizers,
generally priced $10–13, include sautéed crab and steamed

mussels. A typical main dish like Hawaiian swordfish costs around $30, a mixed seafood grill $33, and lobsters $30–47. The same menu is served (until midnight on Fri & Sat) in the less formal, adjoining café, which also has live music. Mon–Thurs & Sun 5.30–10pm, Fri & Sat 5.30–11pm.

Parc Café

Map 3, C7. *Waikīkī Parc*, 2233 Helumoa Rd; ℗921-7272.
Upmarket hotel restaurant boasting the best buffets in Waikīkī. Breakfast buffets ($12.50) are served from 6.30am daily, while the lunchtime choice is either Hawaiian *lū'au* food (Wed & Fri 11.30am–2pm; $16.50), a predictable spread of sandwiches, salads and pasta (Mon, Tues, Thurs & Sat 11.30am–2pm; $13.50), or a full brunch (Sun 11am–2pm; $22). For dinner, the buffets focus on prime rib (Mon–Thurs 5.30–9.30pm; $17.50), or on prime rib with high-quality Japanese, Hawaiian and American seafood (Fri & Sat 5.30–9.30pm; $25.50), plus pastas and salads. À la carte entrees are also available.

Sam Choy's Diamond Head

Map 4, I1. 449 Kapahulu Ave; ℗732-8645.
Very popular, dinner-only "New Hawaiian" restaurant, a mile or so northeast of Waikīkī. TV chef Sam Choy has a reputation for feeding his customers to bursting point, and the portions of the $20–25 entrees such as seafood *laulau* (steamed in *ti* leaves) and veal *ossobucco* are truly enormous, and deliciously flavored with local herbs and spices. The $24 Sunday brunch buffet includes Choy's trademark fried *poke* (diced fish). Mon–Thurs 5.30–9.30pm, Fri & Sat 5–10pm, Sun 10.30am–1pm & 5–10pm.

The Colony

Map 3, G5. *Hyatt Regency Waikīkī*, 2424 Kalākaua Ave; ℗923-1234.
Appetizers at this, the most traditional of the *Hyatt's* restaurants, include a four-onion soup for $4. Steaks, which cost from $19,

WAIKĪKĪ – EXPENSIVE

are available in all sorts of combinations (steak with lobster is $55), and you can also get a delicious seafood brochette for $23. Daily 6–10pm.

DOWNTOWN HONOLULU

Cafe Laniakea
Map 5, G5. YWCA, 1040 Richards St; ℭ524-8789.
Lunch-only downtown cafeteria, run by non-profit adult train-ing organization. Lots of inexpensive vegetarian dishes, such as a $1 mini-*manapua* and a $6 plate lunch with *taro* and sweet potato salad and pesto pasta, plus meat sandwiches and burgers. Mon–Fri 10.30am–2pm.

Centaur Zone
Map 5, E5. 1147 Bethel St; ℭ533-2233.
Chinatown coffee shop, near the Hawaii Theater, which serves espressos, croissants and sandwiches through the day on week-days, and transforms itself into a hot nightspot later on (see p.189). Mon–Fri 6.30am–9.30pm.

Porter Coffee & Tea Co
Map 5, F4. 1117 Union Mall St; ℭ537-1199.
Inexpensive downtown coffee shop and vegetarian bakery/deli. As well as espressos, juices and bagels, you can get *manapua* buns for just $1 – try the apple and banana ones – and takeout salads of *taro* and Molokai sweet potatoes for just $2.75, plus more substantial plate lunches like eggplant parmesan ($5). Mon–Fri 8am–6pm, Sat 9am–6pm.

....

To combine fine food with sightseeing, try the cafés at the Contemporary Museum (p.70) and the Academy of Arts (p.52).

....

CHINATOWN

Buddhist Vegetarian Restaurant
Map 5, B4. 100 N Beretania St #109; ☏532-8218.
Bright, clean Chinese vegetarian restaurant in the heart of
Chinatown, looking out across the Nu'uanu Stream. The
menu features faux beef balls, cuttlefish, pork ribs and tender-
loin – all shaped and flavored out of tofu and other organic
foods to resemble specific meats and fishes. Entrees are priced
well under $10, set meals for four or more work out at under
$10 per person, and there's also a wide selection of vegetarian
dim sum, plus conventional vegetable dishes. No alcohol is
served. Daily except Wed 10.30am–2pm & 5.30–9pm.

Duc's Bistro
Map 5, C5. 1188 Maunakea St; ☏531-6325.
Sophisticated Asian-influenced French restaurant in
Chinatown, which hosts live jazz in the evenings. Appetizers at
$8 include gravadlax, *escargots* and crabcakes; entrees for $20–25
include tiger prawns and crab, duck breast in Grand Marnier,
flambéed steak and lamb brochette. Mon–Fri 11.30am–2pm &
5.30–10pm, Sat 5.30–10pm, closed Sun.

Indigo
Map 5, D5. 1120 Nu'uanu Ave; ☏521-2900.
Chinatown's classiest option serves delicious nouvelle Chinese-
Californian crossover food. Dim sum ranges from *taro*
dumplings or goat's cheese *wontons*, for around $6, to mussels in
black bean and cilantro oil for $10. Dinner entrees, under $20,
include duck confit, *miso*-grilled salmon, cacao bean curried
shrimp and grilled lamb. Mon–Fri 7–10am, 11am–2pm &
5–9.30pm, Sat 11am–2pm & 5–9.30pm, closed Sun.

CHINATOWN

HONOLULU MALL DINING

The *Makai Market Food Court*, downstairs on the ocean side of the **Ala Moana Center**, offers twenty fast-food counters, covering the spectrum through French, Italian, Filipino, Korean, Chinese, Japanese, American and Hawaiian. All share a central seating area, and the standard is generally high. Look out also for *Yami Yogurt*, at street level on the inland side of the mall, which serves amazing fresh-squeezed juices, and the food hall upstairs in the Shirokiya department store, where you can buy delicious hot and cold Japanese specialties. The ten or so restaurants in the mall itself, on the other hand, are deeply unatmospheric.

Both the **Ward Center** and the adjacent **Ward Warehouse**, further west along Ala Moana Boulevard towards downtown, hold several dining options. The former boasts the excellent *Pacific Café* (see p.175) and a good sushi bar – and there's a *Starbucks* across the street from Borders – while the larger Ward Warehouse is geared more towards fast food.

The **Aloha Tower Marketplace** offers eighteen food outlets, among them *Big Island Steak House*, *Scott's Seafood Grill and Bar* and a branch of the tacky *Hooters*, as well as fast food like *Wok & Roll* and *Villa Pizza*. Nearby, **Restaurant Row** is a mall that consists entirely of fully-fledged restaurants; *Jamaican Cuisine*, *Ocean Club*, and *Payao Thai* are reviewed on p.176.

For quick lunches, downtown office workers head for the various takeouts along pedestrian-only **Fort Street**, which can provide anything from *saimin* or Korean sushi to *piroscki* and a cappucino. Chinatown's **Maunakea Marketplace**, off Hotel and Maunakea streets, holds a ravishing assortment of inexpensive fast-food counters, with bargain Thai, Chinese, Vietnamese, Malaysian, Filipino, Japanese and Italian places. A big lunch, say of *saimin* with shrimp, can cost as little as $3.

Legend Seafood Restaurant

Map 5, B4. 100 N Beretania St #108; ©532-1868.

Chinatown seafood specialist, in a modern building whose big plate-glass windows look out over the Nuʻuanu Stream. The lunchtime dim sum trolleys are piled with individual portions at $2–3; full Chinese meals, with entrees at $8–16, are served at both lunch and dinner. Mon, Tues, Thurs & Fri 10.30am–2pm & 5.30–10pm, Sat & Sun 8am–2pm & 5.30–10pm; closed Wed.

Maxime

Map 5, C5. 1134 Maunakea St; ©545-4188.

This bright, clean, pastel-pink Chinatown restaurant is the best place to sample Vietnamese *pho*(noodle soup). Some is served with tripe, but *pho tai*, with thin slices of beef, is a reliable option ($5.50). There are also lots of other noodle dishes for around $7, plus Vietnamese crepes, seafood specials and lemon-grass chicken. Wash it all down with *chanh muoi* (sweet and sour lemon juice), for $1.75. Daily except Wed 9.30am–9pm.

Mei Sum

Map 5, D4. 65 N Pauahi St; ©531-3268.

Small traditional dim sum restaurant, serving a wide assortment of lunchtime snacks at around $2.50 each – tasty options include seafood or mushroom chicken dumplings, turnip cake, and *char siu* buns – plus noodle, rice and wonton entrees later in the day, featuring chicken, prawn, scallops or calamari, for $5–7 per plate. Daily 6am–9pm daily; dim sum until 3pm only.

WATERFRONT HONOLULU

Goma Ichi

Map 2, F4. 631 Keʻeaumoku St; ©951-6666.

Surprisingly formal-looking Japanese noodle bar, not far from the Ala Moana Center, which specializes in giant bowls of *ramen* noodles. The basic choice is between the *shoyu* or the spicier *tan tan* broth, served with vegetables for around $5, chicken or pork for $6, and seafood for $7; you can also get *gyoza* dumplings on the side for $4. Mon–Thurs 11am–2.30pm & 5.15–10pm, Fri & Sat 11am–2.30pm & 5.15–11pm, Sun 11.30am–3pm & 5.15–9pm.

Gordon Biersch Brewery Restaurant

Map 5, J9. Aloha Tower Marketplace, 101 Ala Moana Blvd; ℂ599-4877.

This restaurant with a built-in brewery is one of Aloha Tower's more stylish options. Seating is either outdoors on a large dockside terrace, or indoors, near a long bar that's bursting with beers from around the globe. For lunch ($10–11), try a pizza or calzone, a scallop salad, burger or grill, or steamed clams with *udon* noodles. The dinner menu offers the same pizzas and salads, plus Hawaiian regional dishes such as pan-seared *ahi* ($19) and guava-glazed roast duck ($17), and Japanese, Thai and even German specialties. Mon–Wed 11am–10pm, Thurs–Sat 11am–11pm, Sun 10.30am–10pm; bar open until midnight Mon–Wed & Sun, 1am Thurs–Sat.

Jamaican Cuisine

Map 5, J9. Restaurant Row, 500 Ala Moana Blvd; ℂ521-5855.

Mall restaurant with distinctive Jamaican identity, serving spicy curried goat or shrimp for $10, and subtler and more expensive fish dishes like steamed or marinated snapper. For a non-alcoholic alternative to Red Stripe beer try the *sennel*, a homemade infusion of hibiscus and ginger. Mon–Sat 11am–10pm, Sun 3–10pm, with live reggae Fri & Sat 9.30pm–1am.

La Mariana Sailing Club

Map 2, C3. 50 Sand Island Access Rd; ℂ848-2800.

An atmospheric oceanside restaurant – technically a yacht club – on a *very* obscure stretch of Honolulu's industrial waterfront,

La Mariana is bursting with *tiki* images and South-Seas decor rescued from the ever-dwindling 1950s-style bars and clubs of Waikīkī. The decor is great, and the food's pretty good too, featuring hearty appetizers like *taco poke* (marinated octopus) for $9, full dinners such as seafood brochette or *ahi* Cajun for well under $20, and a good-value $13 buffet brunch on Sundays. However, the real reason to come is for the impromptu semi-professional performances of Hawaiian music on Friday and Saturday evenings, from 9pm until late; for more details, see p.187. Daily 11am–11pm.

Ocean Club

Map 5, J9. Restaurant Row, 500 Ala Moana Blvd; ☎526-9888. Big, loud, and very glitzy bar that's a major hangout for downtown's after-work crowd, and won't admit anyone aged under 23 or wearing a T-shirt. The extensive menu of excellent finger-food (all seafood) is served at well under half-price before 8pm, with coconut shrimp, crab dip or sashimi costing under $4, and *poke* just $2. Tues–Thurs 4.30pm–2am, Fri 4.30pm–3am, Sat 6pm–2am.

A Pacific Café

Map 2, F5. Ward Center, 1200 Ala Moana Blvd; ☎593-0035. Chef Jean-Marie Josselin, owner of thriving *Pacific Cafés* on Kauai and Maui, is working hard to attract Honolulu diners to his second-floor restaurant in this previously unfashionable mall. With its curving walls and wave-like ceiling, it's a very stylish place, painted and lit to suggest that you're dining underwater. Delicious entrees ($20–25) – mostly fish, such as the signature wok-charred *mahi mahi*, but also including *kiawe*-grilled rack of lamb and other meats – abound in fresh-grown Thai herbs and spices, though the four-course Hawaii Regional Cuisine Sampler is good value at $34.50. Mon–Thurs 11.30am–2pm & 5.30–9pm, Fri 11.30am–2pm & 5.30–9.30pm, Sat 5.30–9.30pm & Sun 5.30–9pm.

177

Payao Thai

Map 5, J9. Restaurant Row, 500 Ala Moana Blvd; ⓒ521-3511.
Small but popular restaurant where most of the seating is outside on the mall floor itself; best known for its sticky rice dishes
but also serves Pad Thai noodles and green- and red curries for
$8–10, and fish entrees for $10–13. Mon–Sat 11am–2.30pm &
5–10pm, Sun 5–10pm.

MĀNOA AND THE UNIVERSITY DISTRICT

Canellia Buffet

Map 2, G4. 930 McCully St; ⓒ951-0511.
Korean buffet-restaurant around a mile north of Waikīkī, and
one block south of King Street, with very simple decor; the
few English speakers who venture in have to fend for themselves. Whether at lunch ($13) or dinner ($18), the food is a
treat; you select slices of marinated beef, chicken or pork and
grill them yourself at the gas-fired burners set into each table.
There are also lots of vegetables, which you can cook or not as
you choose, as well as a wide assortment of interesting salads,
including octopus, pickles and delicious tiny dried fish. Daily
11am–2pm & 5.30–9.30pm.

> **Look out for other branches in the *Canellia* chain,
> dotted around Honolulu's more obscure reaches.**

Coffeeline Campus Coffeehouse

Map 2, G4. 1820 University Ave; ⓒ947-1615.
Inconspicuous student café, upstairs in the Atherton YMCA
volunteer center at Seaview Ave, across from the University of
Hawaii campus, and handy for the *Honolulu International Hostel*
(see p.137). It's more of a takeout counter really, with terrace
seating, and serves a small selection of snacks along with espres-

so coffees. There's a ten percent discount on food for Youth Hostel Association members. Mon–Fri 7.30am–4pm.

Down to Earth
Map 2, G4. 2525 S King St; ℘947-7678.
Long-standing wholefood store near the University, which serves a full vegetarian menu of deli dishes, baked pies and pastas – some with tofu, some with cheese – plus a varied salad bar at $5 per pound and a hot bar at $6 per pound. Daily 8am–10pm.

Alan Wong's
Map 2, G4. 1857 S King St; ℘949-2526.
An expensive and hard-to-find restaurant, tucked away on the fifth floor in a nondescript area southwest of the University, *Alan Wong's* has nonetheless rapidly become Honolulu's most fashionable gourmet rendezvous, thanks to its superb food. Besides changing daily specials, appetizers always include the signature "*Da Bag*", a giant foil bag holding clams steamed with *kalua* pig, shiitake mushrooms and spinach ($10.50), and salads such as marinated eggplant with Maui onions and seared *ahi* ($5.50). Typical entrees ($25–35) include ginger-crusted *onaga* (snapper) and a spicy Hawaiian reinterpretation of a seafood paella, and there's a five-course tasting menu each night ($65). Valet parking only. Daily 5–10pm

ELSEWHERE IN HONOLULU

California Pizza Kitchen
Map 2, I6. Kahala Mall, 4614 Kilauea Ave; ℘737-9446.
Brash, yellow-trimmed mall outlet of the national chain also found in Waikīkī (see p.163), serving postmodern, one-person pizzas that boast toppings like tandoori chicken or Peking duck for $10, plus pastas and salads. Mon–Thurs & Sun 11am–10.30pm, Fri & Sat 11am–11pm.

Olive Tree Café

Map 2, I6. 4614 Kilauea Ave; ℂ737-0303.

Simple but tasteful Greek deli, adjoining but not technically within Kahala Mall, with some outdoor seating. The value is unbeatable, and the food is great, ranging from refreshing tomato and feta-cheese-based salads, to a lovely ceviche of New Zealand mussels for $5. Mon–Fri 5–11pm, Sat & Sun 11am–10pm.

Sam Choy's Breakfast, Lunch and Crab

Map 2, D3. 580 N Nimitz Hwy; ℂ545-7979.

Sandwiched between the west- and east-bound carriageways of Nimitz Highway a mile or two west of downtown, this updated version of a local Hawaiian diner looks unenticing from the outside. It's a different story inside, however, where you'll find a full-sized sampan fishing boat, a gleaming microbrewery and mosaic floors, plus crowds of diners seated at the many tables or along the stainless-steel counter facing the vast open-plan kitchen. Plate lunches, at around $10, come very big indeed; the fried *poke* is a must. Evening entrees, at $20 and up, include fresh fish, paella, crabs' legs and roasted or steamed whole crabs. Mon–Fri 6am–4pm & 5.30–10pm, Sat & Sun 6am–4pm & 5pm until late.

HAWAII KAI

Roy's

Map 7, B7. Hawaii Kai Corporate Plaza, 6600 Kalaniana'ole Highway, Hawaii Kai; ℂ396-7697.

Dinner-only gourmet restaurant, off Hwy-72 ten miles east of Waikīkī, which opened in 1988 as chef Roy Yamaguchi's first Hawaiian venture. His innovative Pacific Rim cuisine swiftly became the benchmark for all the top restaurants in Hawaii, and Roy himself has opened branches throughout the state. While renowned as one of Oahu's finest restaurants, it attracts far more locals than tourists; getting here is simply too much of an effort for most Waikīkī-based visitors. It's a noisy, hectic place, where diners can choose between watching the goings-on in the open kitchen or enjoying the views out over Maunalua Bay. The food is consistently excellent, with appetizers including individual pizzas, crab cakes, and blackened *ahi*, and entrees ranging from garlic-mustard short ribs to the *hibachi*-style salmon selected by President Clinton on a recent visit. Mon–Thurs 5.30–10pm, Fri–Sun 5–10pm.

KAILUA

Morning Brew
Map 1, L7. 572 Kailua Rd, Kailua; ☺262-7770.
Friendly local coffee bar in central Kailua, with a full range of coffee drinks, pastries and snacks. Mon–Fri & Sun 6am–9pm, Sat 6am–10pm.

Saeng's Thai Cuisine
Map 1, L7. 315 Hahani St, Kailua; ☺263-9727.
High quality Thai restaurant, where the menu of good-value soups and noodle dishes features plenty of vegetarian options, and they also serve pricier daily specials such as lobster for $10. Mon–Fri 11am–2pm & 5–9.30pm, Sat & Sun 5–9.30pm

Mango's Market & Coffee Loft
Map 1, L7. 319 Hahani St, Kailua.
Well-stocked grocery store, beside Kailua's post office, that also sells smoothies, espressos, *lassi* and authentic Bombay curries for $6–8. Mon–Fri 7am–7.30pm, Sat 8.30am–7.30pm, Sun 10am–4pm.

KAILUA

KA'A'AWA

Crouching Lion Inn
Map 1, I4. Ka'a'awa; ℗237-8511.

The most popular lunch spot for round-island drivers, perched above Hwy-83 immediately below the eponymous windward Oahu landmark (see p.106). Its open-sided *lānai* commands excellent views beyond the tall palms to the open sea, and there's also an extensive indoor seating area. Daily lunch specials cost around $10, with less expensive burgers and fish, pork or steak sandwiches also available; full steak or seafood dinners cost around $20, but they also serve *kālua* pork for $15, and $11 "early bird" meals between 5pm and 6pm. Daily 11am–2pm & 5–10pm.

PUNALU'U

Ahi's
Map 8, H6. Punalu'u; ℗293-5650.

Appealing single-story local restaurant, nestling beneath the palm trees at a curve in Hwy-83 half a mile south of Punalu'u Beach Park, and marked by a vintage delivery truck parked permanently outside. The specialty is delicious fresh shrimp served in a variety of different ways; a $9.50 sampler plate allows you to try four options. Mon–Sat 11am–9pm.

HALE'IWA

Café Hale'iwa
Map 8, B6. Kamehameha Hwy, Hale'iwa; ℗637-5516.

This venerable local diner dates back to the old days of the

Hale'iwa surf scene, and still serves as a rendezvous for surfers to plot the day's events as they look out towards the mountains. Mexican and American breakfasts cost from $4 to $8, while lunch consists of sandwiches, quesadillas or salads, at similar prices. Daily 7am–2pm.

Coffee Gallery

Map 8, B6. North Shore Marketplace, Hale'iwa; ©637-5571. Friendly, funky vegetarian cafe, which offers a nice breezy *lānai*, and sweeping views, though not of the sea. As well as coffees, smoothies and juices, they serve breakfast waffles from $4.50, $6 vegan burgers for lunch, and $7 pasta or curry specials in the evening, when there's often live music. Mon–Fri 6am–9pm, Sat & Sun 7am–9pm.

Jamesons by the Sea

Map 8, B5. 62-540 Kamehameha Hwy, Hale'iwa; ©637-4336. The best of a bunch of conventional steakhouses and tourist haunts located near Hale'iwa harbor. Facing west from the far side of the river, its sunset views are unbeatable. Reserve early if you want an oceanfront table for the Sunset specials (Wed–Sun 5–9pm), when a full shrimp or seafood meal costs $19, and teriyaki chicken, steak or fresh fish is just $13; or just turn up and try to squeeze on to the shaded *lānai* of the bar downstairs, where you can grab a simple snack. Daily 11am–9pm.

Paradise Found Café

Map 8, B6. 66-443 Kamehameha Hwy, Hale'iwa; ©637-4640. Small wholefood snackbar, consisting of a few tables at the back of the Celestial Natural Foods store, where you can pick up breakfast or lunch for about $6, or a big smoothie for $3. Fresh avocado sandwiches and pitta pockets are very much the thing here. Mon–Fri 9am–6.30pm, Sun 10am–6pm, closed Sat.

HALE'IWA

Entertainment and nightlife

Most of Honolulu's **nightlife** concentrates on Waikīkī, where fun-seeking tourists set the tone. On the whole, however, entertainment tends to be bland. Hawaii is usually bypassed by touring mainstream musicians, so if you enjoy **live music** you'll probably have to settle for little-known local performers (even rising stars of contemporary Hawaiian music try to keep their credibility by not playing in Waikīkī too often). As for **bars**, Chinatown has the most raucous in town, but they're way too hair-raising for most tastes.

Various magazines and papers will keep you abreast of what's going on; the best are the free *Honolulu Weekly* newspaper, and the *TGIF* section of Friday's *Honolulu Advertiser*.

Annual events and festivals in Honolulu are listed on p.214.

HAWAIIAN ENTERTAINMENT

The popular image of Hawaiian tourism may still revolve around lilting ukuleles and swaying grass skirts, but it's surprisingly difficult to find good **Hawaiian entertainment** in Waikīkī or Honolulu, and genuine *hula* performances are rare. By far the best idea is to look for events that are arranged for Hawaiian (rather than tourist) audiences, such as the frequent one-off performances and benefit concerts at downtown's beautiful Hawaii Theater (see p.58). Otherwise, settle for evoking bygone days with a sunset cocktail at one of Waikīkī's grander hotels, most of which regularly feature accomplished Hawaiian musicians.

A number of regular **free shows** also take place each week, most of greater appeal to older travelers. In addition to the **Kodak Hula Show** at the Waikīkī Shell (see p.41), there are Polynesian-themed displays at the Royal Hawaiian Shopping Center (Mon, Wed & Fri 6.30pm) and Kūhiō Mall (Mon–Sat 7pm & 8pm). In addition, the **Royal Hawaiian Band** gives free hour-long performances on Fridays at 12.15pm on the lawns of 'Iolani Palace downtown, and on Sundays at 2pm in Waikīkī's Kapi'olani Park.

....

Typical prices in Waikīkī cocktail bars are $4–5 for bottled beer, $6–8 for a Mai Tai.

....

Banyan Court

Map 3, F6. *Sheraton Moana Surfrider*, 2365 Kalākaua Ave, Waikīkī; ✆922-3111.

Open-air beach bar that was home to the nationally syndicated *Hawaii Calls* radio show from the 1930s to the 1970s. Steel guitar and *hula* dancers nightly 5–8pm, followed by a pianist 8–11pm; no cover but a one-drink minimum.

Captain's Table

Map 4, I4. *Hawaiian Waikīkī Beach Hotel*, 2570 Kalākaua Ave, Waikīkī; ℂ922-2511.

Aoia, probably the best of Waikīkī's regular Hawaiian groups, play at 6pm nightly.

Iz: May 20 1959 – June 26 1997

In the summer of 1997, the contemporary Hawaiian music scene lost the man who was in every sense its biggest star. **Israel Kamakawiwoʻole**, who started out singing in the Makaha Sons of Niihau, and then went solo in 1990, died of respiratory difficulties in a Honolulu hospital. During his twenty-year career, "**Iz**" came to epitomize the pride and the power of Hawaiian music. His extraordinary voice adapted equally well to rousing political anthems, delicate love songs, pop standards and Jawaiian reggae rhythms, while his personality, and his love for Hawaii, always shone through both in concert and on record. Like his brother Skippy before him – also a founding member of the Makaha Sons – Iz eventually succumbed to the health problems caused by his immense size. At one point, his weight reached a colossal 757 pounds; he needed a fork-lift truck to get on stage, and could only breathe through tubes. His strength in adversity did much to ensure that he was repeatedly voted Hawaii's most popular entertainer, and after his death he was granted a state funeral, with his body lying in state in the Capitol. His enduring legacy will be the music on his four solo albums – *Ka Anoʻi* (1990), *Facing Future* (1993), *E Ala Ē* (1995), and *ʻn Dis Life* (1996) – while his haunting rendition of *Hawaiʻi 78* (featured on *Facing Future*) has become the signature song of the Hawaiian sovereignty movement.

Duke's Canoe Club

Map 3, E6. *Outrigger Waikīkī on the Beach*, 2335 Kalākaua Ave, Waikīkī; ©922-2268.

Smooth Hawaiian sounds wash over this oceanfront cocktail bar nightly from 4–6pm and 10pm–midnight. On weekends, the afternoon show is usually a big-name "Concert on the Beach"; no cover charge.

House Without a Key

Map 3, C7. *Halekūlani*, 2199 Kālia Rd, Waikīkī; ©923-2311.

A romantic beach bar, named after a Charlie Chan mystery that was written by Earl Derr Biggers after a stay at the hotel. The name of the book and the bar revolves around the fact that no one in Honolulu used to lock their doors. Old-time Hawaiian classics performed nightly 5–8.30pm, with *hula* dancing by a former Miss Hawaii; no cover.

La Mariana Sailing Club

Map 2, C3. 50 Sand Island Access Rd; ©848-2800.

Waterfront restaurant – the food is reviewed on p.176 – with a wonderful 1950s feel, hidden away amid the docks of Honolulu. Pianist Ron Miyashiro and a group of semi-professional singers gather each Fri & Sat, from 9pm onwards, to work their way through a nostalgic set of classic Hawaiian songs. Daily 11am–11pm.

Lobby Bar

Map 4, H4. *Hawaiian Regent Hotel*, 2552 Kalākaua Ave, Waikīkī; ©924-0123.

No-cover hotel cocktail bar where a consistently good roster of Hawaiian musicians perform Sun–Wed 9pm–1am, Thurs 5.30–8.30pm & 9pm–1am, Fri & Sat 5pm–1am. In addition, relatively big-name stars appear most evenings in the hotel's *Ocean Terrace Bar*.

HAWAIIAN ENTERTAINMENT

187

Pier Bar

Map 5, E8. Aloha Tower Marketplace; ©528-5700.

Open-air bar whose waterfront stage features live performances by top Hawaiian musicians until 1am on weekends, and normally a few other nights as well, plus regular lunchtime and sunset entertainment; no cover.

BARS, LIVE MUSIC AND DANCING

There's rarely a clear distinction between **bars**, **live music venues** and **nightclubs** in Honolulu, and many restaurants get in on the act as well. While there's plenty of live music around – especially in Waikīkī – the overall standard tends to be disappointing. In addition, few Waikīkī clubs get to build a regular clientele, so the atmosphere is unpredictable. The biggest touring acts tend to appear at Pearl Harbor's Aloha Stadium (©545-4000); watch for announcements in the local press.

> **You can only drink alcohol in Hawaii if you're over 21, and have the ID to prove it.**

Acqua Lounge

Map 4, H4. *Hawaiian Regent Hotel*, 2552 Kalākaua Ave, Waikīkī; ©924-0123.

Red-hot Latin rhythms, from salsa to samba, with Rolando Sanchez and the Salsa Hawaii Band. Dance lessons Thurs 8pm, club nights Thurs 9pm–2am, Fri & Sat 9.30pm–2am; $3 cover.

Anna Banannas

Map 2, G4. 2440 S Beretania St, Honolulu; ©946-5190.

Reasonable bar in the University district, with live R&B and reggae most nights, and a hectic weekend atmosphere; $4 cover. Daily 9.30pm–2am.

Atomik

Map 4, D2. 1739 Kalākaua Ave, Waikīkī; ℭ949-1739.

Frenzied dance club near the *Hard Rock Café*, where the focus is on DJs rather than live performance, and the music covers the full spectrum from the 1980s onwards, with an emphasis on house and hip-hop; cover varies. Daily 9pm–6am, with alcohol served until 2am only.

Centaur Zone

Map 5, E5. 1147 Bethel St, Honolulu; ℭ533-2233.

This Chinatown coffee shop plays host to live music or performance Mon–Fri 7pm, under the banner "Bethel Street Live!", and often reopens late Saturday night as a jungle music dance den. $5 cover.

Hot Lava Club

Map 2, G4. 2535 Coyne St, Honolulu; ℭ941-5282.

This University-district club, open nightly from 9pm, has something of a split identity; Sun–Wed it focuses on contemporary Hawaiian performers, Thurs–Sat it transforms itself into a venue for alternative rock bands. Cover varies.

Jamaican Cuisine

Map 5, J9. Restaurant Row, 500 Ala Moana Blvd, Honolulu; ℭ521-5855.

Funky Caribbean restaurant in downtown mall – reviewed on p.176 – with live reggae Fri & Sat 9.30pm–1am.

Lewers Lounge

Map 3, C7. *Halekūlani*, 2199 Kalia Rd, Waikīkī; ℭ923-2311.

Sophisticated nightspot that looks more like an English drawing room than a Waikīkī bar. Live jazz nightly 9pm–12.30am, at its best Tues–Sat, when Loretta Ables performs.

BARS, LIVE MUSIC AND DANCING |

Liquid Surf Den

Map 2, G4. 1035 University Ave, Honolulu; ✆942-7873.
University-district bar/club, open nightly from 9.30pm for a
mixed program of punk, reggae, ska and local bands. Reggae
night Mon, college night Tues, ladies' night Thurs. $3 cover.

....

Gay bars and clubs in Honolulu are listed in Chapter 12.

....

Nashville Waikīkī

Map 3, F3. 2330 Kūhiō Ave, Waikīkī; ✆926-7911.
If you're hankering to hoe down in Hawaii, this country music
club below the *Outrigger West* has plenty of room to show off your
rhinestones. There's also pool tables and darts. Daily 4pm–4am.

Ocean Club

Map 5, J9. Restaurant Row, 500 Ala Moana Blvd, Honolulu;
✆526-9888.
Flamboyant, frenetic downtown bar-cum-restaurant, which
serves amazingly inexpensive food in the early evening (see
p.177) and turns into a wild dance club as the night wears on.
Over-22s only; no T-shirts. Open until at least 2am Tues–Sat.

Rose and Crown

Map 3, G4. King's Village, 2400 Koa Ave, Waikīkī.
Not a bad approximation of an English pub; the beer pumps
are fake, but it's appropriately dark and gloomy even at noon.
From 11am until 7.30pm a draught Bud or Miller costs $1.50,
and there's a happy hour 4.30–7.30pm. Daily 11.30am–2am.

Sand Island Restaurant and Bar

Map 2, C3. 197 Sand Island Access Rd, Honolulu; ✆847-4274.
Honolulu's one real blues venue, en route to Sand Island (p.65),
in an area where you're unlikely to see any tourists. Gigs are
usually scheduled for Wed–Sat, starting at 9pm.

Comedy

Waikīkī's principal **comedy** venue is *Coconut's Comedy Club* in the *'Ilikai Hotel Nikko Waikīkī*, 1777 Ala Moana Blvd (℃239-5867), which puts on shows to an irregular schedule, normally including performances on Fri & Sat at 8pm & 10pm; cover $10–15.

Warriors Lounge
Map 4, E4. *Hale Koa Hotel*, 2055 Kālia Rd, Waikīkī; ℃955-0555.
Only military personnel can stay at this seafront hotel, but the no-cover dance floor is open to all, and features country and Latin (Fri & Sat 8.30pm, Sun 8pm), big band music (Mon & Tues 8pm), or contemporary Hawaiian (Wed & Thurs 8pm).

Wave Waikīkī
Map 4, E2. 1877 Kalākua Ave, Waikīkī; ℃941-0424.
In so far as Waikīkī has an alternative rock scene, this is it. Large venue, with a bar upstairs and dance floor down below, and DJs rather than live bands most nights; $5 cover after 10pm. Open nightly 9pm–4am.

SHOWS AND SPECTACULARS

The days when every major Waikīkī hotel put on its own Las-Vegas-style, big-budget show seem to be over. Nonetheless, there are still a few nightly shows on offer. For most of the shows below, specific prices are not listed because you can get much better deals by buying **reduced-price tickets** through "activity centers" (see p.206). Expect to pay $20–25 for the show alone (and bear in mind you'll be expected to drink once you're there), or more like $50 if you opt to eat as well.

Boy-Lesque

Map 3, D5. *Waikīkī Beachcomber*, 2300 Kalākaua Ave, Waikīkī;
©922-2276.

All-singing, all-dancing female impersonators – mostly dressed
as gay icons from Mae West to Madonna – enjoyed over cocktails and/or dinner. Nightly 6.45pm, dinner seating at 5.30pm,
and additional shows Thurs–Sat at 9pm.

Frank DeLima and Glenn Medeiros

Map 3, B5. *Hula Hut*, 286 Beach Walk, Waikīkī; ©923-8411.

If your only doubt about joining Frank DeLima – Hawaii's biggest-
name comedian – in laughing at the islands' ethnic mix is that his
humor may be too locally based, don't worry; it's not exactly sub-
tle. Kauai-born singer Glenn Medeiros co-stars. Fri & Sat 8.45pm.

Legends in Concert

Map 3, D5. Aloha Showroom, Royal Hawaiian Shopping Center,
Waikīkī; ©971-1400.

An enjoyable tribute show of quick-fire impersonations,
though your tastes have to stretch pretty wide to want to see
Elvis, Prince, Jackie Wilson, Michael Jackson, Judy Garland
and Dolly Parton (to name but a few) on the same bill. You
can get the general idea from free "taster" shows on the mall's
open-air stage, at odd times throughout the day. Two shows
nightly at 6.30pm & 9pm; dinner served at 5pm.

Society of Seven

Map 3, E6. *Outrigger* Main Show Room, 2335 Kalākaua Ave,
Waikīkī; ©923-SHOW.

Very long-standing song-and-dance ensemble, which performs
Broadway musical routines and pop hits with amazing energy.
Mon 8.30pm, Tues–Sat 6.30pm & 8.30pm.

SHOWS AND SPECTACULARS

HONOLULU MOVIE THEATERS

The best spot to catch a new **movie** in Honolulu is on one of the nine screens at Restaurant Row, near downtown (☎263-4171). Less mainstream offerings are shown at the Academy of Arts (900 S Beretania St; ☎532-8768) and the Movie Museum (3566 Harding Ave; ☎735-8771). Among options in Waikīkī are the Marina Twins (1765 Ala Moana Blvd; ☎973-5733), and the Waikīkī Theaters (Seaside at Kalākaua Ave; ☎971-5133), though the latter are due to be bulldozed to make way for a new shopping complex.

The giant-screen **Imax Theater** in Waikīkī, 325 Seaside Ave (☎923-4629), has hourly showings of *Ring of Fire* (about volcanoes), *Whales*, or *Hidden Hawaii* (daily 11am–9pm, adults $7.50 one show, $12 two, $15 three; under-12s $5/$8/$10). They also put on laser shows and rock-concert films.

Gay Honolulu

H awaii ranks among the world's most appealing destinations for **gay and lesbian** travelers, and nowhere is the gay presence more conspicuous than in Honolulu. While the social climate of the state is undeniably liberal, recent media attention has tended to exaggerate how much progress has been made in Hawaii on issues such as **same-sex marriage**. A series of court rulings that seemed to clear the way for same-sex unions – which would be of special significance because every US state is obliged by the Constitution to recognize marriages deemed legitimate in any other state – have been consistently thwarted by cautious, conservative state politicians. No such officially sanctioned marriages have yet taken place.

In addition, although Honolulu's gay scene still has plenty to offer visitors, its long-standing epicenter suffered a major blow in 1998. Until recently, a single block of **Kūhiō Avenue** in central Waikīkī housed virtually all Oahu's best-known gay businesses, including the legendary *Hula's Bar and Lei Stand*. That entire block has now been sold to developers, who intend to construct a major shopping complex on the site, and virtually all its former tenants have been obliged to move. At the time of writing, only *Hula's* appears to have found a new home.

The major survivor in the Kūhiō District is Hawaii's one specifically **gay hotel**, the *Hotel Honolulu* at 376 Kai'olu St (see p.139). For gay travelers intending to throw themselves into the Waikīkī scene, reserving a room there is the obvious first step – step two being to join one of the hotel's **sunset dinner cruises**, which take place on Wednesday and Friday evenings. A much lower-key accommodation alternative, in Honolulu itself, would be the *Mango House* (see p.150).

The two most popular **beaches** among gay travelers are **Queen's Surf**, across from Kapi'olani Park at the edge of Waikīkī (see p.34), and **Diamond Head Beach Park**, a mile or so further on (see p.36).

SERVICES FOR GAY TRAVELERS

Pacific Ocean Holidays (PO Box 88245, Honolulu HI 96830-8245; ✆923-2400 or 1-800/735-6600, fax 923-2499; email *poh@hi.net*) organizes all-inclusive **package vacations** in Hawaii for gay and lesbian travelers. It also publishes the thrice-yearly *Pocket Guide to Hawaii*, a useful booklet of gay listings throughout the state (available free in Hawaii, or by mail for $5 per issue, one year's subscription $12).

Other sources of **information** include the monthly magazine *Island Lifestyle* (PO Box 11840, Honolulu HI 96828; ✆737-6400, fax 735-8825; Web site *www.islandlifestyle.com*), which you can pick up at any of Honolulu's gay bars or hotels, and **Web sites** such as *gayhawaii.com*.

Beechman Agencies, #102, 408 Lewers St, Waikīkī (✆923-2433), is a **travel agency** specializing in tickets and activities for gay travelers, while Dave's Island Pride (✆732-6518), operates half- and full-day **bus tours** of Oahu for gay and lesbian visitors. A gay **hiking** club, Likehike (✆455-8193), organizes different group hikes on alternate Sundays.

GAY COMMUNITY RESOURCES

For general information on gay life in Honolulu, contact the **Gay & Lesbian Community Center**, in the YWCA building at 1566 Wilder Ave, Honolulu HI 96822 (✆951-7000), which operates a library and resource center. In addition, the **Life Foundation**, #226, 233 Keawe St, Honolulu, HI 96813 (✆521-2437), offers counseling and support to all persons with HIV/AIDS, and the **Honolulu Gay Support Group** (✆521-6000) provides similar services.

GAY BARS AND CLUBS

Angles Waikīkī
Map 3, D3. 2256 Kūhiō Ave, Waikīkī; ✆926-9766 or 923-1130.
Dance club with lively bar and street-view patio, plus bar sports including pool and darts. Daily 10am–2am.

Fusion
Map 3, D5. 2260 Kūhiō Ave, Waikīkī; ✆924-2422.
Wild, split-level nightclub, open nightly 8pm–4am, with male strippers, female impersonators and special drink discounts.

Hula's Bar and Lei Stand
Map 4, 14. *Waikīkī Grand Hotel*, 134 Kapahulu Ave, Waikīkī; ✆923-0669.
As this book went to press, Waikīkī's most popular gay club had yet to reopen in its new premises, a suite of ocean-view rooms on the second floor of the *Waikīkī Grand*. With 24 years' experience in its former Kūhiō Avenue location, however, it shouldn't take long for both the bar and the associated *Trixx* dance floor to get back to normal.

In-Between
Map 3, B3. 2155 Lau'ula St, Waikīkī; ☏926-7060.
Local gay bar in the heart of Waikīkī, open Mon–Fri
2pm–2am, Sat & Sun 10am–2am.

Michelangelo
Map 4, D3. 444 Hobron Lane, Waikīkī; ☏951-8008.
Club and karaoke bar, open nightly 4pm–2am; the cruiser back
room, *P-10A*(☏942-8536), hosts live erotic entertainment Fri &
Sat. The same complex also houses Max's Gym (☏951-8232), a
24-hour fitness and sauna facility.

Shopping

Despite the millions of dollars invested by big business in the attempt to persuade visitors otherwise, **shopping** is one of the least exciting ways to spend time in Honolulu. The retail scene in both Honolulu and Waikīkī is dominated by large, characterless **malls**, whose primary function is to give Asian customers easy access to the wonders of the American marketplace. Almost nowhere will you find neighborhoods or even streets of traditional independent stores.

According to official figures, the average Japanese tourist in Hawaii spends $113 per day on clothes and accessories; US visitors are reckoned to spend a mere $16 per day. That makes the recent downturn in the Asian economy very bad news indeed for Hawaiian shopkeepers; quite possibly, the frantic race to build ever swankier malls is finally about to collapse.

If you're simply looking for **souvenirs**, the prints, posters and T-shirts piled high along the sidewalks of Waikīkī are all well and good for anyone who thinks that whales are interplanetary voyagers from another dimension, but stores and galleries selling high-quality indigenous arts and crafts are few and far between.

Colorful Hawaiian **clothing**, such as *aloha* shirts and the cover-all "Mother-Hubbard"-style *muʻumuʻu* dress, is on sale everywhere, though classic designs are surprisingly rare and you tend to see the same stylized prints over and over again. The prevailing trend these days is for muted "reverse-print" designs, in which the cloth is effectively worn inside-out; for more stimulating ideas, seek out clothing designed by **Sig Zane** from the Big Island, who depicts spiritually significant Hawaiian plants and animals using traditional colors and dyes, or **Tori Richard**, whose fabrics have a playful, contemporary garishness.

Otherwise, the main **local crafts** to look out for are *lau hala* **weaving**, in which mats, hats, baskets and the like are created by plaiting the large leaves (*lau*) of the spindly legged pandanus (*hala*) tree, and **wood turning**, with fine bowls made from native dark woods such as *koa*.

WAIKĪKĪ SHOPPING

If you want to buy a T-shirt, a beach mat, or a monkey carved out of a coconut, Waikīkī is still definitely the place for you. Kalākaua and Kūhiō avenues especially are lined with cut-price souvenir stores; there are 37 shops in the ABC chain alone, all open daily from 7am to midnight and selling basic groceries along with postcards, sun lotions and other tourist essentials.

Waikīkī's largest malls, the monolithic **Royal Hawaiian Shopping Center** and the five-floor **Waikīkī Shopping Plaza**, across the street at 2250 Kalākaua Ave, are aseptic, upmarket enclaves, packed with designer-clothing outlets, jewelry stores and sunglasses emporiums. They'll shortly be joined, in the same general area, by two more huge ventures, the **Waikīkī Promenade** and the **Waikīkī Royal Walk**.

For the moment, the venerable 1950s-style open-air **International Marketplace**, 2330 Kalākaua Ave, still survives. With its simple wooden stalls scattered among the trees, it has a lot more atmosphere, though it has to be admitted that the "crafts" on sale tend to be essentially made-in-Taiwan.

It's harder than you'd expect to find that quintessential emblem of old Hawaii, the authentic **Aloha shirt**; try Bailey's, 517 Kapahulu Ave (*734-7628).

For eating options in the malls of Waikīkī, see p.161

Honolulu Bookstores and Music Stores

Bookstores

Barnes & Noble, Kahala Mall (*737-3323).
Borders Books & Music, Ward Center (*591-8995).
Honolulu Book Shop, Ala Moana Center (*941-2274).
Rainbow Books & Records, 1010 University Ave at King St (*955-7994).
Rand McNally, Ala Moana Center (*944-6699).
Shop Pacifica, Bishop Museum, 1525 Bernice St (*848-4156).
Waldenbooks, Royal Hawaiian Shopping Center (*926-3200), Waikīkī Shopping Plaza (*922-4154), Waikīkī Trade Center (*924-8330) and several other outlying Honolulu locations.

Music Stores

Barnes & Noble, as above.
Borders Books & Music, as above.
Hungry Ear Records & Tapes, 1518E Makaloa St (*944-5044).
Purple Haze, 2741 S King St (*946-5444).
Rainbow Books & Records, as above.
Tower Records, 2330 Kalākaua Ave (*923-3650), Kahala Mall, and two other outlying Honolulu locations.

HONOLULU SHOPPING

For many years, the **Ala Moana Center**, between down-town Honolulu and Waikīkī, held sway as the premier mall for serious shoppers, but its success has meant that new rivals now seem to be springing up all the time.

Away from the malls, probably the best places to shop for unusual gifts and souvenirs are the stores in Honolulu's major museums and galleries. In the **Bishop Museum** (see p.82), Shop Pacifica and the adjoining Native Books and Beautiful Things stock a wide range of books, cards, clothing and crafts objects. The Academy Shop at the **Honolulu Academy of Arts** (see p.52) specializes in high-quality traditional arts and crafts, including jewelry and fabrics, while the more eclectic Gift Shop at the **Contemporary Museum** (see p.70) carries flamboyant and original gift items, most of them irresistible despite being of little if any practical use.

Ala Moana Center

Map 2, F5. 1450 Ala Moana Blvd; Mon–Sat 9.30am–9pm, Sun 10am–8pm.

The **Ala Moana Center**, a mile west of Waikīkī, has since 1959 been Hawaii's main shopping destination; neighbor-island residents fly to Honolulu specifically in order to shop here. One of the largest open-air malls in the world, it holds several major department stores, including Sears, JC Penney, the Japanese Shirokiya – noteworthy for the amazing food hall upstairs – and Hawaii's own Liberty House. The direct descendant of a ships' chandlery store that opened downtown in 1849, Liberty House has recently hit financial trouble amid accusations of neglecting its traditional customers in pursuit of the tourist dollar.

In addition, the Ala Moana Center is home to a couple of hundred smaller specialty stores, with all the big international names – Emporio Armani, Gucci, Dior, Tiffany, Louis

Vuitton, etc – rubbing shoulders with the likes of The Gap, The Body Shop, and Banana Republic. There's also a new branch of the resolutely downmarket Hilo Hattie's, which specializes in inexpensive aloha wear and souvenirs for tourists – so there's less point than ever in joining the bus parties that trek out to the main Hilo Hattie's, en route to the airport. The whole complex is rounded off by a central performance area, a food court (see p.175), a satellite city hall, and a post office.

Leis

Some of the most attractive products of Hawaii are just too ephemeral to take home. That goes for virtually all the orchids and tropical flowers on sale everywhere, and unfortunately it's also true of *leis*.

Leis (pronounced *lays*) are flamboyant decorative garlands, usually composed of flowers such as the fragrant *melia* (the plumeria or frangipani) or the bright-red *lehua* blossom (from the ʻōhia tree), but sometimes also made from feathers, shells, seeds or nuts. They're worn by both men and women, above all on celebrations or gala occasions – election-winning politicians are absolutely deluged in them, as are the statues of Kamehameha the Great and Queen Liliʻuokalani on state holidays.

The days are gone when every arriving tourist was festooned with a *lei*, but you'll probably be way-*leied* at a *lūʻau* or some such occasion, while if you're around for Lei Day (May 1), everyone's at it. If you want to buy one, **Chinatown** is the acknowledged center of the art, with one or two stores on every street displaying a supply of fresh flower *leis* in refrigerated cabinets. Recommended outlets include Cindy's Flower & Lei Shoppe, 1034 Maunakea St (✆536-6538); Lita's Leis, 59 N Beretania St (✆521-9065); and Aloha Leis, 1145 Maunakea St (✆599-7725).

Victoria Ward Center

Map 2, F5. 1050 Ala Moana Blvd.

Not far west of the Ala Moana Center, the various **Ward**
malls – the Warehouse, Center, Gateway Center, Farmers
Market and Village Shops – have been spruced up considerably in the last few years. Nevertheless, bit by bit, they're
being torn down and replaced by a vast new complex, to be
known as the **Victoria Ward Center**, which will be
anchored by a massive FAO Schwarz toy store and a Saks
Fifth Avenue. New homes will almost certainly be found for
the best of the **Ward Warehouse**'s current crop of interesting
stores, which include the Nohea Gallery, which sells contemporary artworks from paintings and ceramics to woodcarv-
ings, and distinctive clothing boutiques such as Aloha Tower
Traders, Mamo Howell and Pomegranates in the Sun. The
giant Borders bookstore and flamboyant Pacific Café restaurant (see p.177) in the Ward Center should remain intact.

For eating options in the malls of Honolulu, see p.175

Aloha Tower Marketplace

Map 5, E8. Mon–Thurs & Sun 9am–9pm, Fri & Sat 9am–10pm.

Downtown's **Aloha Tower Marketplace** (see also p.62)
has yet to lure significant numbers of tourists away from Ala
Moana, but the dockside setting makes it a fun place to
wander around. Most of the stores are one offs rather than
chain outlets, and shopping opportunities range from the
fake vomit at Monty's World of Magic, to the beautiful and
very expensive koa-wood furniture and Sig Zane aloha
wear at Martin & MacArthur.

Kahala Mall

Map 2, I6. 4211 Waialae Ave; Mon–Sat 10am–9pm, Sun 10am–5pm.

Only a couple of miles from Waikīkī, *mauka* of Diamond

Head, the **Kahala Mall** is almost as chic as – and far less frenzied than – Ala Moana. As well as Liberty House, Longs Drugs, Banana Republic, an eight-screen movie theater, and a fine assortment of restaurants, it holds a large Tower Records and an excellent Barnes & Noble bookstore.

Aloha Flea Market

Map 1, H7. Aloha Stadium, Pearl Harbor; Wed, Sat & Sun 6am–3pm. Over a thousand diverse traders ensure that the **Aloha Flea Market**, held thrice weekly at the Aloha Stadium in Pearl Harbor, provides an entertaining opportunity to look for (mostly second-hand) bargains. The Aloha Flea Market Shuttle Bus (©955-4050) runs there from Waikīkī, charging $6 return, including admission.

Ocean activities

Hawaii's vast tourism industry is rooted in the picture-book appeal of its endless palm-fringed sandy **beaches** and crystal-clear, fish-filled turquoise **ocean**. The opportunities for sea sports on Oahu are almost infinite, ranging from **swimming** through **snorkeling**, **scuba diving**, **fishing** and **whale-watching**, to Hawaii's greatest gift to the world, the art of **surfing**.

....

For landlubbers, a list of Oahu's best golf courses appears on p.219

....

If you're prepared to shop around a little, you can find much lower rates for most activities than those quoted by the island's many activity companies; look out for discount coupons in the free magazines, and the handbills distributed on every street corner. In particular, independent "**activity centers**" throughout Waikīkī sell tickets for every conceivable island activity, including the various waterborne pursuits described in this chapter, as well as land-based tours (see p.18), air trips (p.20), and excursions to *lū'aus* (p.157) and the Polynesian Cultural Center (p.111). They can also offer air tickets and packages to the other Hawaiian islands, and discounts on airport shuttle vans.

Activity Centers

Activities & Attractions of Hawaii, 2270 Kalākaua Ave #203; ℂ971-9700 or 1-800/551-7770.
Affordable, *Waikīkī Park Height Hotel*, 2440 Kūhiō Ave; ℂ922-5522.
Aloha Express, *Waikīkī Circle Hotel*, 2464 Kalākaua Ave; ℂ924-4030.
Horizon Discount Tours, 159 Ka'iulani Ave and 1833 Kalākaua Ave; ℂ955-0877.
Magnum Tickets & Tours, 2134 Kalākaua Ave; ℂ923-7825.
Pacific Monarch Travel, *Pacific Monarch Hotel*, 142 Uluniu Ave; ℂ924-7717.
Polynesian Express, Kūhiō Mall, 2301 Kūhiō Ave #222; ℂ922-5577 or 1-800/222-5024.

Aim to pay perhaps $20 per person for a basic cruise (including a buffet dinner), increasing to as much as $90 for a submarine or a better standard of food, and perhaps $50 for anything like jet-skiing or scuba diving. For activities not based in central Waikīkī, the price should include round-trip transport to the departure point.

Ocean Safety

It's all too easy to forget that Hawaiian beaches can be deadly as well as beautiful; Hawaii is the remotest archipelago on earth, so waves have two thousand miles of the misnamed Pacific Ocean to build up their strength before they come crashing into the islands. People born in Hawaii are brought up with a healthy **respect for the sea** and learn to watch out for all sorts of signs before they swim. You'll be advised to throw sticks into the waves to see how they move, or to look for disturbances in the surf that indicate powerful currents; unless you have local expertise, however, you're better off sticking to the official beach parks and most popular spots, especially those that are shielded by offshore reefs. Not all beaches have lifeguards and warning flags, and unattended beaches are not necessarily safe. Look for other bathers, but whatever your experience elsewhere, don't assume you'll be able to cope with the same conditions as the local kids. Always ask for advice, and above all follow the cardinal rule – **Never turn your back on the water**.

The beaches that experience the most accidents and drownings are those where waves of four feet or more break directly onto the shore. This varies according to the season, so beaches that are idyllic in summer can be storm-tossed death traps between October and April. If you get caught in a rip current or undertow and find yourself being dragged out to sea, stay calm and remember that the vast majority of such currents disappear within a hundred yards of the shore. Never exhaust yourself by trying to swim against them, but simply allow yourself to be carried out until the force weakens, and swim first to one side and then back to the shore.

Sea creatures to avoid include *wana* (black spiky **sea urchins**), Portuguese man-o-war **jellyfish**, and **coral** in general, which can give painful, infected cuts. **Shark attacks** are much rarer than popular imagination suggests; those which do occur are usually due to "misunderstandings", such as spear-fishers inadvertently keeping sharks from their catch or surfers idling on their boards looking a bit too much like turtles from below.

Emergency Numbers

Police, Fire and Ambulance   ℂ911
Ocean Search and Rescue   ℂ1-800/552-645

ACTIVITY CENTERS

DINNER AND SIGHTSEEING CRUISES

Dream Cruises

℡592-2000

Lunch and sunset cruises, plus snorkel equipment. They also offer whale-watching in winter. Based at Kewalo Basin.

Leahi Catamaran

℡922-5665 or 1-800/462-7975

Sightseeing cruises in a sailing catamaran that leaves from Waikīkī Beach, ranging from one-hour trips for under $20 to snorkel, scuba, whale-watching and cocktail cruises.

Navatek I

℡848-6360 or 1-800/852-4183

Giant catamaran, operated by Royal Hawaiian Cruises and based at Pier 6 in Honolulu, which prides itself on offering the smoothest sailing experience on Oahu. Snorkeling, scuba, sightseeing and deluxe dinner cruises.

Paradise Cruise

℡593-2493

The *Star of Honolulu* cruises between Diamond Head and Pearl Harbor, from Kewalo Basin. Inexpensive morning sightseeing excursions, with whale-watching in winter, and sunset cruises up to $200 a person. Also trips in the glass-bottomed *Holo Holo Kai* catamaran.

Windjammer

℡537-1122 or 1-800/367-5000

Tall pseudo-sailing ship, with a buffet and a fine-dining restaurant. Sunset cruises from Pier 7A near Aloha Tower.

SUBMARINES

Atlantis Submarines
℡973-9811 or 1-800/548-6262
Passengers leave Waikīkī's *Hilton Hawaiian Village* by motorboat, then transfer onto a genuine submarine out in the ocean for a 45-min dive down to the seabed, which includes circling a shipwreck.

Nautilus
℡591-9199
The *Nautilus*, which is based at Kewalo Basin, does not actually submerge, but the experience is similar; passengers simply descend to the underwater viewing cabin once the *Nautilus* reaches open ocean.

Voyager Submarines
℡592-7850
After a five-minute catamaran trip from Kewalo Basin, passengers rendezvous with the "yellow submarine" above a natural reef, and take a 35-min tour along the ocean floor.

SURFING

The nation that invented **surfing** – long before the foreigners came – remains its greatest arena. A recurring theme in ancient legends has young men frittering away endless days in the waves rather than facing up to their duties; now young people from all over the world flock to Hawaii to do just that. The sport was popularized early in the twentieth century by champion Olympic swimmer **Duke Kahanamoku**, the original Waikīkī Beach Boy; see p.38. He toured the world with his sixteen-foot board, demonstrating his skills to admiring crowds and was responsible for introducing surfing to Australia.

Waikīkī lost its best surf breaks when it was relandscaped at the start of the tourist boom, but with advances in techniques and technology, surfing has never been more popular. Oahu's fabled **North Shore** – see p.117 onwards – is a Mecca for surf bums, who ride the waves around Waimea Bay and hang out in the coffee bars of Hale'iwa. However, surfing at such legendary sites is for experts only. Whatever your surfing experience at home, you need to be very sure you're up to it before you have a go in Hawaii, so start by sampling conditions at lesser surf-spots to be found on all the islands.

Concession stands near the Duke Kahanamoku statue in central Waikīkī rent out surfboards for around $10 per hour, and offer **surfing lessons** for beginners costing more like $25 per hour, including board rental. Lessons are great fun, and they really work; with the aid of a friendly push at the right moment, almost everyone manages to ride a wave within the hour. An equally exhilarating way to get a taste for the surf is to start out by using a smaller **boogie board**, which you lie on.

WINDSURFING

Since Oahu's Robbie Naish won the first world championships in the 1970s, at the age of 13, Hawaii has also been recognized as the spiritual home of **windsurfing**. Maui tends to be regarded as the prime goal for enthusiasts from around the world, but Oahu also has some excellent spots, not least Kailua Beach on the windward shore (see p.101). Once again, be warned that Hawaiian waters present challenges on a vastly different scale to what you may be used to at home.

Naish himself now operates Naish Windsurfing Hawaii at 155-C Hamakaua Drive, Kailua Beach (©261-3539), offering equipment rental from $25 per half-day and private lessons from $55. A similar service on the North Shore is provided by Surf'n'Sea, 62-595 Kamehameha Hwy, Hale'iwa (℗637-9887 or 1-800/899-SURF); see p.119.

SNORKELING

Probably the easiest ocean activity for beginners is **snorkeling**. Equipped with mask, snorkel and fins, you can while away hours and days having face-to-face encounters with the rainbow-colored populations of Hawaii's reefs and lava pools. A description of Oahu's best-known site, **Hanauma Bay**, appears on p.94. Conditions in the waters close to Waikīkī tend to be less enticing. The best spot among Waikīkī's beaches, however, is Sans Souci Beach (see p.35).

Operators of snorkel cruises and similar activities provide equipment to their customers, and there's a concession stand at Hanauma Bay, but you may prefer to **rent** better stuff from a specialist such as Snorkel Bob's, 700 Kapahulu Ave, Waikīkī (℗735-7944), or Surf'n'Sea in Hale'iwa (see above). Typical rates start at $5 per day, or $20 per week.

SCUBA AND SNUBA

Scuba diving is both expensive and demanding, but with endless networks of submarine lava tubes to explore, and the chance to get that bit closer to some amazing marine life forms, Hawaii is one of the planet's greatest diving destinations. Aficionados do not usually rank Oahu as highly as the Big Island or Maui, in part because there are few stellar dives accessible directly from the shoreline. Nonetheless, there are still some superb sites a short distance offshore, particularly in the southeast. Note that for medical reasons you shouldn't dive within 24 hours of flying.

A typical rate for a two-tank dive trip should be around $90. Operators include the Aloha Dive Shop at Koko

Marina, not far from Hanauma Bay (℃395-5922); Aaron's Dive Shop, 692 Kailua Rd, Kailua (℃262-2333); and Waikīkī Diving Center, 1734 Kalākaua Ave, Waikīkī (℃395-5922).

For a taste of what it's all about, you might like to try **snuba**, which is basically snorkeling from a boat equipped with a longer breathing tube. Many snorkel cruises offer snuba for an extra charge, or you could contact Snuba Tours of Oahu (℃396-6163), which organizes specialist snuba cruises to Hanauma Bay and other destinations for around $85.

KAYAKING

Kayaks for inshore expeditions can readily be rented in both Waikīkī (Prime Time Sports; ℃949-8952) and Kailua (Karel's Fiberglass; ℃261-8424). The best organized **kayak tours**, at $50 for two hours, are run by Kayak Oahu Adventure, which has bases in Waikīkī at the *New Otani Kaimana Beach Hotel*, adjoining Sans Souci Beach (℃923-0539), and on the North Shore at Waimea Park (℃638-8189).

WATER-SKIING AND PARASAILING

Traditional **water-skiing** is available in southeast Oahu's Koko Marina with Suyderhoud's Waterski Center (℃395-3773), who charge around $50 per half-hour. For a similar price, you can also try **parasailing**, where you soar several hundred feet up into the air beneath a parachute. Companies operating brief flights off Waikīkī include Aloha Parasail (℃521-2446) and Hawaiian Parasail (℃847-6229).

FISHING

Big-game **fishing**, for marlin especially, is a year-round attraction for many visitors to Hawaii. Most of Oahu's wide range of charter vessels are based at Koko Marina in the southeast. Rates for a day's expedition with outfits such as Kono Fishing Charters (✆536-7472) and Ku'u Huapala (✆596-0918) vary from $50 per person up to as much as $1000 for a whole boat.

Details on fishing regulations, and thirty-day licenses for freshwater fishing ($3.75), can be obtained from the Department of Land and Natural Resources, 1151 Punchbowl St, Room 311, Honolulu HI 96813 (✆587-0077).

WHALE-WATCHING

A large proportion of the North Pacific's three thousand **humpback whales** winter in Hawaiian waters between late November and early April. They're especially fond of the shallow channels between Maui, Molokai and Lanai, and prefer not to linger in the rougher seas off Oahu. The only Oahu-based boat to run regular **whale-watching** expeditions in season is the *Navatek 1* (see p.208; ✆848-6360 or 1-800/852-4183), which is stable enough to give passengers a comfortable ride even in adverse ocean conditions. A 2hr 30min cruise from Pier 6 in Honolulu costs around $40.

Festivals and holidays

The following calendar includes all federal and state holidays celebrated in Hawaii, together with Oahu's major annual festivals and sporting events. Note that the exact dates of **surfing** contests, and in some cases the venues as well, depend on the state of the waves.

Jan 1	New Year's Day; public holiday
Jan	Morey Bodyboards World Championships, Banzai Pipeline
3rd Mon in Jan	Dr Martin Luther King Jr's Birthday; public holiday
Feb	Mākaha World Surfing Championship, Mākaha Beach
Feb	Big Board Surfing Classic, Mākaha Beach
3rd Mon in Feb	Presidents Day; public holiday
March 17	St Patrick's Day Parade, Waikīkī
March 26	Prince Kūhiō Day; public holiday, state-wide celebrations

late March	Hawaii Longboard Surfing Association Contest, Sunset Beach
Easter Sunday	Easter Sunrise Service at dawn, Punchbowl, Honolulu
Easter Monday	public holiday
April	Hawaiian Professional Championship Rodeo, Waimānolo
May 1	May Day, *Lei* Day; public holiday, state-wide celebrations
May 2	*Lei* ceremony at Royal Mausoleum, Honolulu
late May	Molokai–Oahu kayak race ends at Hawaii Kai
late May	Maui–Oahu Bankoh Ho'omana'o canoe race ends at Waikīkī Beach
Last Mon in May	Memorial Day; public holiday
late May/early June	State Fair, Aloha Stadium, Honolulu
June 11	Kamehameha Day; public holiday, state-wide celebrations, Honolulu to Waikīkī parade
mid-June	Matsuri in Hawaii Festival; Japanese parade in Waikīkī
late June	King Kamehameha *Hula* Festival, Blaisdell Center, Honolulu
June 11	Kamehameha Day; public holiday
July 4	Independence Day; public holiday
early July	Nā Wāhine O Hawaii; Hawaiian women performers, Ala Moana Park
mid-July	Prince Lot *Hula* Festival, Moanalua Gardens, Honolulu

FESTIVALS AND HOLIDAYS |

July	Hawaiian Pro Am Surfing Contest, South Shore
late July	Hawaii International Jazz Festival, Honolulu
early Aug	Kāneʻohe Bay Fest, Kāneʻohe
mid-Aug	Floating Lantern Ceremony, Waikīkī
mid-Aug	Hawaiian Slack Key Guitar Festival, Honolulu
mid-Aug	Ka Hīmeniʻana; traditional singing contest, University of Hawaii
3rd Fri in Aug	Admission Day; public holiday
1st Mon in Sept	Labor Day; public holiday
early Sept	Polynesian Festival, Kāneʻohe
early Sept	Outrigger Hotels Hawaiian Oceanfest; island-wide watersports
mid-Sept	Aloha Festival, island-wide
late Sept	Molokai–Oahu women's outrigger canoe race ends at Waikīkī
late Sept	Makahiki Festival, Waimea Falls Park
early Oct	Molokai–Oahu men's outrigger canoe race ends at Waikīkī
2nd Mon in Oct	Columbus Day; public holiday
Oct 31	Halloween parade, Waikīkī
early Nov	World Invitation *Hula* Festival, Honolulu
Nov 11	Veterans' Day; public holiday
Nov	Hawaii International Film Festival, Honolulu
mid-Nov	Triple Crown of Surfing; Hawaiian Pro, Aliʻi Beach Park, Haleʻiwa

Last Thurs in Nov	Thanksgiving; public holiday
late Nov/early Dec	Triple Crown of Surfing; World Cup, Sunset Beach
late Nov/early Dec	Menehune Meet; kids' surfing contest, Mākaha Beach
early Dec	Triple Crown of Surfing; Pipe Masters, Banzai Pipeline
early Dec	Honolulu Marathon
mid-Dec	Mākaha Longboard Pro-Am; surfing contest, Mākaha Beach
Dec 25	Christmas Day; public holiday. Aloha Bowl Football Classic, Aloha Stadium, Honolulu

Directory

AREA CODE The telephone area code for the whole state of Hawaii is ☏808.

BANKS For details of banks in Honolulu and Waikīkī, see p.24.

CLIMATE For details of the climate on Oahu, see the *Introduction* on p.xiii.

CONSULATES Neither Britain, New Zealand nor Canada has a consulate in Honolulu. There is, however, an Australian consulate, at 1000 Bishop St, Honolulu HI 96813 (☏524-5050).

DENTISTS Oahu dental practitioners can be recommended by the Hawaii Dental Association (☏536-2135).

DOCTORS All Waikīkī hotels keep a list of doctors to recommend to guests requiring minor medical help; Doctors on Call (☏971-6000) maintains a 24-hr clinic at the *Outrigger Waikīkī on the Beach*, 2335 Kalākaua Ave.

ELECTRICITY Hawaii's electricity supply, like that on the US mainland, uses 110 volts AC. Plugs are standard American two-pins.

FISHING For full details on Hawaii's fishing regulations write to Division of Aquatic Resources, Dept of Land and Natural Resources, Kalanimoku Building, 1151 Punchbowl St, Room 330, Honolulu HI 96813.

GOLF The annual *Hawaii Golf Guide*, published by the Aloha Section PGA (#715, 770 Kapiʻolani Blvd, Honolulu HI 96813; ©593-2232) carries complete listings and details of all Hawaii's golf courses. Stand-By Golf (©1-888/645-2265) is a company that specializes in finding discounted and short-notice golfing opportunities on all the Hawaiian islands.

OAHU'S GOLF COURSES

Ala Wai Golf Course, Honolulu; $40; ©733-7387
Bayview Golf Links, Kaneʻohe; $75; ©247-0451
ʻEwa Beach Golf Club, ʻEwa Beach; $80; ©689-8351
Hawaii Country Club, Wahiawa; $37; ©621-5654
Hawaii Kai Golf Course
   Championship Course, Hawaii Kai; $100; ©395-2358
   Executive Course, Hawaii Kai; $37; ©395-2358
Hawaii Prince Golf Club, ʻEwa Beach; $90; ©944-4567
Honolulu Country Club, Honolulu; $125; ©833-4541
Kahuku Golf Course, North Shore; $20; ©293-5842
Kapolei Golf Course, Ko ʻOlina; $75; ©674-2227
Ko ʻOlina Golf Club, Ko ʻOlina; $145; ©676-5300
Koʻolau Golf Course, Kāneʻohe; $80; ©236-4653
Luana Hills Country Club, Kailua; $80; ©262-2139
Mākaha Valley Country Club, Mākaha; $75; ©695-9578
Mid-Pacific Country Club, Kailua; $140; ©261-9765
Mililani Golf Club, Mililani; $84; ©623-2222
Moanalua Golf Club, Honolulu; $40; ©839-2411
Oahu Country Club, Honolulu; $125; ©595-3256
Olomana Golf Links, Waimānalo; $90; ©259-7926

Pali Golf Course, Kāneʻohe; $40; ✆296-7254
Pearl Country Club, ʻAiea; $75; ✆487-3802
Sheraton Makaha Golf Club, Mākaha; $160; ✆695-9544
Ted Makalena Golf Course, Waipahu; $40; ✆675-6052
Turtle Bay Hilton Country Club
   The Links at Kuilima, Kahuku; $125; ✆293-8574
   Turtle Bay Country Club, Kahuku; $60; ✆293-8574
Waialae Country Club, Kahala; $120; ✆732-1457
Waikele Golf Club, Waipahu; $75; ✆676-9000
West Loch Golf Course, ʻEwa Beach; $47; ✆676-2210

HOSPITALS Honolulu hospitals providing 24-hour assistance include Kuakini Medical Center, 347 Kuakini St (✆536-2236); Moanalua Medical Center, 3288 Moanalua Rd (✆834-5333); the Queens Medical Center, 1301 Punchbowl St (✆538-9011); and the Straub Clinic and Hospital, 888 S King St (✆522-4000). In emergencies call ✆911.

INOCULATIONS No inoculations or vaccinations are required by law in order to enter Hawaii, though some authorities suggest a polio vaccination.

LAUNDROMATS Among public laundromats in Waikīkī are those at the *Outrigger Coral Seas*, 250 Lewers St; the *Outrigger Waikīkī on the Beach*, 2335 Kalākaua Ave; and the *Outrigger West*, 2330 Kūhiō Ave.

LIBRARY Honolulu's main public library is at Punchbowl and S King St downtown (Mon, Fri & Sat 9am–5pm; Tues & Thurs 9am–8pm; Wed 10am–5pm; ✆586-3500).

POST OFFICES The major post offices in Honolulu and Waikīkī are listed on p.26.

PUBLIC TOILETS Some public toilets are labeled in Hawaiian: *Kanes* means Men, *Wahines* means Women.

QUARANTINE Very stringent restrictions apply to the importation of all plants and animals into Hawaii. Cats and dogs have to stay in quarantine for 120 days; if you were hoping to bring an alligator or a hamster into the state, forget it. For full regulations call ✆871-5656.

SENIOR TRAVELERS US residents aged 50 or over can join the American Association of Retired Persons, 601 E St NW, Washington DC 20049 (✆1-800/424-3410), for discounts on accommodation and vehicle rental.

TIME Hawaii switches to Daylight Saving Time at 2am on the last Sunday in April until 2am on the last Sunday in October. Between those dates the difference between Hawaii and the West Coast is three hours, not the usual two; the difference from the mountain region is four hours not three, and from the East Coast it's six hours not five. Hawaii varies from ten to eleven hours behind the UK.

TIPPING Waiting staff in restaurants expect tips of fifteen percent, in bars a little less. Hotel porters and bellhops should receive around $1 per piece of luggage and housekeeping staff $1 per night.

TRAVELERS WITH DISABILITIES Copies of the *Aloha Guide to Accessibility in the State of Hawaii*, and additional information on facilities for travelers with disabilities on Oahu, can be obtained from the State Commission on Persons with Disabilities, 919 Ala Moana Blvd, #101, Honolulu HI 96814 (✆586-8121). Both HandiVans (✆832-0777) and Handi-Cabs of the Pacific (✆524-3866) provide transportation for disabled visitors, and most TheBus vehicles are adapted to suit passengers with physical disabilities.

WEDDINGS To get married in Hawaii, you need to have a valid state licence, which costs $25 from the Department of Health, Marriage License Office, 1250 Punchbowl St, Honolulu HI 96813 (✆586-4545), and is valid for thirty days. You also need proof of rubella immunizations or screening, which can be arranged through the Department of Health. The HVB's *Weddings in Hawaii* booklet lists companies that arrange weddings; most resorts offer their own marriage planners, or you can contact wedding specialists such as Aloha Wedding Planners (✆1-800/943-2711), Affordable Weddings of Hawaii (✆923-4876 or 1-800/942-4554), or Traditional Hawaiian Weddings (✆671-8420 or 1-800/884-9505).

WORK For details on finding paid employment in Hawaii – an option only open to US citizens – contact the State Department of Labor & Industrial Relations, 830 Punchbowl St, Honolulu HI 96813.

CONTEXTS

A brief history

Until less than two thousand years ago, Oahu remained an unknown speck in the vast Pacific, populated by the few organisms that had been carried here by wind or wave. Exactly when and where its first human settlers arrived remains unknown, in part because rising water levels have almost certainly submerged the very earliest settlements. However, carbon dating of sites at Kahana Valley and Bellows Field on the windward coast suggests that there were people on Oahu by around 200 AD.

These first inhabitants were **Polynesians**, probably from the Marquesas Islands. Except perhaps for their first chance landfall, they came equipped to colonize, carrying goats, dogs, pigs, coconut palms, bananas and sugar cane among other essentials. Their ancestors had spread from Asia to inhabit Indonesia and the Solomon Islands 30,000 years ago. Such migrations, across coastal waters shallower than they are today, involved hopping from island to island without crossing open ocean. There then followed a 25,000-year hiatus, while the techniques were acquired to venture farther. Just over three thousand years ago, the voyagers reached Fiji; they then spread via Tahiti to populate the "Polynesian Triangle", extending from Easter Island in the east to Hawaii in the north and New Zealand in the south.

Waves of settlers came to Hawaii at widely spaced intervals, each possibly violently supplanting its predecessors. Marquesas Islanders continued to arrive until the eighth century, and were followed by Tahitians between the eleventh and fourteenth centuries. Little subsequent two-way voyaging occurred between Hawaii and the South Pacific, and the era of the long-distance migrations had been over for around five hundred years by the time the Europeans appeared.

Before the coming of the foreigners, Oahu was probably the least significant of the four major Hawaiian islands. Nonetheless, the windward valleys of the east coast are thought to have held sizeable agricultural populations, while the sheltered coastline of Pearl Harbor supported an intricate network of fishponds. Not until the eighteenth century, however, did any individual chief become powerful enough to subdue the whole island, and by that time the rulers of Maui and Hawaii (the Big Island) were capable of launching successful invasions.

The coming of the foreigners

No Western ship is known to have chanced upon Hawaii before **Captain James Cook** in January 1778; the first European to sail across the Pacific, Magellan, did so without seeing a single island. However, **Spanish** mariners may have been shipwrecked in Hawaii during the sixteenth century. Spanish vessels disappeared in the northern Pacific as early as the 1520s, and from 1565 onwards the "Manila Galleons" made annual voyages across the Pacific between Mexico and the Philippines. A map captured by the British in 1742 shows a group of islands, labeled "La Mesa", in the correct location. That might explain the similarity of the red and yellow feather head-dresses of Hawaiian warriors to the helmets of Spanish soldiers, and account for the Hawaiians familiarity with iron.

When Cook first encountered Hawaii, on his way to the north Pacific in search of the Northwest Passage, he missed Maui and the Big Island altogether, and only glimpsed Oahu before making his first footfall upon Kauai. When he returned to the "**Sandwich Islands**" at the end of the year, he again bypassed Oahu en route to the Big Island, where he met his death in a skirmish in Kealakekua Bay on February 14, 1779.

Shortly after Cook's death, one of his ships, the *Resolution*, put in at Waimea Bay on Oahu's North Shore to collect water for the long voyage north. The new Captain Clerke described the first spot on Oahu to be visited by foreigners as "by far the most beautiful country we have yet seen among the Isles... bounteously cloath'd with verdure, on which were situate many large villages and extensive plantations."

By the time the next foreign expedition reached Oahu in 1792, led by Cook's former midshipman George Vancouver, the island had been conquered by Chief **Kahekili** of Maui. Kahekili's ferocious *pahupu* or "cut-in-two" warriors, who tattooed half of their bodies completely black, killed two of Vancouver's crew in Waimea Valley.

After news of Cook's discoveries reached the outside world, the Sandwich Islands became a port of call for traders of all kinds, especially those carrying furs from the Pacific Northwest to China. In 1793, Captain William Brown, a British fur trader in command of HMS *Butterworth*, noted the existence of a safe anchorage near the spot where the Nu'uanu Stream had created a gap in the coral reef fringing southeastern Oahu. The Hawaiians knew this as *He Awa Kou*, "the harbor of Kou", but Brown renamed it "fair haven", which was soon translated into Hawaiian as **Honolulu**. That name in turn attached itself to the small fishing village that stood nearby, which until then had been too insignificant even to deserve its own name.

The rise and fall of the Hawaiian monarchy

The acquisition of European military technology made it possible for a single chief to conquer the entire archipelago. The first to do so was the astute young Big Island warrior **Kamehameha**, who was by some accounts Kahekili's own bastard son. Kahekili himself died at Waikīkī in 1794, and Kamehameha won control of Oahu the following year, defeating the armies of Kahekili's heir Kalanikūpule in an epic battle at Nu'uanu Valley (see p.228).

Kamehameha originally based himself in a grass hut beside the beach at Waikīkī. Within ten years, however, Honolulu had turned into a cluster of shacks surrounding the semi-permanent adobe homes of sixty foreigners, and Kamehameha had built himself a palace, known as *Halehui*, at what is now the foot of Bethel Street. Another ten years on – by which time Kamehameha had moved his capital back to the Big Island, and then died – Honolulu was a thriving port, complete with bars and taverns.

Kamehameha was succeeded as King by two of his sons – Liholiho or **Kamehameha II**, who died of measles during a visit to England, and Kauikeaouli or **Kamehameha III**. Under both rulers, Kamehameha's widow Queen Ka'ahumanu was the real power behind the throne. She was largely responsible for the overthrow of the ancient *kapu* system of Hawaiian religion (see p.241) – motivated to some extent by the fact that the *kapu* denied women any political authority – and her subsequent conversion to Christianity was a principal factor in the success of Hawaii's first Christian **missionaries**.

In the years that followed, **whaling** ships en route between the Arctic and Japan began to call in twice-yearly to pick up provisions, drop off their haul, and catch up on a little entertainment. In Honolulu, the whalers were originally hauled in by Hawaiians standing on the reef; later on, teams of oxen did the job, and for many years an immense rope reached up Alakea Street to loop around a capstan at the foot of Punchbowl. By 1830, the city had a population of ten thousand, with a dominant American presence, and the basic grid of downtown streets was in place. Tensions between the missionaries and the lawless whaling crews were high, and both the seat of Hawaiian government, and the epicenter of the whaling industry, moved back and forth between Honolulu and Lahaina on Maui. Only in the 1840s did Honolulu become definitively established as the capital of Hawaii.

The Great Mahele

Kamehameha III's government was dominated by foreign-born fortune-seekers. Fourteen of the King's closest advisers were white, including his three most important ministers. The various foreign powers jostled for position; it is easy to forget now that it was not inevitable that the islands would become American. In 1843, a British commander captured Honolulu, claiming all Hawaii for Queen Victoria, and it was six months before word arrived from London that it had all been a mistake. A French admiral did much the same thing in 1849, but this time everyone simply waited until he got bored and sailed away again.

The most important obstacle to the advance of the foreigners was that they could not legally own land. In the old Hawaii there was no private land; all was held in trust by the chief, who apportioned it to individuals at his continued pleasure only. After a misunderstanding with the British consul almost resulted in the islands' permanent cession to Britain, the king was requested to "clarify" the situation. A land commission was set up, under the direction of a missionary, and its deliberations resulted in the **Great Mahele**, or "Division of Lands", in 1848. In theory all the land was parceled out to native Hawaiians only, with sixty percent going to the crown and the government, 39 percent to just over two hundred chiefs, and less than one percent to eleven thousand commoners. Claiming and keeping the land involved complex legal procedures, and required expenditures that few Hawaiians, paid in kind not cash, were able to meet. In any case, within two years the *haoles* (non-Hawaiians) too were permitted to buy and sell land. The much-repeated jibe that the missionaries "came to

THE GREAT MAHELE

Hawaii to do good – and they done good" stems from the speed with which they amassed vast acreages; their children became Hawaii's wealthiest and most powerful class.

Many Hawaiians were denied access to the lands they had traditionally worked, arrested for vagrancy, and used as forced labor on the construction of roads and ports for the new landowners. Meanwhile, a simultaneous **water-grab** took place, with new white-owned plantations diverting water for their thirsty foreign crops from the Hawaiian farmers downstream.

The sugar industry

At the height of the whaling boom, many newly rich entrepreneurs began to put their money into **sugar**. Hawaii's first sugar plantation started in 1835 in Kōloa on Kauai, and it swiftly became clear that this was an industry where large-scale operators were much the most efficient and profitable. By 1847 the field had narrowed to five main players, four of whom had started out by provisioning whale ships. These **Big Five** were Hackfield & Co (later to become Amfac), C Brewer & Co, Theo Davies Co, Castle & Cooke (later Dole) and Alexander & Baldwin. Thereafter, they worked in close co-operation with each other, united by common interests and, often, family ties.

Hawaii was poised to take advantage of the coming of Civil War, when the markets of the northern US began to cast about for an alternative source of sugar to the Confederate South. The consequent boom in the Hawaiian sugar industry, and the ever-increasing integration of Hawaii into the American economic mainstream, was the major single factor in the eventual loss of Hawaiian sovereignty.

The Civil War also coincided with the decline of the whaling industry. Several ships were bought and deliberately sunk to blockade Confederate ports, while the discovery of petroleum had diminished the demand for whale oil. The final disaster came in 1871, when 31 vessels lingered in the Arctic too long at the end of the season, became frozen in, and had to be abandoned.

By the 1870s, canefields were spreading across all the islands. The ethnic mixture of modern Hawaii is largely the product of the search for laborers prepared to submit to the draconian conditions on the plantations. Once the Hawaiians had demonstrated their unwillingness to knuckle under, agents of the Hawaiian Sugar Planters Association scoured the world in search of peasants eager to find new lives.

As members of each ethnic group in turn got their start on the plantations, and then left to find more congenial employment or establish their own businesses, a new source of labor had to be found. It soon became clear that few single men chose to stay on the plantations when their contracts expired – many left for California to join the Gold Rush – so the planters began to try to lure families to Hawaii, which meant providing better housing than the original basic dormitories.

First came the **Chinese** (see p.56), recruited with a $10 inducement in Hong Kong, shipped over for free, and then signed to five-year contracts at $6 or less per month. The **Portuguese** followed, brought from Madeira and the Azores from 1878 onwards by planters who thought they might adjust more readily than their Asian counterparts to the dominant *haole*-Hawaiian culture. **Koreans** arrived during the brief period between 1902, when they were first allowed to leave their country, and 1905, when it was invaded by the **Japanese**, who themselves came in great numbers until 1907, when the Gentleman's Agreement banned further immigration. **Filipinos**, whose country had been annexed by the US in 1898, began to arrive in their stead, to find the climate, soil and crops were all similar to their homelands.

THE SUGAR INDUSTRY

The end of the Kingdom of Hawaii

Hawaii is ours. As I look back upon the first steps in this miserable business, and as I contemplate the means used to complete the outrage, I am ashamed of the whole affair.

US President Grover Cleveland, 1893

After sugar prices dropped at the end of the Civil War, the machinations of the sugar industry to get favorable prices on the mainland moved Hawaii inexorably towards **annexation** by the US. In 1876 the Treaty of Reciprocity abolished all trade barriers and tariffs between the US and the Kingdom of Hawaii; within fifteen years sugar exports to the US had increased tenfold.

By now, the Kamehameha dynasty had come to an end, and the heir to the Hawaiian throne was chosen by the national legislature. The first such king, William Lunalilo, died in 1874, after barely a year in office. In the ensuing

The Hawaiian Monarchy

Kamehameha I	1791–1819
Kamehameha II (Liholiho)	1819–1824
Kamehameha III (Kauikeaouli)	1825–1854
Kamehameha IV (Alexander Liholiho)	1854–1863
Kamehameha V (Lot Kamehameha)	1863–1872
William C. Lunalilo	1873–1874
David Kalākaua	1874–1891
Liliʻuokalani	1891–1893

elections, **Queen Emma**, the Anglophile widow of Kamehameha IV (see p.78), lost to **King David Kalākaua**. The "Merrie Monarch" is affectionately remembered today for his role in reviving traditional Hawaiian pursuits such as *hula* and surfing, but he was widely seen as being pro-American, and a riot protesting his election in 1874 virtually destroyed Honolulu's Old Court House. King Kalākaua was to a significant extent the tool of the plantation owners. In 1887 an all-white (and armed) group of "concerned businessmen" forced through the "Bayonet Constitution", in which he surrendered power to an assembly elected by property owners (of any nationality) as opposed to citizens. The US government was swiftly granted exclusive rights to what became Pearl Harbor.

Kalākaua died in San Francisco in 1891, shortly after recording a farewell address to his people on a newly invented Edison recording machine. In his absence, he had appointed his sister **Lili'uokalani** to serve as his regent, and she now became queen. When she proclaimed her desire for a new constitution, the same group of businessmen, who had now convened themselves into an "**Annexation Club**", called in the US warship *Boston*, then in Honolulu, and declared a provisional government. President Grover Cleveland (a Democrat) responded that "Hawaii was taken possession of by the United States forces without the consent or wish of the government of the islands. . . . [It] was wholly without justification . . . not merely a wrong but a disgrace." With phenomenal cheek, the provisional government rejected his demand for the restoration of the monarchy, saying the US should not "interfere in the internal affairs of their sovereign nation". They found defenders in the Republican US Congress, and declared themselves a **republic** on July 4, 1894, with **Sanford Dole** as their first President.

Following an abortive coup attempt in 1895, Liliʻuokalani was charged with **treason**. She was placed under house arrest, first in ʻIolani Palace, and later at her Honolulu home of Washington Place (see p.48). Though she lived until 1917, hopes of a restoration of Hawaiian independence were dashed in 1897, when a Republican president, McKinley, came to office claiming "annexation is not a change. It is a consummation." The strategic value of Pearl Harbor was emphasized by the Spanish–American War in the Philippines; and on August 12, 1898 Hawaii was formally **annexed** as a territory of the United States.

The twentieth century

At the moment of annexation there was no question of Hawaii becoming a state; the whites were outnumbered ten to one, and had no desire to afford the rest of the islanders the protection of US labor laws, let alone to give them the vote. Furthermore, as the proportion of Hawaiians of Japanese descent (*nisei*) increased (to 25 percent by 1936), Congress feared the prospect of a state whose inhabitants might consider their primary allegiance to be to Japan. Consequently, Hawaii remained for the first half of this century the virtual fiefdom of the Big Five, who, through their control of agriculture (they owned 96 percent of the sugar crop), dominated transport, banks, utilities, insurance and government.

Things began to change during World War II. The Japanese offensive on Pearl Harbor, detailed on p.86, meant that Hawaii was the only part of the United States to be attacked in the war, and it demonstrated just how crucial the islands were to the rest of America. Military bases and training camps were established throughout Hawaii, many of which remain operational to this day. In addition, Hawaiian troops played an active role in the war. Veterans of the much-decorated 442nd Regimental Combat Team –

composed of Japanese Hawaiians and, for obvious reasons, sent to fight in Europe – have been a leading force in Hawaiian politics ever since.

The main trend in Hawaiian history since the war has been the slow decline of agriculture and the rise of **tourism**. Strikes organized along ethnic lines in the sugar plantations had consistently failed in the past, but from 1937, labor leaders such as Jack Hill and Harry Bridges of the International Longshoremen's and Warehousemen's Union began to organize workers of all races and all crafts, in solidarity with mainland unions. In September 1946, the plantation workers won their first victory. Thanks to the campaigns that followed, the long-term Republican domination of state politics ended, and Hawaii's agricultural workers became the highest paid in the world. Arguably, this led to the eventual disappearance of all their jobs in the face of Third World competition, and fifty years on almost all the sugar mills have closed.

Hawaii finally became the fiftieth of the United States in 1959, after a plebiscite showed a 17-to-1 majority in favor, with the only significant opposition coming from the few remaining native Hawaiians. **Statehood** coincided with the first jet flight to Hawaii, which halved the previous nine-hour flight time from California. These two factors triggered a boom in tourism – many visitors had had their first sight of Hawaii as GIs in the war – and also in migration from the mainland to Hawaii. As detailed on p.30, Waikīkī, has been repeatedly relandscaped and rebuilt to cope with its emergence as the main focus of the tourist industry.

Official figures showing the growth of the Hawaiian economy since statehood conceal a decline in living standards for many Hawaiians. Consumer prices in the state went up by 73 percent during the 1980s, while wages rose by only 13 percent. Real-estate prices in particular have rocketed, so that many islanders are obliged to work at two

235

jobs, others end up sleeping on the beaches, and young Hawaiians emigrate in droves with no prospect of being able to afford to return.

The sovereignty movement

In the last decade, broad-based support has mushroomed for the concept of **Hawaiian sovereignty**, meaning some form of restoration of the rights of native Hawaiians. Pride in the Polynesian past has been rekindled by such means as the voyages of the *Hōkūleʻa* canoe, and the successful campaign to claim back the island of Kahoolawe of Maui, which had been used since the war as a Navy bombing range.

The movement has reached the point where everyone seems sure that sovereignty is coming, but no one knows what form it will take. Of the three most commonly advanced models, one sees Hawaii as an independent nation once again, recognized by the international community, with full citizenship perhaps restricted either to those born in Hawaii or prepared to pledge sole allegiance to Hawaii. Another possibility would be the granting to native Hawaiians of nation-within-a-nation status, as with Native American groups on the mainland, while others argue that it would be more realistic to preserve the existing political framework within the context of full economic reparations to native Hawaiians.

Even the US government has formally acknowledged the illegality of the US overthrow of the Hawaiian monarchy with an official **Apology to Native Hawaiians** signed by President Clinton in November 1993. In 1996, the state of Hawaii organized a plebiscite, open to anyone of Hawaiian ancestry, to decide whether to elect a constitutional convention to discuss the alternatives. Almost three quarters voted in favor, but funding for the elections themselves has yet to be allocated.

A separate but related problem, indicative of the difficulties faced in resolving this issue, is the failure by both federal and state government to manage 200,000 acres set aside for the benefit of native Hawaiians in 1921. The state has now agreed to pay Hawaiians more than $100 million compensation, though disputes remain over where the money will come from and to whom it will go.

With dozens of different groups claiming to speak on behalf of native Hawaiians – including the self-proclaimed King Kamehameha VI, in jail in Colorado for refusing to pay US taxes – there's a real danger of the sovereignty movement dissolving into factionalism. There may even turn out to be a parallel with events of a century ago, with a sympathetic Democrat President (Cleveland then, Clinton now) being replaced in office by a Republican for whom the interests of the federal government come first.

Ancient culture and society

No written record exists of the centuries between the arrival of the Polynesians and the first contact with Europeans. However, sacred chants, passed down through the generations, show a history packed with feuds and forays between the islands, and oral traditions provide a detailed picture of the day-to-day life of ordinary Hawaiians.

Developing a civilization on the most isolated islands in the world, without metals and workable clays, presented many challenges. Nevertheless, by the late eighteenth century, Hawaii was home to around a million people. Two hundred years later, the population has climbed back to a similar level, though its distribution is utterly different. The Big Island probably held several hundred thousand, and Maui perhaps 200,000, compared to around 100,000 each today, while Oahu, which formerly sheltered well under 100,000 inhabitants, now boasts around 900,000. Furthermore, virtually no pure-blooded Hawaiians remain, and the islands are not even close to being self-sufficient in food.

Daily life

In a sense, ancient Hawaii had no economy, not even barter. Although, then as now, most people lived close to the coast, each island was organized into wedge-shaped land divisions called *ahupua'a*, stretching from the ocean to the mountains. The abundant fruits of the earth and sea were simply shared out among the inhabitants within each *ahupua'a*.

There's some truth in the idea of pre-contact Hawaii as a leisured paradise, but it had taken a lot of work to make it that way. Coconut palms had to be planted along the seashore to provide food, clothing and shade for coastal villages, and bananas and other food plants distributed inland. Crops such as sugar cane were cultivated with the aid of complex systems of terraces and irrigation channels. *Taro*, whose leaves were eaten as "greens" and whose roots were mashed to produce *poi*, was grown in the windward valleys.

Most **fishing** took place in shallow inshore waters. Fish-hooks made from human bone were believed to be especially effective; the most prized hooks of all were made from the bones of chiefs who had no body hair, so those unfortunate individuals were renowned for their low life expectancy. Nets were never cast from boats, but shallow bays might be dragged by communal groups of wading men drawing in *hukilau* nets (Elvis did it in *Blue Hawaii*, and you occasionally see people doing it today). In addition, the art of **aquaculture** – fish-farming – was more highly developed in Hawaii than anywhere in Polynesia.

Ordinary commoners – the **maka'āinana** – lived in simple windowless huts known as *hales*. Most of these were thatched with *pili* grass, though in the driest areas they didn't bother with roofs. Buildings of all kinds were usually raised on platforms of stone, using rounded boulders taken from river beds. Matting covered the floor, while the pounded tree bark called *kapa* (known as *tapa* elsewhere in the Pacific, and decorated with patterns) served as clothing and bedding. Lacking pottery, households made abundant use of gourds, wooden dishes and woven baskets.

The ruling class, the **ali'i**, stood at the apex of Hawaiian society. In theory, heredity counted for everything, and great chiefs demonstrated their fitness to rule by the length of their genealogies. In fact the *ali'i* were educated as equals, and chiefs won the very highest rank largely through physical prowess and force of personality. To hang on to power, the king had to be seen to be devoutly religious and to treat his people fairly.

DAILY LIFE

The most popular pastime was **surfing**. Ordinary people surfed on five- to seven-foot boards known as *alaia*, and also had *paipus*, the equivalent of the modern boogie board; only the *ali'i* used the thick sixteen-foot *olo* boards, made of dark oiled *wiliwili* wood. On land the *ali'i* raced narrow sleds on purpose-built, grass-covered *hōlua* slides and staged boxing tournaments.

Religion

It's all but impossible now to grasp the subtleties of ancient Hawaiian **religion**. So much depends on how the chants and texts are translated; if the word *akua* is interpreted as meaning "god", for example, historians can draw analogies with Greek or Hindu legends by speaking of a pantheon of battling, squabbling "gods" and "goddesses" with magic powers. Some scholars however prefer to translate *akua* as "spirit consciousness", which might correspond to the soul of an ancestor, and argue that the antics of such figures are peripheral to a more fundamental set of attitudes regarding the relationship of humans to the natural world.

The **Kumulipo**, Hawaii's principal creation chant, has been preserved in full. It tells how after the emergence of the earth "from the source in the slime . . . [in] the depths of the darkness", more complicated life forms developed, from coral to pigs, until finally men, women and "gods" appeared. Not only was there no Creator god, but the gods were much of a kind with humans. It took a hundred generations for Wākea, the god of the sky, and Papa, an earth goddess, to be born; they were the divine ancestors of the Hawaiian people.

Not all Hawaiians necessarily shared the same beliefs; different groups sought differing ways of augmenting their *mana*, or spiritual power. Only the elite *ali'i* may have paid much attention to the bloodthirsty warrior god Kū, while ordinary families, and by extension villages and regions,

owed their primary allegiance to their personal *'aumākua* –
a sort of clan symbol, possibly a totem animal such as a
shark or owl, or a more abstract force, such as that embod-
ied by Pele, the volcano goddess.

Spiritual and temporal power did not lie in the same
hands, let alone in the same places. Hawaiian "priests" were
known as **kahunas** ("men who know the secrets"), and
were the masters of ceremonies at temples called **heiaus**. A
heiau consisted of a number of separate structures set on a
rock platform (*paepae*). These might include the *hale mana*
or "house of spiritual power"; the *hale pahu* or "house of
the drum"; and the *anu'u*, the "oracle tower", from the top
of which the *kahunas* conversed with the gods. Assorted *ki'i
akua*, wooden images of different gods, stood on all sides,
and the whole enclosure was fenced or walled off. In addition to the two main types of *heiau* – **luakinis**, dedicated to
the war god Kū, which held *leles* or altars used for human
sacrifice; and **māpeles**, peaceful temples to Lono – there
were also *heiaus* to such entities as Laka, goddess of the *hula*.
Devotees of Pele, on the other hand, did not give their pro-
tectress formal worship at a *heiau*. Most *heiaus* were built for
some specific occasion, and did not remain in constant use;
the largest on Oahu was the **Pu'u O Mahuka Heiau**,
overlooking Waimea Valley on the North Shore (see p.122).

Hawaiian religion in the form encountered by Cook was
brought to the islands by the Tahitian warrior-priest Pa'ao,
who led the last great migration to Hawaii. Pa'ao is also
credited with introducing the complex system of **kapu** –
the Hawaiian version of the Polynesian *tabu*, or *taboo* –
which circumscribed the daily lives of all Hawaiians. Some
of its restrictions served to augment the power of the kings
and priests, while others regulated domestic routine or
attempted to conserve natural resources. Many had to do
with food. Women were forbidden to prepare food, or to
eat with men; each husband was obliged to cook for him-

RELIGION

self and his wife in two separate ovens, and to pound the *poi* in two distinct calabashes. The couple had to maintain separate houses, as well as a *Hale Noa*, where a husband and wife slept together. Women could not eat pork, bananas or coconuts, or several kinds of fish. Certain fish could only be caught in specified seasons; and a *koa* tree could only be cut down once two more were planted in its place.

No one could tread on the shadow of a chief; the highest chiefs were so surrounded by *kapus* that some would only go out at night. The ruling chiefs did not necessarily possess the highest spiritual status. One of Kamehameha's wives was so much his superior that he could only approach her naked and on all fours.

The only crime in ancient Hawaii was to break a *kapu*, and the only punishment was death. It was possible for an entire *ahupua'a* to break a *kapu* and incur death, but that penalty was not always exacted. One way guilty parties could avoid execution was by hotfooting it to a *pu'uhonua*, or "place of refuge".

Books

An extraordinary quantity of books have been written about Hawaii and all matters Hawaiian, though you're only likely to come across most of them on the islands themselves. Honolulu bookstores are listed on p.200.

Unless otherwise specified, all the publishers below are based in the US.

History

Gavan Daws, *Shoal of Time* (University of Hawaii Press). Definitive if dry single-volume history of the Hawaiian Islands, tracing their fate from European contact to statehood.

Greg Dening, *The Death of William Gooch* (University of Hawaii Press). Elaborate anthropological and metaphysical speculations spun around the 1792 murder of three European sailors in Oahu's Waimea Valley.

Michael Dougherty, *To Steal a Kingdom: Probing Hawaiian History* (Island Style Press). An eccentric and entertaining look at Hawaiian history, which focuses on the famous names of the nineteenth century and pulls no punches.

Bob Dye (ed), *Hawaii Chronicles* (University of Hawaii Press). A collection of entertaining short essays on little-known aspects of Hawaiian history, culled from *Honolulu* magazine.

Glen Grant, *Waikiki Yesteryear* (Mutual Publishing). Short but well-illustrated history of Hawaii's premier playground.

Lili'uokalani, *Hawaii's Story by Hawaii's Queen* (Mutual Publishing). Autobiographical account by the last monarch of Hawaii of how her kingdom was taken away. Written in 1897 when she still cherished hopes of a restoration.

Jeannette Peek, *Stepping Into Time* (Mutual Publishing).
Attractively presented volume of historical accounts of Honolulu's
major landmarks, ably illustrated by the author.

Gordon W. Prange, *At Dawn We Slept* and *The Verdict of History*
(Penguin). Definitive best-selling analysis of the attack on Pearl
Harbor. Over two volumes, Prange exhaustively rebuts revisionist
conspiracy theories.

A Grenfell Price (ed), *The Explorations of Captain James Cook in
the Pacific* (Dover). Selections from Cook's own journals,
including his first landfall on Kauai and his ill-fated return to the
Big Island.

Luis I. Reyes, *Made in Paradise* (Mutual Publishing). Lovingly
prepared coffee-table history of how Hollywood has depicted
Hawaii, with some great illustrations.

Ronald Takaki, *Pau Hana* (University of Hawaii Press). Moving
history of life on the sugar plantations, and the trials experienced
by generations of immigrant laborers.

Ancient Hawaii

Nathaniel B Emerson, *Unwritten Literature of Hawaii – The Sacred
Songs of the Hula* (Charles E Tuttle Co). Slightly dated account of
ancient Hawaii's most important art form. Published in 1909, its
wealth of detail ensures that it remains required reading for all
students of the hula.

Samuel M Kamakau, *The People of Old* (Bishop Museum Press, 3
vols). Anecdotal essays, published in Hawaiian as newspaper
articles in the 1860s. Packed with fascinating information, they
provide a compendium of Hawaiian oral traditions. Kamakau's
longer *Ruling Chiefs of Hawaii* (Bishop Museum Press) details all
that is known of the deeds of the kings.

Patrick Kirch, *Feathered God and Fishhooks* and *Legacy of the Past* (both University of Hawaii Press). The former is the best one-volume account of ancient Hawaii, though non-specialists may find the minutiae of specific archeological digs hard going; the latter, an excellent guide to specific Hawaiian sites.

David Malo, *Hawaiian Antiquities* (Bishop Museum Press). Nineteenth-century survey of culture and society, written by a Maui native who was brought up at the court of Kamehameha the Great.

Contemporary Hawaii

Michael Kioni Dudley and Keoni Kealoha Agard, *A Call for Hawaiian Sovereignty* (Na Kane O Ka Malo, 2 vols). The first of these short books attempts to reconstruct the world view of the ancient Hawaiians; the second is the clearest imaginable account of their dispossession.

Randall W Roth (ed), *The Price of Paradise* (Mutual Publishing, 2 vols). Assorted experts answer questions about life and society in Hawaii, in short essays that focus on economic and governmental issues. Of most interest to local residents or prospective migrants.

Travelers' tales

Isabella Bird, *Six Months In the Sandwich Islands* (University of Hawaii Press). The enthralling adventures of an Englishwoman in the 1870s, whose escapades on the Neighbor Islands are interspersed with acute observations of the Honolulu social scene.

James Macrae, *With Lord Byron at the Sandwich Islands in 1825* (Petroglyph Press). Short pamphlet of extracts from the diary of a Scottish botanist, including descriptions of Honolulu as a small village and the first-known ascent of Mauna Kea

Andy Martin, *Walking on Water* (Minerva, UK). An English journalist attempts to immerse himself in the surfing culture of Oahu's North Shore.

Robert Louis Stevenson, *Travels in Hawaii* (University of Hawaii Press). The Scottish novelist spent several months in Hawaii in the late nineteenth century, and struck up a close friendship with King David Kalākaua.

Mark Twain, *Letters from Hawaii* (University of Hawaii Press). Colorful and entertaining accounts of nineteenth-century Hawaii; much of the best material was reworked for inclusion in *Roughing It* (Penguin UK and US).

Hawaii in fiction

Herman Melville, *Typee* (Penguin). Largely set in the Marquesas Islands, but with echoes of his time in Hawaii, Melville's wildly romanticized version of the South Seas – originally published as non-fiction – makes a perfect escapist read.

James Michener, *Hawaii* (Random House). Another romanticized romp, whose success was a major factor in the growth of Hawaiian tourism.

Richard Tregaskis, *The Warrior King* (Falmouth Press). This fictionalized biography of Kamehameha the Great serves as a readable introduction to a crucial period in Hawaiian history.

Kathleen Tyau, *A Little Too Much is Enough* (Farrar, Straus & Giroux US, The Women's Press UK). Atmospheric and amusing account of growing up as a Chinese-Hawaiian, with an appetizing emphasis on food.

Natural sciences

Gordon A. Macdonald and Agatin A. Abbott, *Volcanoes in the Sea* (University of Hawaii Press). Thorough technical examination – sadly not illustrated in color – of how fire and water have shaped the unique landscapes of Hawaii.

Frank Stewart (ed), *A World Between Waves* (Island Press). Stimulating collection of essays by authors such as Peter Matthiessen and Maxine Hong Kingston, covering all aspects of Hawaiian natural history.

A Hawaiian glossary

The Hawaiian language is an offshoot of languages spoken elsewhere in Polynesia, with slight variations that arose during the centuries when the islands had no contact with the rest of Polynesia. Among its most unusual features is the fact that there are no verbs "to be" or "to have", and that, although it lacks a word for "weather", it distinguishes between 130 types of rain and 160 types of wind.

Although barely two thousand people speak Hawaiian as their mother tongue, it remains a living language and has experienced a revival in recent years. While visitors to Hawaii are almost certain to hear Hawaiian-language songs, it's rarely spoken in public, and there should be no need to communicate in any language other than English. However, everyday conversations tend to be sprinkled with Hawaiian words, and you'll also spot them in many local place names.

The Hawaiian alphabet

Hawaiian only became a written language when a committee of missionaries gave it an alphabet. The shortest in the world, it consists of just twelve letters – a, e, h, i, k, l, m, n, o, p, u, and w – plus two punctuation marks. When the missionaries were unable to agree on the precise sounds of the language, they simply voted on which letter to include – thus k beat t, and l beat r.

Hawaiian may look hard to **pronounce**, but in fact with just 162 possible syllables – as compared to 23,638 in Thai – it's the least complicated on earth. The letters h, l, m and n are pronounced exactly as in English; k and p are pronounced approximately as in English but with less aspiration; *w* is like the English *v* after an *i* or an *e*, and the English *w* after a *u* or an *o*. At the start of a word, or after an *a*, *w* may be pronounced like a *v* or a *w*.

The **glottal stop** (') creates the audible pause heard in the English "oh-oh". Words without macrons (⁻), to indicate stress, are pronounced by stressing alternate syllables working back from the penultimate syllable. Thanks to the frequent repetition of syllables it's usually easier than this may sound. "Kamehameha" for example breaks down into the repeated pattern *Ka–meha–meha*, pronounced *Ka–mayha–mayha*.

a	*a as in above*
e	*e as in bet*
i	*y as in pity*
o	*o as in hole*
u	*u as in full*
ā	*a as in car*
ē	*ay as in day*
ī	*ee as in bee*
ō	*o as in hole (but slightly longer)*
ū	*oo as in moon*

Note that, strictly speaking, the word Hawaii should be written Hawai'i, with the glottal stop to show that the two "i"s are pronounced separately. However, this book follows the convention that words in common English usage are written without their Hawaiian punctuation. Maui itself is unique among the islands in that its correct name features neither a macron nor a glottal stop, while all the other island names – Hawaii, Oahu, Kauai, and so on – appear in their familiar English form.

Glossary

'A'Ā rough lava

AHUPUA'A basic land division, a "slice of cake" from ocean to mountain

'ĀINA land, earth

AKUA god, goddess, spirit, idol

ALI'I chief, chiefess, noble

ALOHA love, hello, goodbye.

'AUMĀKUA personal god or spirit, totem animal

HALA tree (pandanus, screw pine)

HALĀU long house used for *hula* tuition; also a *hula* group

HALE house, building

HANA work

HAOLE (white) non-native Hawaiian, whether foreign or American resident

HAPA half, as in *hapa haole*, or half-foreign

HĀPU'U tree fern

HEIAU ancient place of worship

HONUA land, earth

HUI group, club

HULA dance/music form (*hula 'auana* is a modern form, *hula kahiko* is traditional)

IMU pit oven

KAHUNA priest(ess) or someone particularly skilled in any field; *kahuna nui* chief priest

KAI sea

KĀLUA To bake in an *imu* (underground oven)

KAMA'ĀINA Hawaiian from another island; state resident

KĀNE man

KAPA the "cloth" made from pounded bark, known elsewhere as *tapa*

KAPU forbidden, taboo, sacred

KAUKAU food

KEIKI child

KIAWE thorny tree, mesquite
KI'I temple image or petroglyph
KOA dark hardwood tree
KŌKUA help
KONA leeward (especially wind)
LĀNAI balcony, terrace, patio
LAU leaf
LEHUA or **'ŌHI'A LEHUA** native red-blossomed shrub/tree
LEI garland of flowers, feathers, shells or other material
LILIKO'I passion fruit
LIMU seaweed
LOMI LOMI massage or raw salmon dish
LUAKINI temple of human sacrifice
LŪ'AU traditional Hawaiian feast
MAHALO thank you
MAKAI direction: away from the mountain, towards the sea
MALIHINI newcomer, visitor
MANA spiritual power
MAUKA direction: away from the sea, towards the mountain
MELE ancient chant
MENEHUNE in legend, the most ancient Hawaiian people, supposedly dwarfs
MU'UMU'U long loose dress
NĒNĒ Hawaiian goose – the state bird
NUI big, important
'OHANA family
'ŌHELO sacred red berry
'ŌHI'A LEHUA see *lehua*
'ONO delicious
'ŌPAE shrimp
PĀHOEHOE smooth lava
PALI sheer-sided cliff
PANIOLO Hawaiian cowboy
PAU finished
PILI grass; used for thatch

POI staple food made of *taro* root
POKE raw fish dish
PUA flower, garden
PŪPŪ snack
PU'U hill, lump
TARO Hawaiian food plant
TSUNAMI tidal wave
TŪTŪ grandparent, general term of respect
WAHINE woman
WAI water
WIKIWIKI hurry, fast

INDEX

Stay in touch with us!

ROUGH*NEWS* **is Rough Guides' free newsletter.**
In three issues a year we give you news, travel issues, music reviews, readers' letters and the latest dispatches from authors on the road.

I would like to receive ROUGH*NEWS*: please put me on your free mailing list.

NAME . . . .

ADDRESS . . . .

Please clip or photocopy and send to: Rough Guides, 62-70 Shorts Gardens, London WC2H 9AB, England

or Rough Guides, 375 Hudson Street, New York, NY 10014, USA.

Backpacking through **Europe**?
Cruising across the **US of A**?
Clubbing in **London**?
Trekking through **Costa Rica**?

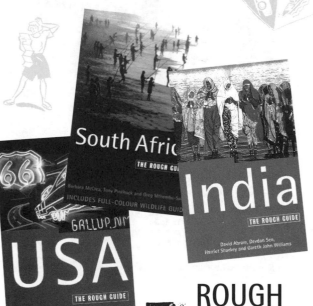

South Afri
THE ROUGH GUI
Barbara McCrea, Tony Pinchuck and Greg Mthembu-S
INCLUDES FULL-COLOUR WILDLIFE GUID

India
THE ROUGH GUIDE
David Abram, Devdan Sen,
Harriet Sharkey and Gareth John Williams

USA
THE ROUGH GUIDE
Samatha Cook, Jamie Jensen,
Tim Perry & Greg Ward

ROUGH
Travel Guides to more than
from Amsterdam...

Wherever you're headed, **Rough Guides** tell you what's happening – the history, the people, the politics, the best beaches, nightlife and entertainment on your budget

GUIDES

100 destinations worldwide
...to Zimbabwe.

MAP LIST

MAP SYMBOLS

═══378═══	Highway	◆	Ancient site
═══════	Road	▲	Peak
────────	Waterway	✈	Airport
── ── ──	Trail	◉	Accommodation
⊠	Post office	△	Campground
⊤	Public gardens	■	Building
⚑	Waterfall	✚	Church
⚓	Shipwreck	▦	Park
♛	Museum		

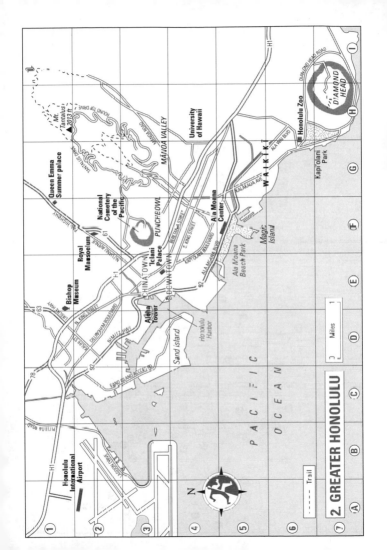

2. GREATER HONOLULU

- - - - Trail

Miles

Honolulu International Airport

PACIFIC OCEAN

Sand Island

Honolulu Harbor

Aloha Tower

Bishop Museum

CHINATOWN

DOWN TOWN

'Iolani Palace

Royal Mausoleum

National Cemetery of the Pacific

PUNCHBOWL

Queen Emma Summer palace

Mt. Tantalus 2013 ft

ROUND TOP DRIVE

TANTALUS DRIVE

MĀNOA VALLEY

University of Hawaii

A'la Moana Center

Ala Moana Beach Park

Magic Island

WAIKIKI

KALAKAUA AVE.

Kapi'olani Park

Honolulu Zoo

DIAMOND HEAD

DIAMOND HEAD ROAD

Ala Wai Canal

PALI HIGHWAY

NUUANU AVENUE

MOANALUA ROAD

S. KING STREET

BERETANIA STREET

KAPIOLANI BOULEVARD

ALA MOANA BLVD.

N. NIMITZ HWY.

SAND ISLAND ACCESS RD.

N. KING STREET

MOANALUA FWY.

LIKELIKE HWY.

H-1

N

PACIFIC OCEAN

61

92

78

63

1 2 3 4 5 6 7

A B C D E F G H I

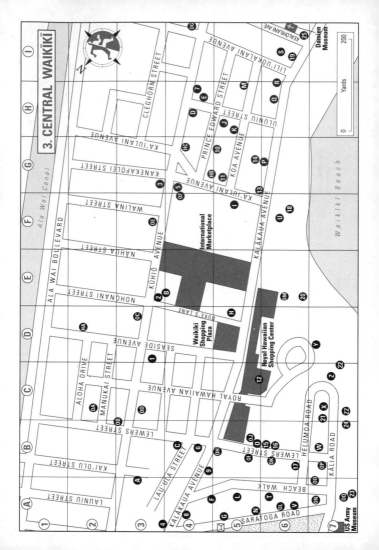

3. CENTRAL WAIKĪKĪ

N

Ala Wai Canal

Waikīkī Beach

| 0 | 200 | Yards

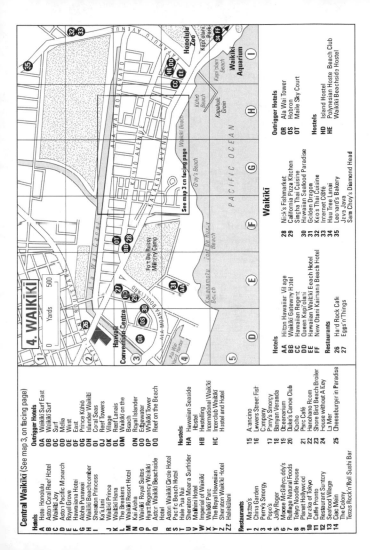

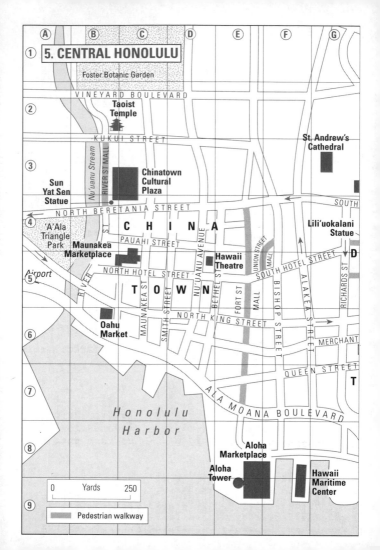

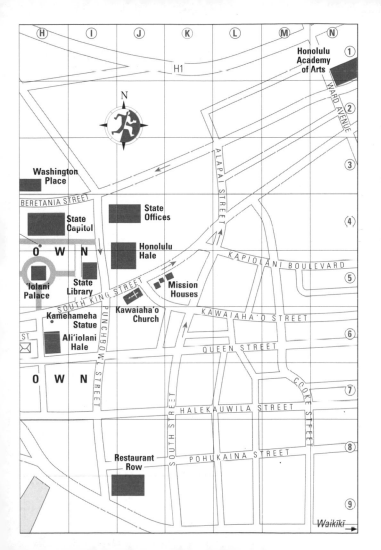

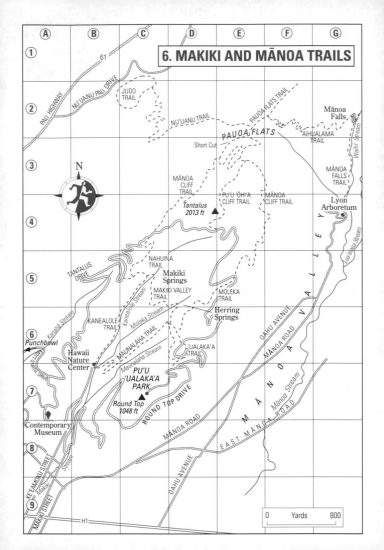

6. MAKIKI AND MĀNOA TRAILS

A **B** **C** **D** **E** **F** **G**

1

2
61
PALI HIGHWAY
NU'UANU PALI DRIVE
JUDD TRAIL
NU'UANU TRAIL
PAUOA FLATS TRAIL
Mānoa Falls

3
NU'UANU TRAIL
PAUOA FLATS
Short Cut
MĀNOA CLIFF TRAIL
AIHUALAMA TRAIL
MĀNOA FALLS TRAIL
Waihi Stream

N

4
Tantalus 2013 ft
PU'U 'ŌHI'A CLIFF TRAIL
MĀNOA CLIFF TRAIL
Lyon Arboretum

5
TANTALUS DRIVE
NAHUINA TRAIL
Makiki Springs
MAKIKI VALLEY TRAIL
MOLEKA TRAIL
Kanealole Stream
Kanealole Stream

6
Punchbowl
KANEALOLE TRAIL
Moleka Stream
Herring Springs
MAUNALAHA TRAIL
'UALAKA'A TRAIL
Hawaii Nature Center
Maunalaha Stream
OAHU AVENUE
MĀNOA ROAD
MĀNOA VALLEY
Liʻa-laʻa Stream
Mānoa Stream

7
Smith Drive
PU'U 'UALAKA'A PARK
Round Top 1048 ft
ROUND TOP DRIVE
Mānoa Stream
EAST MĀNOA ROAD

8
Contemporary Museum
KEʻEAMOKU STREET
Makiki Stream
MĀNOA ROAD
OAHU AVENUE
EAST MĀNOA ROAD

9
MAKIKI STREET
H1
0   Yards   800

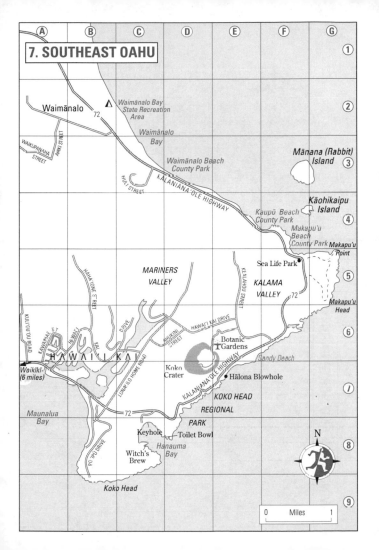

7. SOUTHEAST OAHU

8. WINDWARD AND NORTH OAHU

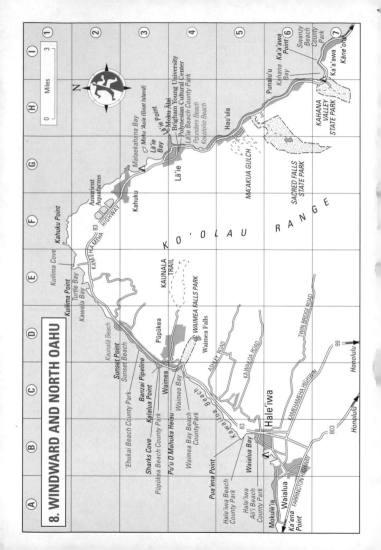